THE COMIC BOOK STORY OF BEER

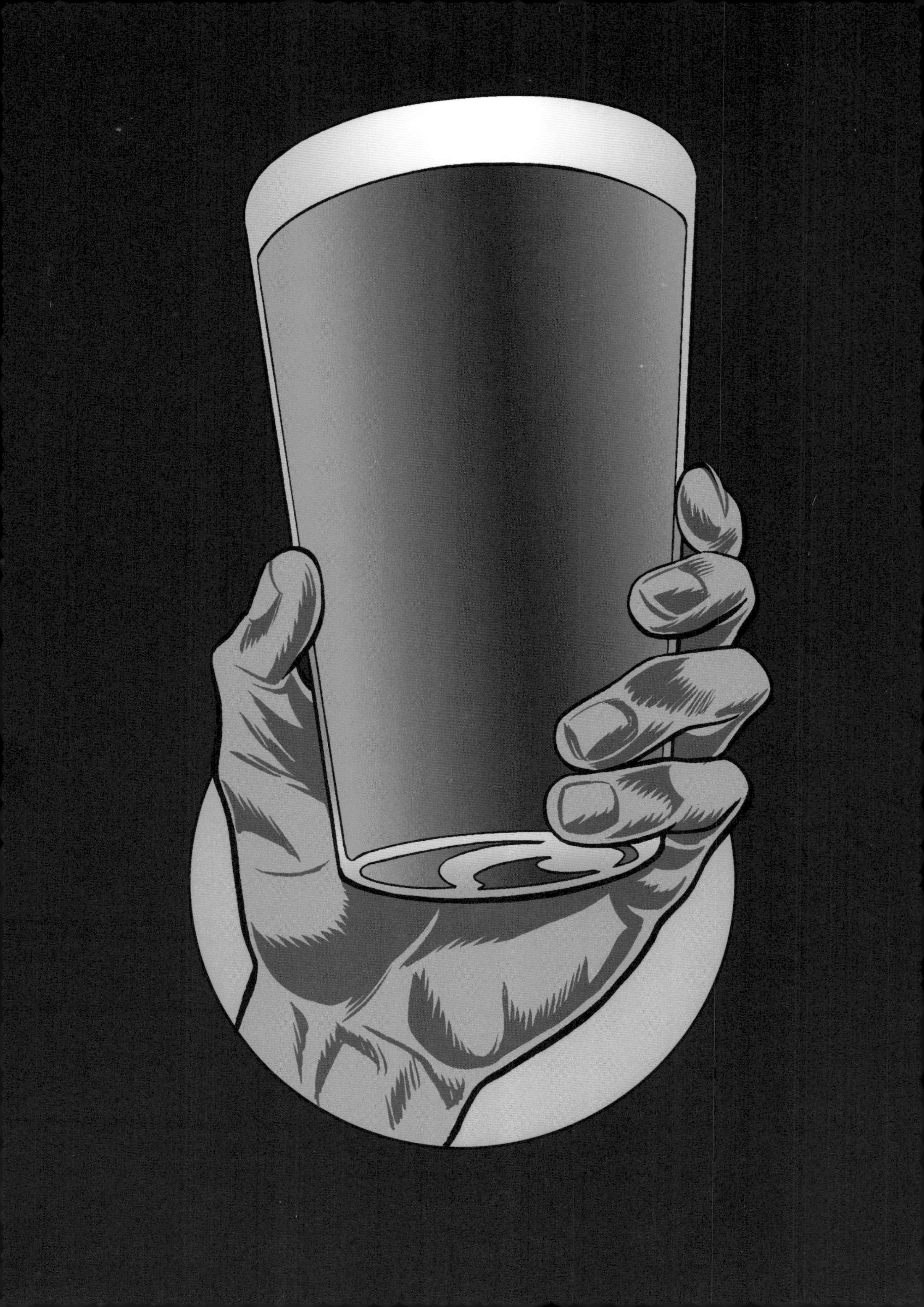

THE
COMIC BOOK STORY OF
BEER

The World's Favorite Beverage
from 7000 BC to Today's
Craft Brewing Revolution

Jonathan Hennessey and Mike Smith

Art by Aaron McConnell
Lettering by Tom Orzechowski

TEN SPEED PRESS
Berkeley

INTRODUCTION **The World's Favorite Beverage** 1

CHAPTER ONE **Beer in the Ancient World** 11

CHAPTER TWO **The Brewing Process** 33

CHAPTER THREE **Dark Ages and Medieval Beer** 50
Meet the Beer: Lambic 60
Meet the Beer: Trappist Dubbel 65

CHAPTER FOUR **The Hops Revolution: Beer Becomes a Commodity** 69
Meet the Beer: Bock 83

CHAPTER FIVE **Empire and Industry: Beer Goes Big** 85
Meet the Beer: Porter 94
Meet the Beer: India Pale Ale 97

CHAPTER SIX **Science and Politics Transform Beer—But for the Better?** 100
Meet the Beer: Pilsner 108

CHAPTER SEVEN **Prohibition and Homogenization Blues: Beer Goes Stale** 118
Meet the Beer: American Lager 135

CHAPTER EIGHT **Drinking on the Shoulders of Giants: Beer Today** 138
Meet the Beer: American Pale Ale 146
Meet the Beer: Belgian Wit 157

Acknowledgments 171

Index 172

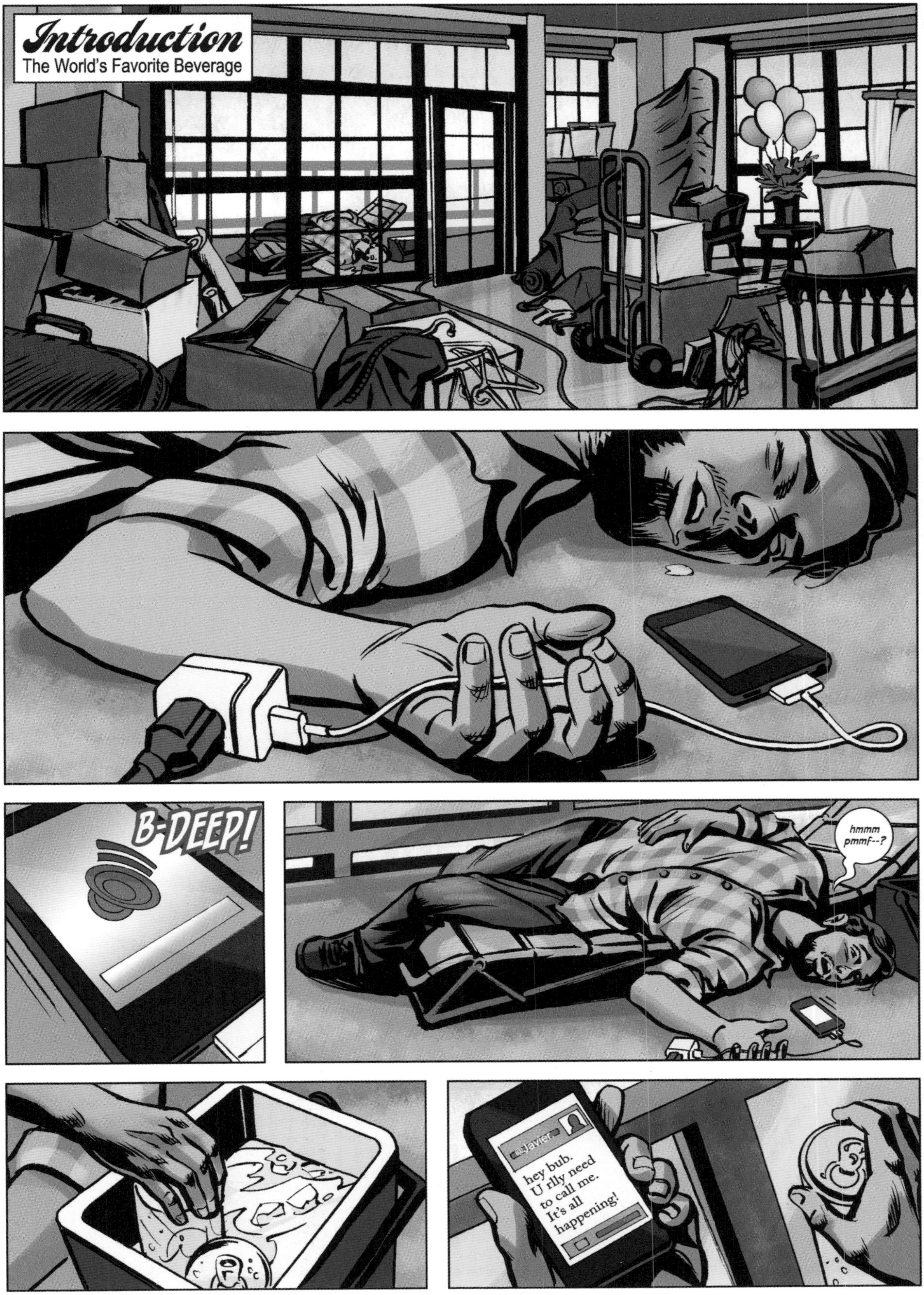
Introduction
The World's Favorite Beverage
B-DEEP!
hmmm pmmf--?
@Javier
hey bub. U rlly need to call me. It's all happening!

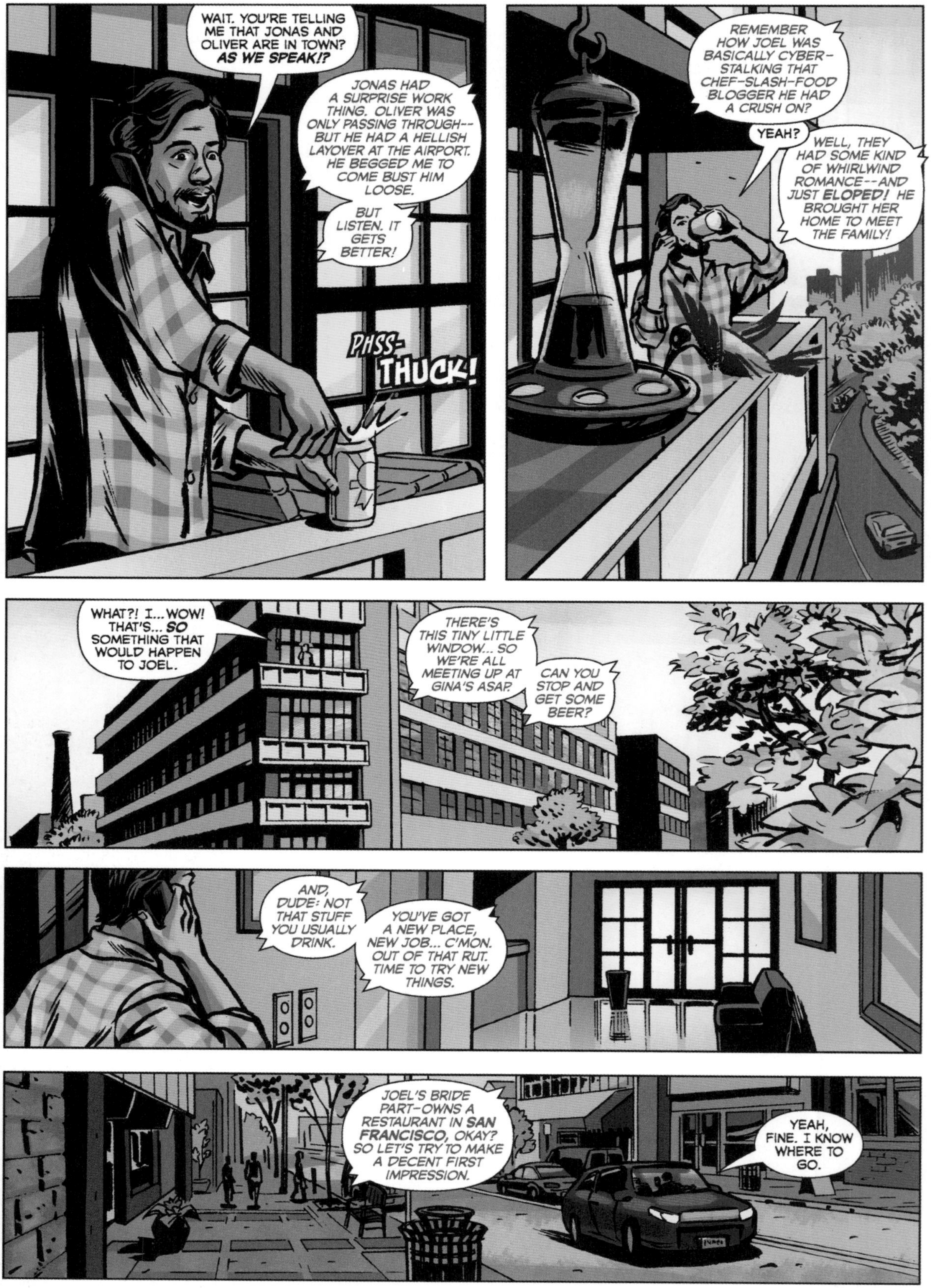
WAIT. YOU'RE TELLING ME THAT JONAS AND OLIVER ARE IN TOWN? AS WE SPEAK!?
JONAS HAD A SURPRISE WORK THING. OLIVER WAS ONLY PASSING THROUGH--BUT HE HAD A HELLISH LAYOVER AT THE AIRPORT. HE BEGGED ME TO COME BUST HIM LOOSE.
BUT LISTEN. IT GETS BETTER!
PHSS-THUCK!
REMEMBER HOW JOEL WAS BASICALLY CYBER-STALKING THAT CHEF-SLASH-FOOD BLOGGER HE HAD A CRUSH ON?
YEAH?
WELL, THEY HAD SOME KIND OF WHIRLWIND ROMANCE--AND JUST ELOPED! HE BROUGHT HER HOME TO MEET THE FAMILY!
WHAT?! I...WOW! THAT'S... SO SOMETHING THAT WOULD HAPPEN TO JOEL.
THERE'S THIS TINY LITTLE WINDOW... SO WE'RE ALL MEETING UP AT GINA'S ASAP.
CAN YOU STOP AND GET SOME BEER?
AND, DUDE: NOT THAT STUFF YOU USUALLY DRINK.
YOU'VE GOT A NEW PLACE, NEW JOB... C'MON. OUT OF THAT RUT. TIME TO TRY NEW THINGS.
JOEL'S BRIDE PART-OWNS A RESTAURANT IN SAN FRANCISCO, OKAY? SO LET'S TRY TO MAKE A DECENT FIRST IMPRESSION.
YEAH, FINE. I KNOW WHERE TO GO.

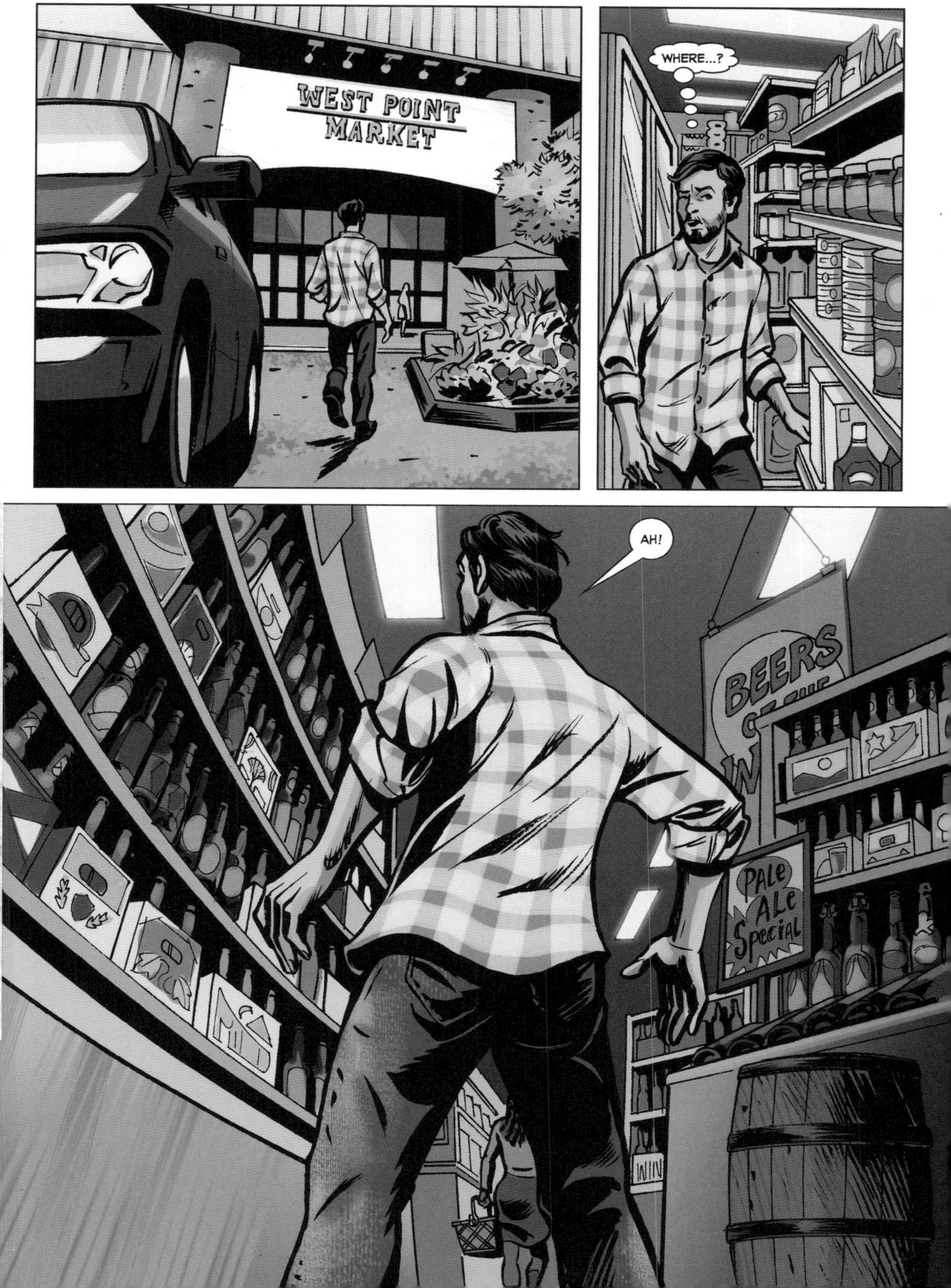
WEST POINT MARKET
WHERE...?
AH!
BEERS
Pale Ale Special

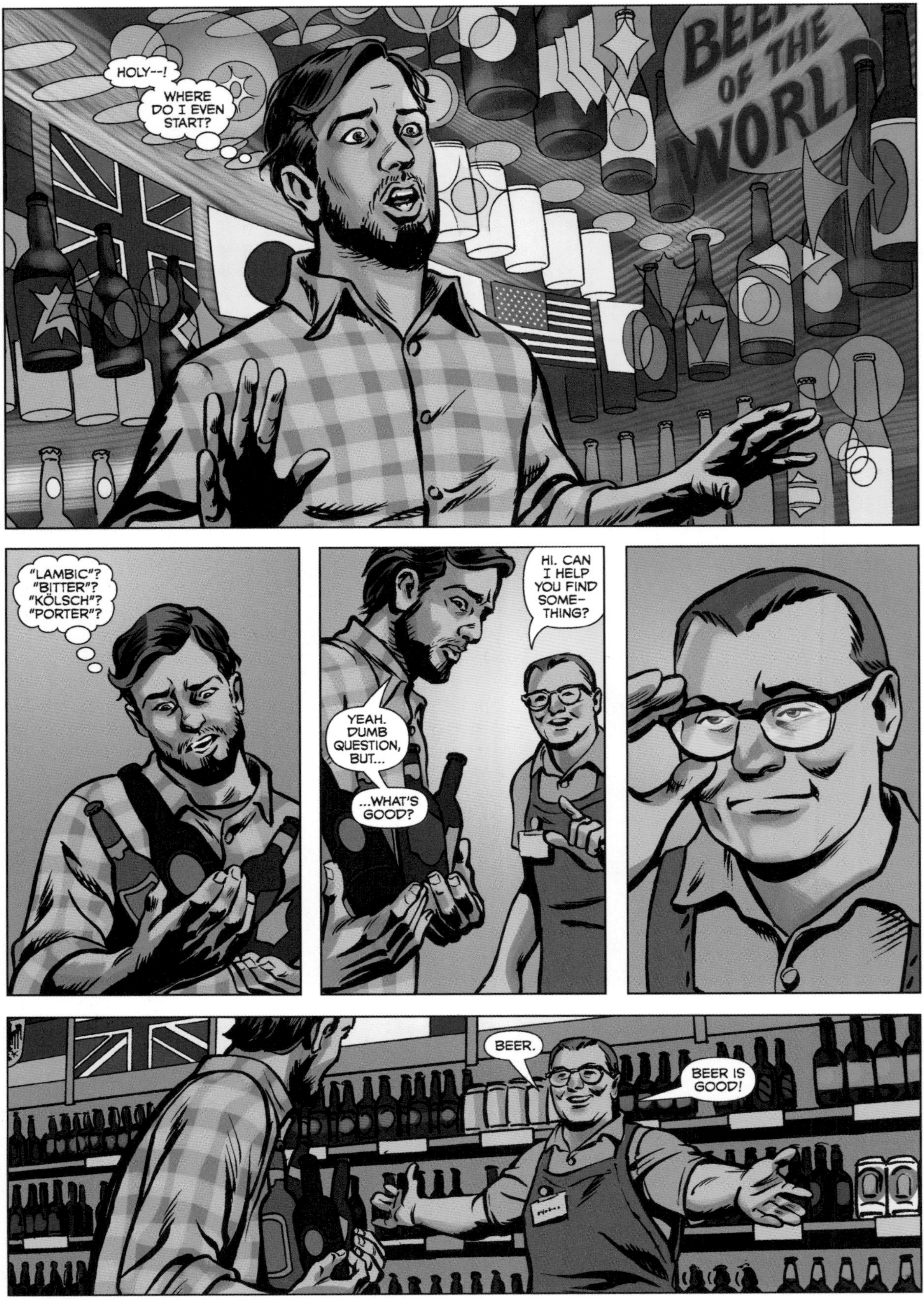
HOLY--!
WHERE DO I EVEN START?
"LAMBIC"? "BITTER"? "KÖLSCH"? "PORTER"?
HI. CAN I HELP YOU FIND SOME-THING?
YEAH. DUMB QUESTION, BUT...
...WHAT'S GOOD?
BEER.
BEER IS GOOD!

NO DRINK INSPIRES PASSION LIKE BEER.

AROUND THE GLOBE, PEOPLE CONSUME MORE BEER THAN COFFEE, WINE, AND EVEN COCA-COLA.

BEER IS THE QUINTESSENTIAL BEVERAGE.

IT LIKELY GETS ITS NAME FROM *BIBERE*, THE ANCIENT LATIN WORD THAT MEANS "TO DRINK."

SO BEER IS **SYNONYMOUS** WITH THE ACT OF **DRINKING** ITSELF!

BIBERE

SOME MIGHT DISMISS BEER AS NOTHING MORE THAN A THROWAWAY CONSUMER ITEM.

BUT MAKE NO MISTAKE...

BEER IS NOT ONLY UBIQUITOUS.

...IT IS ANCIENT.

This tablet records beer rations given to temple workers. Ancient Sumeria: 3300-3100 BC.

AND IT HAS PLAYED A FAR MORE VITAL ROLE IN THE STORY OF HUMANITY THAN MOST PEOPLE REALIZE.

NOWADAYS, WE TEND TO THINK OF BEER AS A RECREATIONAL DRINK...

...SOMETHING TO ACCOMPANY FOOD.

BUT FOR UNTOLD CENTURIES BEER *WAS* FOOD.

THINK ABOUT IT: GRAIN, YEAST, WATER...

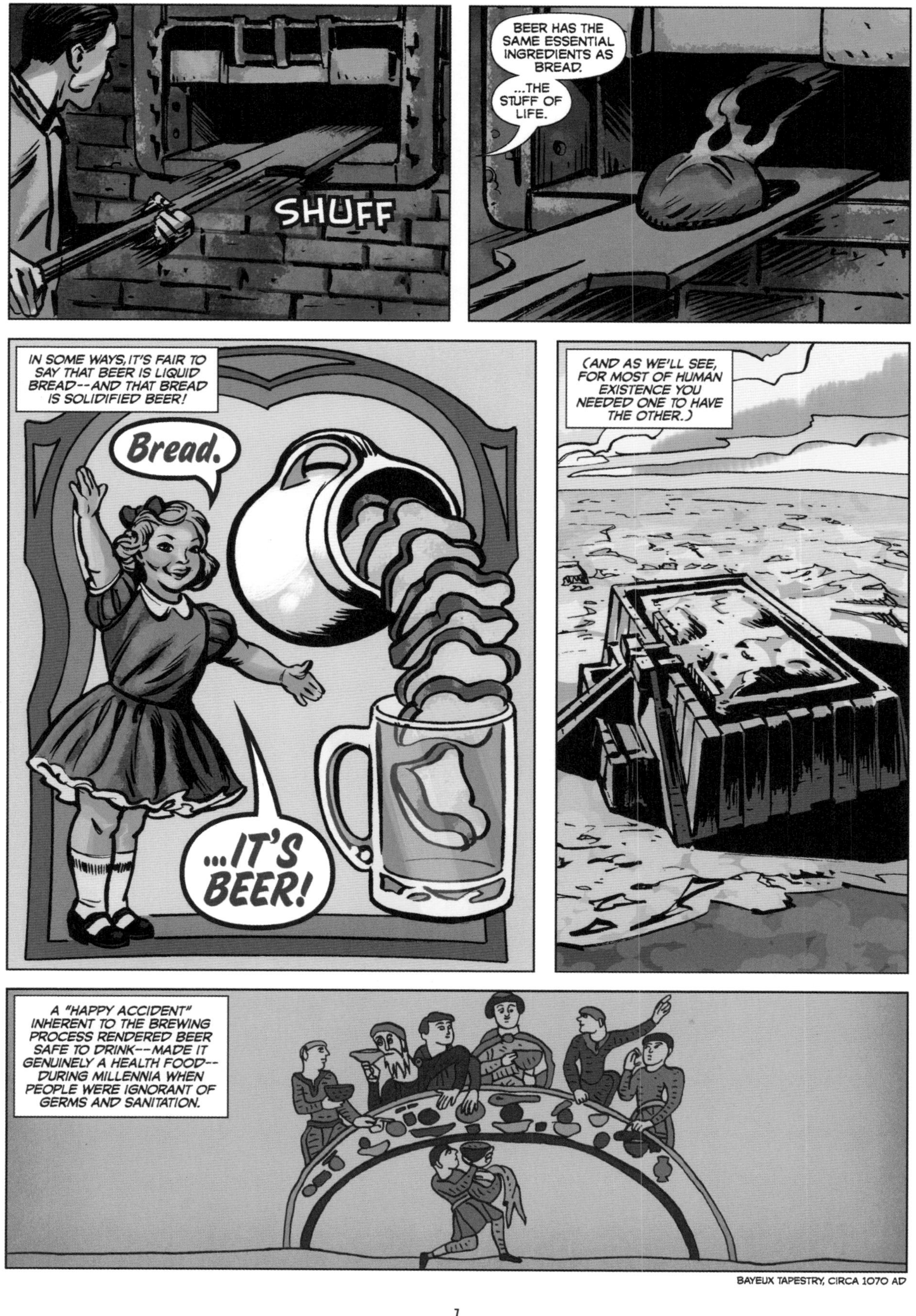
SHUFF
BEER HAS THE SAME ESSENTIAL INGREDIENTS AS BREAD.
...THE STUFF OF LIFE.
IN SOME WAYS, IT'S FAIR TO SAY THAT BEER IS LIQUID BREAD--AND THAT BREAD IS SOLIDIFIED BEER!
Bread.
...IT'S BEER!
(AND AS WE'LL SEE, FOR MOST OF HUMAN EXISTENCE YOU NEEDED ONE TO HAVE THE OTHER.)
A "HAPPY ACCIDENT" INHERENT TO THE BREWING PROCESS RENDERED BEER SAFE TO DRINK--MADE IT GENUINELY A HEALTH FOOD--DURING MILLENNIA WHEN PEOPLE WERE IGNORANT OF GERMS AND SANITATION.

BAYEUX TAPESTRY, CIRCA 1070 AD

BEER HAS LITERALLY HELPED HUMANITY TO SURVIVE. ...TO FLOURISH.

MANY THINGS INSPIRE OUR LOVE AFFAIR WITH THIS DRINK.

GERMAN-JEWISH PAINTER MAX LIEBERMANN'S *MUNICH BEER GARDEN*, 1884.

UNDENIABLY, ONE OF THEM IS THE FACT THAT BEER IS A SUPREME SOCIAL LUBRICANT.

ALE... PROVOKES MEN TO [SINGING] AND MIRTH...

IT WILL SET A BASHFULL SUITER A [WOOING...]

IT WILL PUT COURAGE INTO A COWARD, AND MAKE HIM SWAGGER AND FIGHT...

IT WILL MAKE THE PHILOSOPHER TALKE PROFOUNDLY, THE SCHOLLER LEARNEDLY, AND THE LAWYER ACUTE AND FEELINGLY...

ENGLISH POET JOHN TAYLOR, 1637.

AND SO WE HAVE GRANTED IT A REVERENTIAL STATUS.

WE HAVE MADE IT PART OF OUR MOST IMPORTANT RITUALS.

A *SANGOMA'S* HEALING RITUAL, ACCOMPANIED BY TRADITIONAL ZULU SORGHUM BEER, OR *UTSHWALA*--SOUTH AFRICA.

BEER HAS ANOINTED WEDDINGS AND BIRTHS.

IT HAS HELPED BROKER PEACE BETWEEN WARRING FACTIONS.

IT HAS AFFIRMED FRIENDSHIPS AND SEALED CONTRACTS.

IT HAS INSPIRED ARTISTS.

PICASSO

BASS

PABLO PICASSO'S *PIPE AND A BOTTLE OF BASS,* 1913–1914.

EN EL CIELO NO HAY CERVEZA QUE BEBER POR ESO ANDO TOMANDO NOCHE Y DÍA...

IT HAS BEEN A CAPTIVATING MUSE FOR WRITERS OF POETRY, PROSE, AND SONG.

THIS HEADY CONCOCTION OF FERMENTED GRAIN AND WATER HAS CHANGED US.

AND WE HAVE CHANGED IT.

OUR APPRECIATION OF BEER CAN ONLY DEEPEN BY LEARNING MORE ABOUT IT--MORE ABOUT ITS STORY.

THAT STORY, MOREOVER, IS OUR STORY.

BEER HAS ALWAYS BEEN THE DRINK OF THE PEOPLE.

IT HAS SHAPED AND BEEN SHAPED BY EACH OF THE MANY CULTURES THAT HOLD IT DEAR.

BEER REFLECTS WHAT MAKES US GREAT...

...AS WELL AS WHAT MAKES US, WELL...

...FLAWED.

BEER'S STORY ENCOMPASSES LOVE, WAR, FAMILY, FANATICISM, SCIENCE, SUPERSTITION, THEFT, RIVALRY, FREEDOM, TYRANNY...

...THE COLDEST AND MOST RATIONAL OF INTELLECT, AND THE MERRIEST OF DEBAUCHERY.

EVEN THOUGH WE CAN'T PIN DOWN THE EXACT DATE, THE BEST SCIENTIFIC EVIDENCE PROVES THAT BEER'S STORY BEGAN AT LEAST 9,000 YEARS AGO.

Chapter One
BEER IN THE ANCIENT WORLD

JIAHU.

...AN EARLY STONE AGE SITE IN THE YELLOW RIVER BASIN OF CHINA.

CLAY JARS EXCAVATED HERE WERE FOUND TO CONTAIN A BEER-LIKE DRINK MADE FROM FERMENTED RICE, HONEY, AND FRUIT.

CHATEAU JIAHU, A RE-CREATION OF THIS STONE-AGE BEER, WON A GOLD MEDAL* AT THE 2009 GREAT AMERICAN BEER FESTIVAL.

Dogfish Head

CHATEAU JIAHU

*IN THE "SPECIALTY BEER" CATEGORY.

RADIOCARBON ANALYSIS DATES THESE DRINKING JARS FROM AS EARLY AS 7000 BC.

Bone flute -
    a miracle in the history of Chinese music
Early Peiligang Culture, Neolithic Age (about 8700-8200 years ago)
Excavated at Jiahu village, Wuyang county

THIS MORE THAN 9,000-YEAR-OLD "BEER" WAS DISCOVERED IN THE COMPANY OF RELIGIOUS ITEMS AND SOME OF THE EARLIEST MUSICAL INSTRUMENTS EVER FOUND.

11

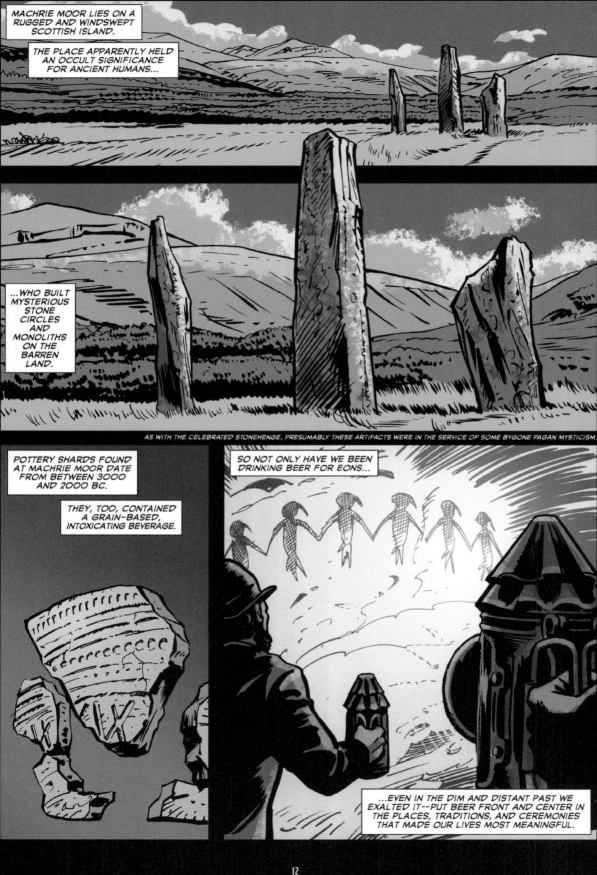

MACHRIE MOOR LIES ON A RUGGED AND WINDSWEPT SCOTTISH ISLAND.

THE PLACE APPARENTLY HELD AN OCCULT SIGNIFICANCE FOR ANCIENT HUMANS...

...WHO BUILT MYSTERIOUS STONE CIRCLES AND MONOLITHS ON THE BARREN LAND.

AS WITH THE CELEBRATED STONEHENGE, PRESUMABLY THESE ARTIFACTS WERE IN THE SERVICE OF SOME BYGONE PAGAN MYSTICISM.

POTTERY SHARDS FOUND AT MACHRIE MOOR DATE FROM BETWEEN 3000 AND 2000 BC.

THEY, TOO, CONTAINED A GRAIN-BASED, INTOXICATING BEVERAGE.

SO NOT ONLY HAVE WE BEEN DRINKING BEER FOR EONS...

...EVEN IN THE DIM AND DISTANT PAST WE EXALTED IT--PUT BEER FRONT AND CENTER IN THE PLACES, TRADITIONS, AND CEREMONIES THAT MADE OUR LIVES MOST MEANINGFUL.

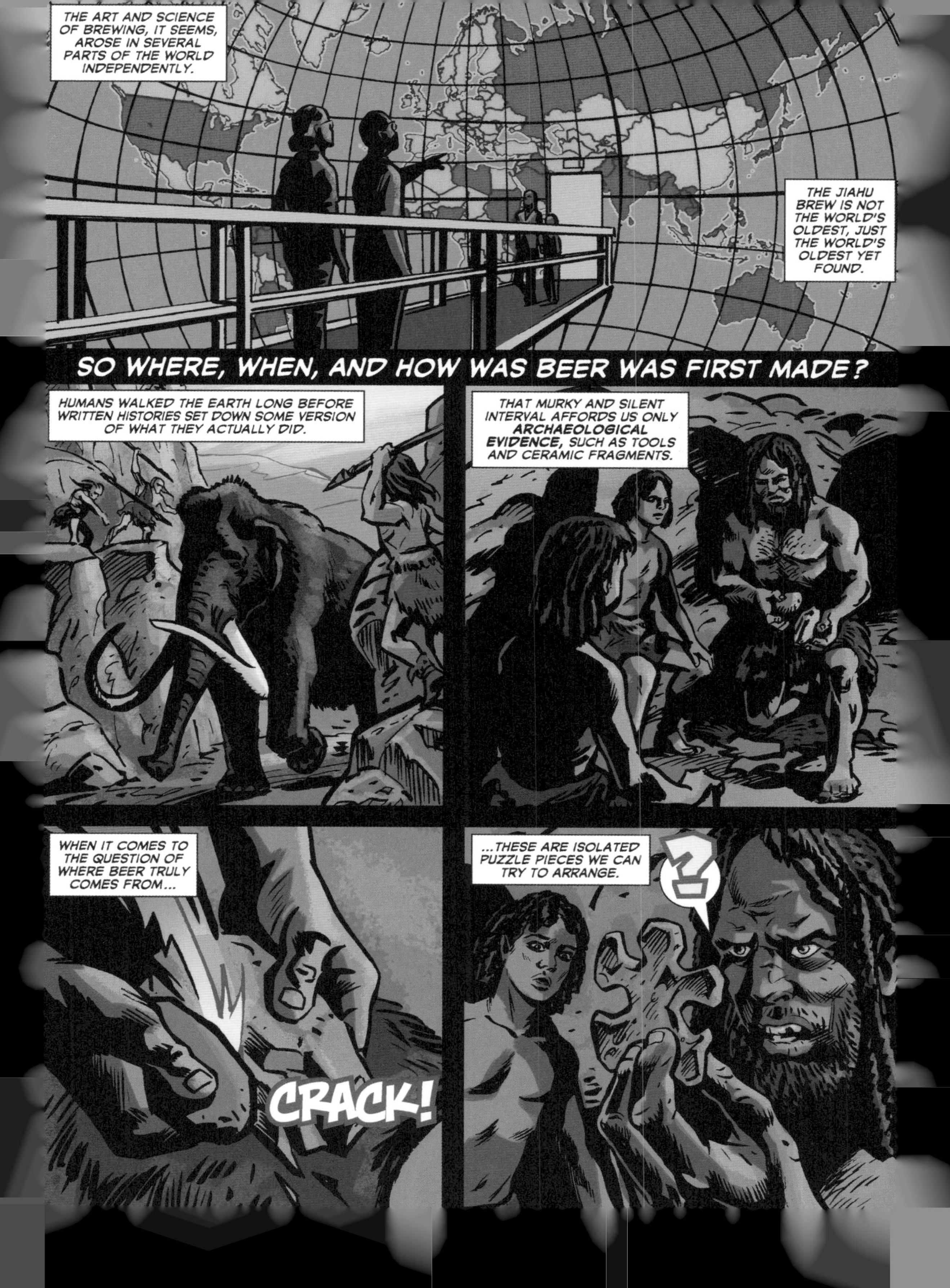
THE ART AND SCIENCE OF BREWING, IT SEEMS, AROSE IN SEVERAL PARTS OF THE WORLD INDEPENDENTLY.
THE JIAHU BREW IS NOT THE WORLD'S OLDEST, JUST THE WORLD'S OLDEST YET FOUND.
SO WHERE, WHEN, AND HOW WAS BEER WAS FIRST MADE?
HUMANS WALKED THE EARTH LONG BEFORE WRITTEN HISTORIES SET DOWN SOME VERSION OF WHAT THEY ACTUALLY DID.
THAT MURKY AND SILENT INTERVAL AFFORDS US ONLY ARCHAEOLOGICAL EVIDENCE, SUCH AS TOOLS AND CERAMIC FRAGMENTS.
WHEN IT COMES TO THE QUESTION OF WHERE BEER TRULY COMES FROM...
CRACK!
...THESE ARE ISOLATED PUZZLE PIECES WE CAN TRY TO ARRANGE.
?

THESE PUZZLE PIECES, HOWEVER, ARE AS PROBLEMATIC AS THEY ARE INTRIGUING. WHY?

POTTERY MAY PRESERVE TRACES OF ITS LIQUID CONTENTS VERY WELL...

...AND LEAVE ENCOURAGING CLUES FOR TODAY'S SCIENTISTS.

BUT POTTERY ITSELF IS A CONSIDERABLY ADVANCED TECHNOLOGY...

...INITIALLY SURFACING IN CHINA ABOUT 20,000 YEARS AGO.

THE VERY FIRST BEER WAS PROBABLY BREWED IN AN ORGANIC CONTAINER LIKE AN ANIMAL SKIN OR WOODEN VESSEL. MATERIALS LIKE THIS WOULD HAVE DECAYED LONG BEFORE ARCHAEOLOGISTS COULD DISCOVER THEM, THEREBY LEAVING BEHIND NO TRACE IN THE ARCHAEOLOGICAL RECORD.

SO WE DON'T KNOW--WE PROBABLY CAN'T KNOW--THE FULL DETAILS OF BEER'S GENESIS.

BUT WE DO KNOW THAT, AT SOME POINT THIS SIDE OF 9000 BC, HUMAN CIVILIZATION TOOK A QUANTUM LEAP FORWARD WITH THE INVENTION OF AGRICULTURE.

AGRICULTURE LED TO THE FIRST PERMANENT VILLAGES AND TOWNS-- OR AT LEAST MADE PREEXISTING SETTLEMENTS MORE SECURE AND SOPHISTICATED. THESE COMMUNITIES BECAME LAUNCHING PADS FOR BOOMS IN POPULATION, CULTURE, AND TECHNOLOGY.

WITH MORE FIXED AND RELIABLE SOURCES OF FOOD, PEOPLE--ONCE NOMADIC WANDERERS-- COULD STAY PUT FOR A CHANGE.

THIS GRANTED THEM THE CHANCE TO SPECIALIZE IN SKILLS OTHER THAN BASIC SURVIVAL.

WITHOUT THE DEVELOPMENT OF AGRICULTURE, CIVILIZATION...

...THE BOOK IN YOUR HAND, THE LIGHT SHINING ON IT....

CONCEIVABLY EVEN WRITTEN LANGUAGE ITSELF MIGHT NEVER HAVE DEVELOPED.

WOULD WE EVEN HAVE AGRICULTURE--AND THE CIVILIZATION IT MADE POSSIBLE-- IF NOT FOR BEER?

AND SOME SCHOLARS POSE A PROVOCATIVE QUESTION:

THE STONE AGE SETTLEMENT OF ÇATALHÖYÜK, NEAR MODERN KONYA, TURKEY.

15

THRONGS OF STONE AGE HUMANS ABANDONED THEIR HUNTER-GATHERER LIFESTYLE AND LEARNED TO GROW CROPS.

DID HUNGER DRIVE THEM TO THIS?

OR WAS IT THIRST?

IT MAY VERY WELL BE THAT HUMANKIND SO CLAMOROUSLY DESIRED BEER THAT AGRICULTURE WAS, AT FIRST, ALL ABOUT BREWING.

HERE'S HOW THAT ARGUMENT GOES:

INGREDIENTS: HULLED BARLEY, EMMER WHEAT, SEDGE SEEDS, EINKORN WHEAT, ASSORTED TUBERS.

LONG BEFORE HUMANS FIGURED OUT HOW, BY THEIR TOIL, TO COAX CROPS OUT OF THE GROUND...

...THEY STILL HAD WAYS TO EAT MANY CEREALS.

PRODUCT OF: (MODERN-DAY) SYRIA, IRAN, IRAQ, JORDAN, EGYPT, PALESTINE, ISRAEL...

UNDOMESTICATED, WILD VERSIONS OF CEREAL GRAINS WERE COMMON IN THE NEAR EAST.

PEOPLE SCAVENGED FOR THIS STURDY SOURCE OF CALORIES.

AND HOW THEY ATE THESE GRAINS PROBABLY LED TO THE CREATION OF THE VERY FIRST BEER...

THE ACCIDENTAL CREATION OF THE VERY FIRST BEER, THAT IS!

IN ALL LIKELIHOOD, WHEN PREHISTORIC PEOPLE GATHERED WILD BARLEY OR WHEAT, THEY MADE NOT BREAD BUT GRUEL...

...GRAIN STEEPED IN AND SOFTENED BY WATER.

IN THE NEAR EAST'S HOT SUN, THIS GRAIN MIGHT SOON GERMINATE.

GRUEL NEGLECTED OR POORLY STORED MAY THEN HAVE ATTRACTED AIRBORNE YEASTS.

THIS WOULD SET FERMENTATION IN MOTION.

(FOR MUCH MORE ABOUT ALL THIS, SEE CHAPTER TWO.)

WITH FERMENTATION SET IN MOTION, THE GRUEL WOULD BECOME SWEET--AND DEVELOP A LOW ALCOHOLIC CONTENT.

THIS BLAND FOOD-STUFF WOULD HAVE BEEN TRANSFORMED INTO SOMETHING AMAZING.

THE INTOXICATING EFFECT OF THE "BEER"--ITS IMPACT ON THE HUMAN STATE OF MIND-- WAS WONDROUS AND ENTHRALLING.

MAGIC.

THIS ARCHAIC "BEER" WOULD HAVE BEEN PRIZED-- EXTREMELY DESIRABLE.

IN FACT, IT WOULD HAVE BEEN DEEMED SO EXTRAORDINARY THAT IT'S EASY TO IMAGINE IT QUICKLY BEING GIVEN A SPIRITUAL SIGNIFICANCE OR OTHER- WISE BEING USHERED INTO THE CULTURE AND RITUALS OF THE GROUP.

WHAT'S MORE, ALTHOUGH THEY WOULDN'T HAVE REALIZED IT, THOSE EARLY DRINKERS OF BEER WERE BENEFITING FROM ALL KINDS OF NUTRITIONAL BONUSES. FERMENTED, THE GRAIN WOULD HAVE BECOME RICH IN B VITAMINS, LYSINE, AND PHYTATES. THE VITAMINS AND MINERALS WOULD INJECT THE BEER DRINKERS, AND BY EXTENSION THEIR OFFSPRING, WITH CONSIDERABLE HEALTH ADVANTAGES.

ALTHOUGH THESE DIETARY BENEFITS COME MOSTLY

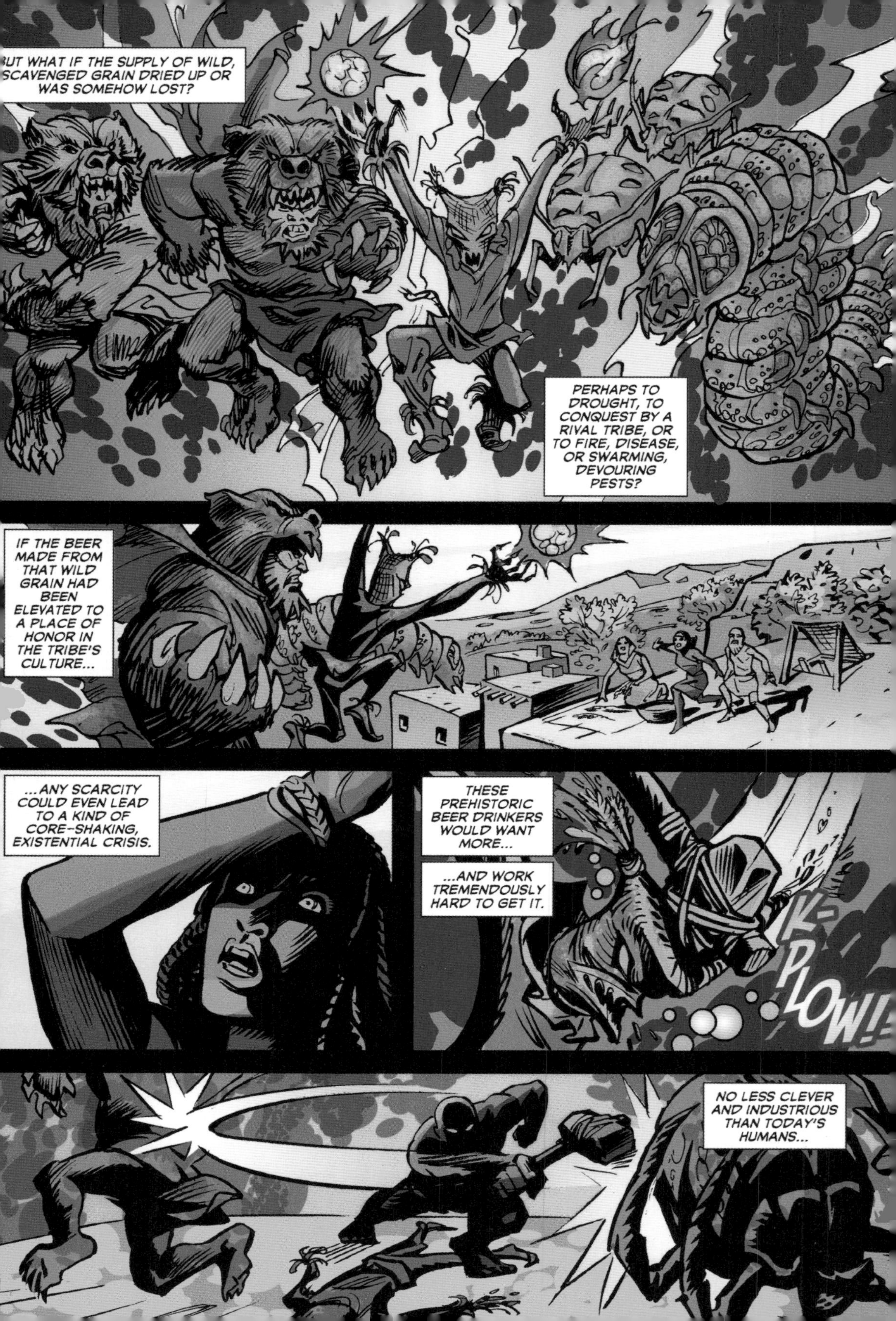
BUT WHAT IF THE SUPPLY OF WILD, SCAVENGED GRAIN DRIED UP OR WAS SOMEHOW LOST?
PERHAPS TO DROUGHT, TO CONQUEST BY A RIVAL TRIBE, OR TO FIRE, DISEASE, OR SWARMING, DEVOURING PESTS?
IF THE BEER MADE FROM THAT WILD GRAIN HAD BEEN ELEVATED TO A PLACE OF HONOR IN THE TRIBE'S CULTURE...
...ANY SCARCITY COULD EVEN LEAD TO A KIND OF CORE-SHAKING, EXISTENTIAL CRISIS.
THESE PREHISTORIC BEER DRINKERS WOULD WANT MORE...
...AND WORK TREMENDOUSLY HARD TO GET IT.
K-PLOW!!
NO LESS CLEVER AND INDUSTRIOUS THAN TODAY'S HUMANS...

...PRIMEVAL PEOPLE WOULD HAVE FUNNELED A GREAT DEAL OF INGENUITY TOWARD THIS GOAL.

THE SPECULATION GOES THAT THEY WOULD HAVE EXPERIMENTED WITH ANY STRANDS OF WILD GRAIN THEY COULD FIND--AND ACHIEVED THE SKILL TO GROW BARLEY AND WHEAT BY TRIAL AND ERROR.

YET PIONEER FARMERS, SCARCELY KNOWING WHAT THEY WERE DOING, AND LACKING THE BEST TOOLS AND PRACTICES FOR THE JOB...

...WOULD HAVE PRODUCED VERY LITTLE.

THEY COULD HARDLY HAVE HARVESTED ENOUGH--AT LEAST AT FIRST--TO ACTUALLY FEED AND SUSTAIN A SUBSTANTIAL NUMBER OF PEOPLE.

AND SO--THE BACKBREAKING, FRUSTRATING WORK OF FARMING...

...WHY WOULD THEY HAVE BOTHERED WITH IT AT ALL?

AGRICULTURE MAY ONLY HAVE BEEN WORTH ALL THE EFFORT IF IT PAID OFF IN THIS FLAVORFUL, MYSTICAL, AND SOCIALLY IMPORTANT BEVERAGE.

AS TWO NOTED PROPONENTS OF THIS "BEER THEORY" OF AGRICULTURE PRAGMATICALLY PUT IT, "GIVEN A CHOICE OF GRUEL, BREAD, OR BREW, WHICH WOULD YOU RATHER HAVE?"

THERE ARE, HOWEVER, WORTHY ARGUMENTS AGAINST THE "BEER THEORY" OF AGRICULTURE. FOR EXAMPLE, WE KNOW IT WOULD HAVE BEEN EXTREMELY DIFFICULT TO HEAT AND STORE FERMENTING GRAIN WITHOUT THE CERAMIC VESSELS THAT ONLY LATER ADVANCES WOULD BRING.

LIKE A LANDSCAPE VEILED BY A SANDSTORM, THE DISTANT PAST IS OFTEN OBSCURE TO US.

ARCHAEOLOGICAL EVIDENCE OF THE FIRST BEER IS PROBABLY AN UNRECOVERABLE HOLY GRAIL.

BUT AS WE TREK FORWARD THROUGH THE WINDS OF TIME...

...DOCUMENTARY EVIDENCE ENTERS AND UNCLOUDS THE PICTURE.

THE ANCIENTS WROTE ABOUT BEER AND CREATED ART INSPIRED BY IT.

WATER AND GRAIN COMBINING TO INDUCE AN ALTERED STATE, EVEN ECSTASY? WE KNOW IT SEEMED A MIRACLE TO PEOPLE OF THE ANCIENT WORLD--THE WORK OF THE GODS.

IN ANCIENT SUMERIA, A BEWITCHING DIVINE BEING WAS BELIEVED TO BE RESPONSIBLE FOR THIS TRANSFORMATION:

NINKASI

HER NAME MEANS "YOU WHO FILL MY MOUTH SO FULL." AND THANKS TO HER WORSHIPPERS, TODAY WE HAVE A KEEN INSIGHT ON HOW BEER WAS MADE IN THAT ERA.

ARCHAEOLOGISTS WORKING IN PRESENT-DAY IRAQ DISCOVERED THE "HYMN TO NINKASI" CARVED IN CLAY TABLETS. THOUGH DATING FROM 1800 BC, THE HYMN IS LIKELY FAR OLDER.

BESIDES SINGING THE BREWING GODDESS'S PRAISES, THE HYMN INTRIGUINGLY GOES MUCH FURTHER. ENCODED IN ITS VERSES IS AN ACTUAL MILLENNIA-OLD RECIPE FOR BEER!

"NINKASI, YOU ARE THE ONE WHO HANDLES THE DOUGH [AND] WITH A BIG SHOVEL, MIXING IN A PIT, THE BAPPIR WITH [DATE] HONEY"

THIS PARTICULAR LINE FROM THE HYMN IS CRITICAL.

SUMERIAN **BAPPIR** WAS A TYPE BAKED BARLEY FLOUR BREAD. THIS BREAD WAS THEN SOAKED WITH WATER IN A JAR, COMBINED WITH OTHER INGREDIENTS, AND ALLOWED TO FERMENT.

THIS IS THE METHOD BY WHICH BEER MAY HAVE BEEN PRODUCED FOR THOUSANDS OF YEARS...

...ESSENTIALLY BY THROWING BREAD INTO WATER!

THIS ONCE STATE-OF-THE-ART BREWING PRACTICE FELL OUT OF FAVOR LONG AGO. BUT KVASS, A TYPE OF FERMENTED DRINK POPULAR IN RUSSIA AND EASTERN EUROPE, IS STILL MADE BY SOAKING RYE BREAD IN WATER.

A PASSAGE IN THE HEBREW SCRIPTURE QOHELETH (ECCLESIASTES), FROM THE THIRD CENTURY BC, CAN EVEN BE INTER-PRETED AS TESTAMENT TO THIS PERENNIAL MODE OF BREWING:

THROW YOUR BREAD UPON THE FACE OF THE WATER, BECAUSE IN MANY DAYS YOU WILL ACQUIRE [BEER].

THE GREAT ADVANTAGE OF USING BREAD AS A KEY INGREDIENT FOR BEER IS THAT BEER CAN BE STORED.

BAPPIR WAS SELDOM EATEN AS BREAD. INSTEAD, IT WAS KEPT AS A KIND OF "STARTER"--BOTH TO MAKE BEER AND TO MAKE MORE **BAPPIR**--IN A PROCESS SIMILAR TO THE WAY SOURDOUGH BREAD AND YOGURT ARE STILL MADE TO THIS DAY.

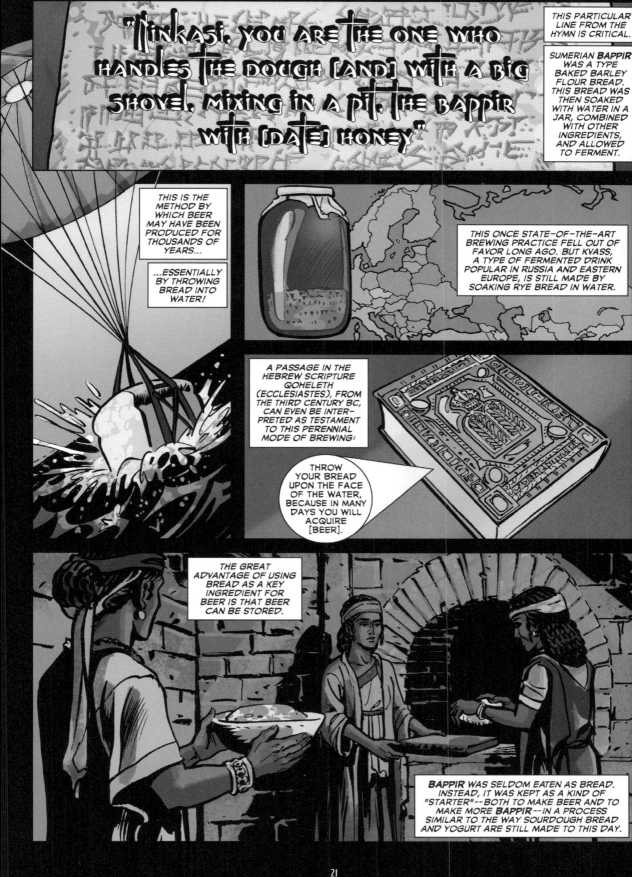

BREAD'S STORAGE ASPECT IS CRUCIAL.

IT HAS TO DO WITH TWO OF THE ALL-TIME DOWNERS ABOUT ANCIENT BEER.

YOU CAN'T FERMENT GRAIN WITHOUT AN ORGANISM LIKE YEAST.

BREWERS BACK THEN COULD NOT HAVE REALIZED IT, BUT THE MICROBES THEY DEPENDED ON WERE EITHER IN THE AIR...

...OR ADHERING TO THE SKINS OF FRUITS THAT BREWERS ADDED FOR FLAVOR.

AND AS SUCH, THOSE MICROBES WERE NOT AVAILABLE YEAR-ROUND.

SO DOWNER NUMBER ONE IS THAT DRINKERS HAD TO COPE WITH THEIR FAVORITE BEVERAGE BEING SEASONAL!

DOWNER NUMBER TWO IS THAT ANCIENT BEER SPOILED QUICKLY.

THINK ABOUT IT: THE ANCIENTS LACKED REFRIGERATION, PASTEURIZATION, CANNING, BOTTLING, AND THE WHOLE HOST OF MODERN NATURAL AND ARTIFICIAL PRESERVATIVES. IF THEY WERE SO BLIND TO THE NUTS AND BOLTS OF MICROBIOLOGY THAT FERMENTATION SEEMED LIKE MAGIC TO THEM, WE CAN BET THEIR BREWING GEAR WAS NEVER STERILIZED.

THE UPSHOT OF ALL THIS IS THAT ANCIENT NEAR EASTERN BEER PROBABLY LASTED A WEEK AT MOST.

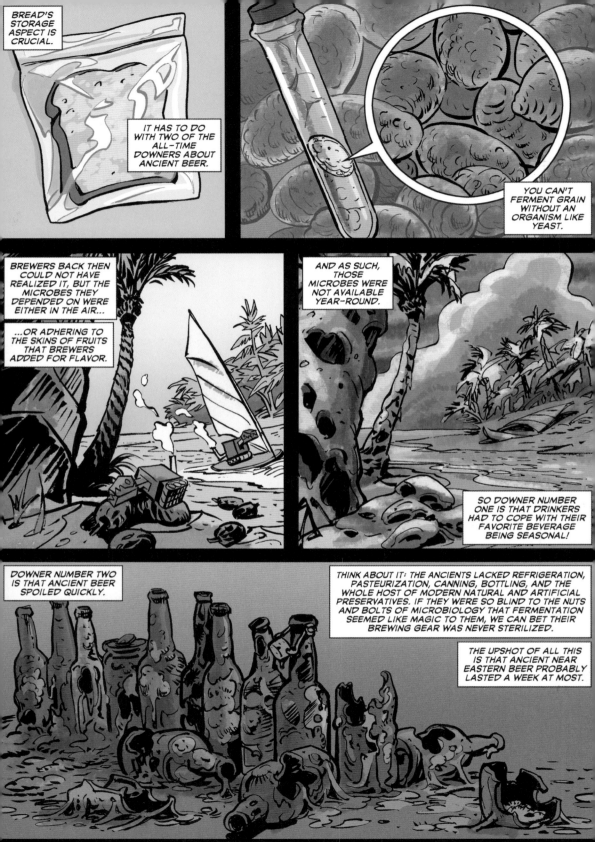

IN SOUTHERN AND EASTERN ASIA, AS WE'VE SEEN IN THE CASE OF JIAHU...

...BEER WAS MADE WITH RICE.

RICE BEER HAS A STRONGER ALCOHOLIC CONTENT.

SINCE ALCOHOL IMPEDES THE GROWTH OF UNWANTED MICROBES, THE ANCIENT BEERS OF CHINA, INDIA, BANGLADESH, AND ENVIRONS KEPT LONGER.

DURING CHINA'S TANG DYNASTY (907-618 BC), BREWERS EVEN LEARNED TO BOIL THEIR BEER AND SEAL THE JARS WITH BEESWAX. THIS PROTOTYPICAL TYPE OF PASTEURIZATION AND "BOTTLING" ALLOWED RICE BEERS TO BE SAFELY DRINKABLE FOR A YEAR OR MORE.

Ninkasi, you are the one who pours out the filtered beer of the collector vat. it is [like] the onrush of [the] Tigris and Euphrates.

IF YOU CHECK OUT NINKASI'S DRINKING VESSEL, ANOTHER PECULIAR THING ABOUT ANCIENT BEER MIGHT STRIKE YOU:

IT WAS DRUNK WITH "STRAWS"-- TUBES MADE OF BONE, CLAY, REEDS, OR, FOR THE WEALTHY, EVEN PRECIOUS METALS.

SUMERIAN BREWS, LIKE THOSE OF SO MUCH OF THE ANCIENT WORLD, WERE THICK AND STEWY. THEY HAD HUSKS OF SOGGY BREAD AND EVEN BITS OF BARLEY HULLS AND STALKS! THE DRINK NEEDED TO BE FILTERED BEFORE ENTERING THE MOUTH.

ANOTHER BENEFIT OF STRAWS HAS BEEN POINTED OUT: THEY WOULD BE NEEDED TO KEEP INSECTS OUT OF A DRINKER'S MOUTH--

ESPECIALLY AT NIGHT!

BEER WAS THE NATIONAL DRINK OF THE ANCIENT EGYPTIANS.

THE EARLIEST VERIFIABLE BREWERY ARCHAEOLOGISTS HAVE DISCOVERED IS AT HIERAKONPOLIS, DATING FROM 3500 TO 3400 BC.

THE ANCIENT EGYPTIANS CREDITED THE GOD OSIRIS WITH BRINGING CIVILIZATION TO THE WORLD.

BREWING WAS PART OF THIS GIFT.

ANOTHER ANCIENT EGYPTIAN MYTH TELLS OF THE FEROCIOUS LION-HEADED GODDESS SEKHMET.

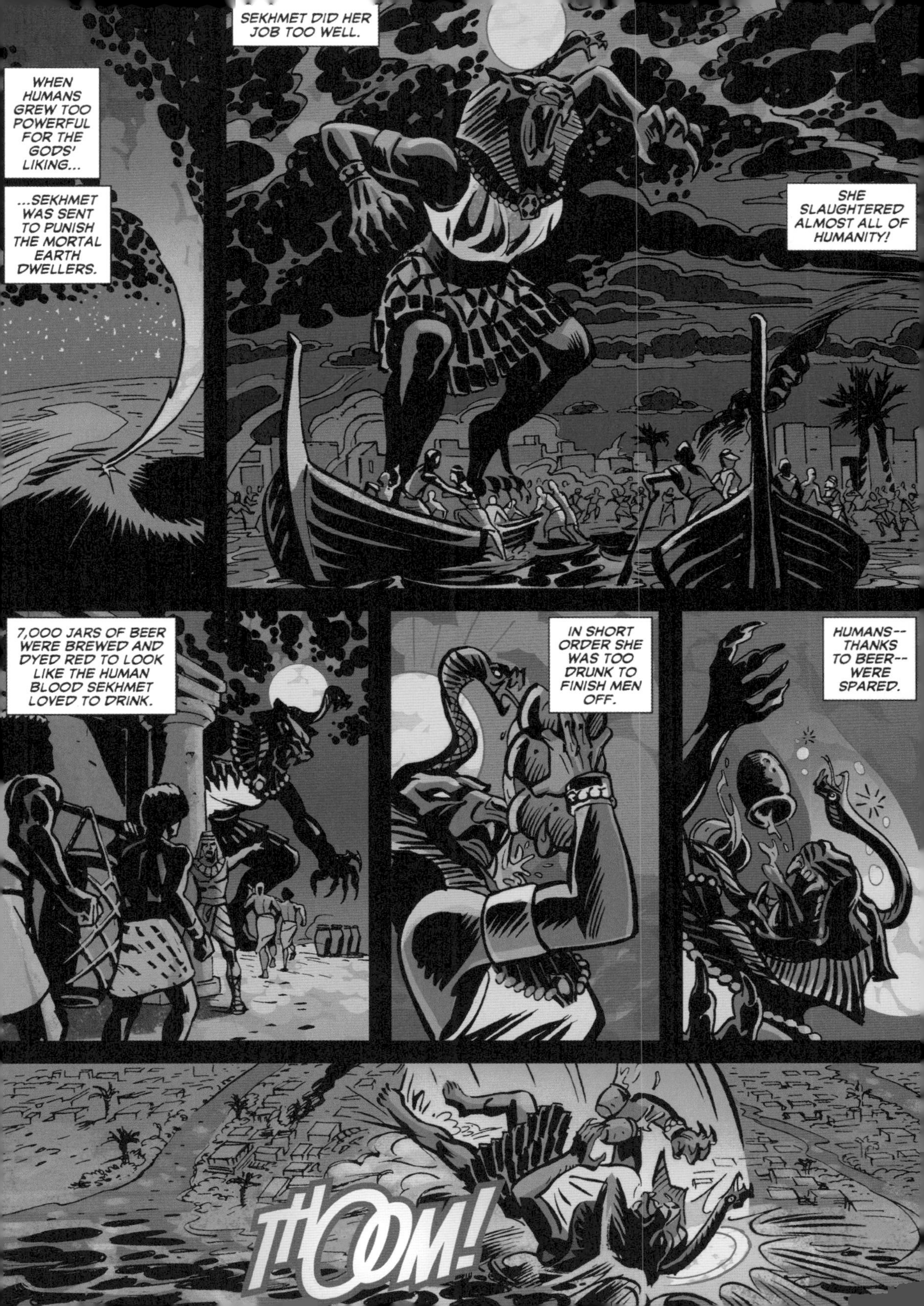
WHEN HUMANS GREW TOO POWERFUL FOR THE GODS' LIKING...
...SEKHMET WAS SENT TO PUNISH THE MORTAL EARTH DWELLERS.
SEKHMET DID HER JOB TOO WELL.
SHE SLAUGHTERED ALMOST ALL OF HUMANITY!
7,000 JARS OF BEER WERE BREWED AND DYED RED TO LOOK LIKE THE HUMAN BLOOD SEKHMET LOVED TO DRINK.
IN SHORT ORDER SHE WAS TOO DRUNK TO FINISH MEN OFF.
HUMANS--THANKS TO BEER--WERE SPARED.
THOOM!

HIEROGLYPHIC RECORDS TELL US THAT THE LABORERS WHO BUILT EGYPT'S PYRAMIDS, LIKE THE GREAT PYRAMID OF GIZA (BUILT AROUND 2500 BC), WERE PAID IN BEER.

THE BEER WAS FOOD, DRINK, AND REWARD ALL IN ONE.

ARCHAEOLOGIST PATRICK McGOVERN ASSERTS THAT IF YOU WERE A PYRAMID-BUILDING PHARAOH, AND YOUR BEER SUPPLY RAN OUT...

...YOU WOULD HAVE HAD A REBELLION ON YOUR HANDS.

IN THE ABSENCE OF BEER, THESE WONDERS OF THE WORLD MIGHT NEVER HAVE BEEN COMPLETED.

THE BABYLONIAN *EPIC OF GILGAMESH* IS ONE OF HUMANITY'S OLDEST WRITTEN STORIES.

ARGUABLY DRAWN FROM EVEN EARLIER STORIES, IT DATES FROM ABOUT 1700 BC.

IN IT, A GODDESS RE-CREATES A THOROUGHLY PRIMORDIAL MAN, LIKE THE BIBLICAL ADAM.

ENKIDU IS PHYSICALLY SUPERHUMAN. YET IN HIS BEHAVIOR, HE IS BEAST-LIKE.

26

A MAN UNLIKE ANY OTHER ROAMS THE PASTURES.

HE IS AS STRONG AS A STAR FROM HEAVEN.

ENKIDU POSED A THREAT TO THE SITTING KING.

THE KING SENT SHAMHAT, A SEDUCTRESS, TO SUBDUE ENKIDU.

THE TWO EUPHORICALLY COPULATED FOR AN ENTIRE WEEK.

THEN...

"They led him to their table, they put bread and beer in front of him. [Shamhat told him]..."

'Go ahead, Enkidu.'
'This is food. We humans eat and drink this.'

"[Enkidu]... drank seven pitchers of beer, his heart grew light, his face glowed, and he sang out with joy."

MAKING LOVE, EATING BREAD, AND DRINKING BEER. THESE ACTS MAKE ENKIDU BECOME "FULLY HUMAN." IN OTHER WORDS, DRINKING BEER WAS EVEN THEN AS THOROUGHLY HUMAN AN ACTIVITY AS THERE CAN BE.

SHAMHAT, NINKASI, SEKHMET...

...NOT FOR NOTHING DO THESE FEMALE FIGURES KEEP TURNING UP IN ANCIENT BEER STORIES.

FOR NEARLY ALL OF BEER'S HISTORY, BREWING AND SERVING BEER HAS BEEN AN ALMOST EXCLUSIVELY FEMALE ENTERPRISE!

BREWING WAS SOMETHING DONE IN THE KITCHEN: TRADITIONALLY THE WOMAN'S DOMAIN.

BEER IS ALSO NOURISHING--LIKE A MOTHER'S CARE, LIKE A MOTHER'S MILK.

AND THIS IS PRECISELY WHY, THE WORLD OVER, BUXOM WOMEN CONTINUE TO BE USED TO MARKET BEER.

Now for the first time in India, from the makers of London Pilsner...London Diet, the Slim Beer.

London Diet

THE HEBREW WORD **SHEKAR**-- RELATED TO THE BABYLONIAN TERM SHIKARU, MEANING "BEER"--MAKES MANY APPEARANCES IN THE BIBLE.

IN THE BOOK OF NUMBERS, YAHWEH TELLS MOSES THAT THE ISRAELITES SHOULD SACRIFICE ABOUT TWO QUARTS OF BEER A DAY TO THEIR GOD:

"In the holy place you shall pour out a drink offering of [beer] to the Lord."

FOR OTHER BIBLICAL MENTIONS OF BEER, SEE PROVERBS 31:6, ISAIAH 5:11, 24:9, AND 28:7, PROVERBS 20:1 AND 31:4, AND ECCLESIASTES 11:1.

YOUR MOTEL ROOM EDITION OF THE BIBLE MAY NOT BE ALL THAT FORTHCOMING WITH BEER REFERENCES, THOUGH.

BEER DRINKERS HAVE OFTEN BEEN CHARACTERIZED AS LOUTISH AND COARSE.

THIS HAS BEEN THE CASE LITERALLY FOR MILLENNIA.

IT'S VERY POSSIBLE THAT THE MANY ACADEMICS WHO HAVE WORKED TO TRANSLATE THE BIBLE EXPUNGED FROM IT ALL MENTION OF BEER.

...EVEN IN THE FACE OF OVERWHELMING EVIDENCE THAT THE STUFF WAS UBIQUITOUS IN BIBLICAL PLACES AND TIMES.

WHAT'S THIS ANTIBEER AGENDA ALL ABOUT?

ARGUABLY, THE INTELLECTUAL ELITES OF WESTERN CIVILIZATION INHERITED A PREJUDICE AGAINST BEER DRINKING FROM THE VERY SAME PEOPLE TO WHOM WE STILL OFTEN TURN FOR HIGHBROW IDEAS ABOUT TRUTH, BEAUTY, JUSTICE, AND SOPHISTICATION:

THE ANCIENT GREEKS AND ROMANS.

THE PEOPLE OF BOTH ANCIENT GREECE AND ANCIENT ROME WERE DECIDED DISCIPLES OF WINE...

...NOT BEER.

GRAPEVINES GREW MUCH MORE READILY IN THEIR PART OF THE WORLD THAN CEREALS LIKE BARLEY AND WHEAT.

IN FACT, THERE'S NO EVIDENCE THAT BEER BREWING WAS EVER CARRIED OUT IN ITALY IN ITS ANCIENT HISTORY!

FURTHER-MORE, BOTH GREECE AND (CENTURIES LATER) ROME WERE SURROUNDED BY HOSTILE, BEER-DRINKING PEOPLES.

THE GREEKS TERMED THESE BEER DRINKERS **BARBARIANS**-- TRIBESPEOPLE LIKE THE THRACIANS, SCYTHIANS, IBERIANS, AND CELTS.

"ALL THESE BEING WARLIKE RACES"...

...AS PLATO PUT IT.

SO THE GREEKS CAME TO VIEW DRINKING BEER AS A BARBARIC ACT.

THE GREEK PLAYWRIGHT AESCHYLUS DEPICTED LYCURGUS OF THRACE, "THE KING OF THE BARBARIANS," KILLING THE DISCIPLES OF DIONYSUS, THE GOD OF WINE.

AS PAYBACK, AESCHYLUS LATER HAS LYCURGUS BEING BLINDED BY THE GODS AND EVENTUALLY SLAIN.

IN THE FIRST CENTURY AD, ROMAN PHYSICIAN DIOSCORIDES WROTE THAT BEER...

...ENDANGERS THE BRAIN MEMBRANE, AND CAUSES BLOATING, BAD PHLEGMS, AND ELEPHANTITIS.

THEOPHRASTUS, THE GREEK FATHER OF BOTANY, DESCRIBED BEER AS "WINES FROM BARLEY OR WHEAT."

HE TAUGHT HIS COUNTRYMEN THAT BEER WAS NOTHING BUT A REVOLTING, UNNATURAL BY-PRODUCT OF PLANT ROT.

ROMAN SOLDIERS TRAMPED OVER THE ALPS AND CROSSED SPEARS WITH MANY A BARBARIAN TRIBE.

JULIUS CAESAR HIMSELF DESCRIBED THE "BRAVEST" BARBARIANS AS THE ONES WHO WERE UNTAINTED BY ROMAN WINES AND OTHER ALLURING LUXURIES.

CURIOUSLY, CAESAR CLAIMED THE BRAVEST OF THE BARBARIANS WERE "THE BELGAE"-- IN OTHER WORDS, BELGIANS, WHO CONTINUE TO BE AMONG THE WORLD'S PREEMINENT BEER LOVERS.

BEFORE ITS FALL, MIGHTY ROME CONQUERED AND ABSORBED MANY OF ITS NEIGHBORS. THE ELITES OF GAUL AND EVEN OF EGYPT APED THE PRETENSIONS OF THEIR NEW MASTERS. SOON THE RICH, REFINED, AND POWERFUL AMONG THEM PREFERRED WINE TO BEER.

BEER WAS REDUCED IN STATUS TO THE DRINK OF EVERYDAY FOLK...

...LIKE THOSE OF THE LOWER CLASSES WHOSE BEST OPPORTUNITIES, THEY DECIDED IN DROVES, LAY IN JOINING UP WITH THE ROMAN MILITARY.

THE BEER-DRINKING WAYS OF THESE FOEDERATI... MERCENARY OUTSIDERS... WERE TOLERATED JUST FINE, IT SEEMS.

IN FACT, THE CONQUERORS MAY EVEN HAVE PROFITED FROM IT!

ROMAN HEADSTONES FOUND NEAR TRIER, GERMANY, INDICATE THE BURIAL SITES OF SEVERAL PROFESSIONAL BREWERS: MAKERS OF CERVESA.

D·M·
SATTONIVS
CAPVRILLVS
CERVESARIVS
SIBI ET SVIS VF

AND ROMANS THEMSELVES, IN FAR-FLUNG PARTS OF THE EMPIRE WHERE PASSABLE WINE GRAPES JUST WOULDN'T GROW, MAY HAVE LEARNED TO PINCH THEIR NOSES AND DRINK BEER.

THE ROMAN WAY OF LIFE, WITH ITS LUXURIOUS VILLAS, GRAND PUBLIC WORKS, AND HIGH CULTURE, SPREAD OVER MUCH OF NORTHERN EUROPE.

AND HERE, THE EVIDENCE WOULD SEEM TO INDICATE, A DAZZLING ADVANCEMENT WAS MADE IN BREWING TECHNOLOGY.

RECALL THE MILLENNIA-OLD, STANDARD OPERATING PROCEDURE OF BREWING BEER BY SOAKING LOAVES OF BREAD?

IN EXCAVATED ROMAN RUINS IN BELGIUM AND GERMANY, THERE IS CONVINCING EVIDENCE OF A WELCOME DEPARTURE FROM THE STEWY, CLOUDY, CHUNKY BEER OF OLD.

BEER, IN THE DAYS OF IMPERIAL ROME, STARTED TO LOOK LIKE BEER.

BUT IF THE TECHNIQUES AND PRODUCTS OF BREWING CAN CHANGE SO DRASTICALLY AND STILL BE, TO SOME DEGREE, THE SAME, WE MUST ASK OURSELVES A QUESTION.

HOW DO WE MAKE IT IN THE FIRST PLACE? AND JUST WHAT IS BEER?

BEER

End of Chapter One

Chapter Two
THE BREWING PROCESS

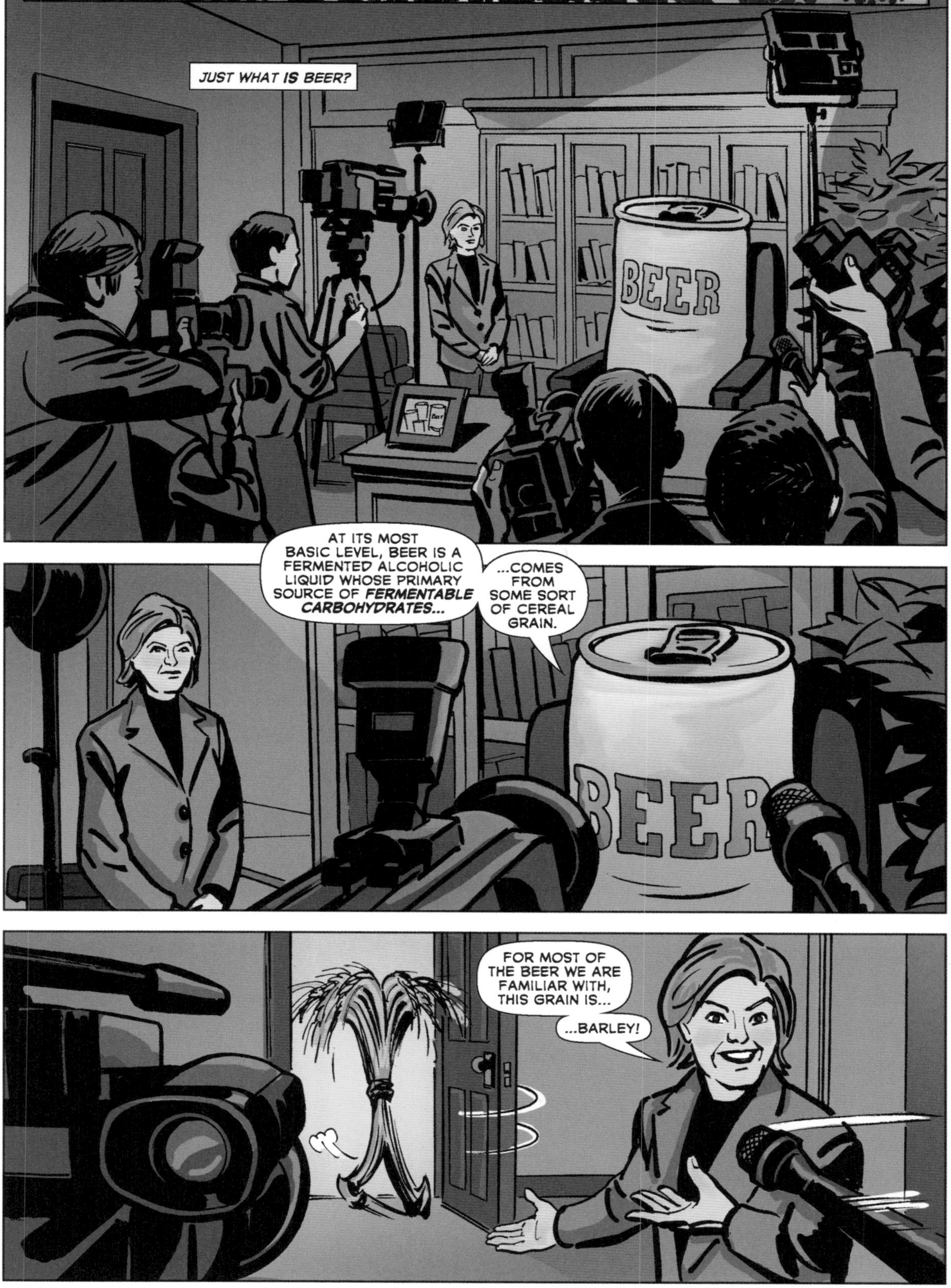
JUST WHAT IS BEER?
BEER
AT ITS MOST BASIC LEVEL, BEER IS A FERMENTED ALCOHOLIC LIQUID WHOSE PRIMARY SOURCE OF FERMENTABLE CARBOHYDRATES...
...COMES FROM SOME SORT OF CEREAL GRAIN.
BEER
FOR MOST OF THE BEER WE ARE FAMILIAR WITH, THIS GRAIN IS...
...BARLEY!

CONSIDER OTHER FERMENTED DRINKS, SUCH AS WINE, CIDER, MEAD,* OR EVEN KEFIR OR KUMISS.**

THE BASE INGREDIENTS OF THOSE DRINKS-- FRUIT JUICE, HONEY, AND MILK--ARE ALREADY *TEEMING* WITH *FERMENTABLE SUGARS.*

*AN ALCOHOLIC DRINK MADE FROM HONEY AND WATER. **ALCOHOLIC DRINKS MADE FROM MILK.

FRUCTOSE

BUT BEER? BEER TAKES A LITTLE MORE WORK.

BEER REQUIRES A *TWO-STEP PROCESS* TO RELEASE SUGARS FROM ITS BASE INGREDIENT: *STARCHES,* USUALLY THOSE FOUND IN CEREAL GRAINS.

TO PRODUCE BEER, THESE STARCHES MUST FIRST BE BROKEN DOWN...

...AND THEN THOSE SUGARS ARE CONVERTED INTO ALCOHOL.

STARCH

SIMPLE SUGARS

ALCOHOL (ETHANOL)

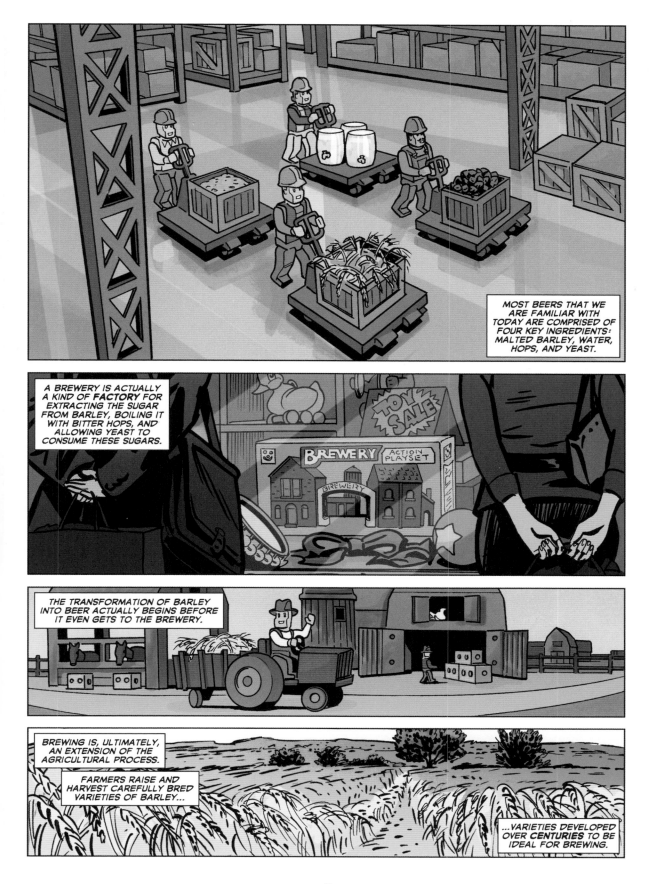

MOST BEERS THAT WE ARE FAMILIAR WITH TODAY ARE COMPRISED OF FOUR KEY INGREDIENTS: MALTED BARLEY, WATER, HOPS, AND YEAST.

A BREWERY IS ACTUALLY A KIND OF **FACTORY** FOR EXTRACTING THE SUGAR FROM BARLEY, BOILING IT WITH BITTER HOPS, AND ALLOWING YEAST TO CONSUME THESE SUGARS.

THE TRANSFORMATION OF BARLEY INTO BEER ACTUALLY BEGINS BEFORE IT EVEN GETS TO THE BREWERY.

BREWING IS, ULTIMATELY, AN EXTENSION OF THE AGRICULTURAL PROCESS.

FARMERS RAISE AND HARVEST CAREFULLY BRED VARIETIES OF BARLEY...

...VARIETIES DEVELOPED OVER **CENTURIES** TO BE IDEAL FOR BREWING.

THE NEXT PART OF THIS PROCESS OCCURS WITH THE **MALTSTER**.

THE MALTSTER IS IN CHARGE OF PREPARING HARVESTED BARLEY FOR BREWING.

NOTED MALTSTER DR. E.S. BEAVEN, 1857–1941.

AT THE MALTSTER'S **MALT HOUSE,** THE BARLEY IS ALLOWED TO **GERMINATE.**

INSIDE THE SEED, PROTECTED BY A TOUGH **SEED COAT,** IS AN **EMBRYO**-- AN EMBRYO FOR A NEW BARLEY PLANT.

WHEN GERMINATION OCCURS, THIS NEW BARLEY PLANT BEGINS TO GROW.

TO GROW, THE BABY PLANT NEEDS FOOD. AND MOTHER NATURE HAS PROVIDED IT.

GROWS

FEEDS

PACKED RIGHT INTO THE SEED COAT NEXT TO THE EMBRYO IS THE **ENDOSPERM**--A STORED-UP RATION OF ENERGY-RICH STARCH. THE STARCH PROVIDES SUSTENANCE FOR THE BARLEY SPROUT UNTIL IT'S MATURE ENOUGH TO DEVELOP LEAVES. FROM THAT POINT FORWARD, IT GETS MOST OF ITS NOURISHMENT FROM PHOTOSYNTHESIS.

THIS STARCH IS A VALUABLE COMMODITY.

IT'S MONEY IN THE BANK FOR THE BABY PLANT.

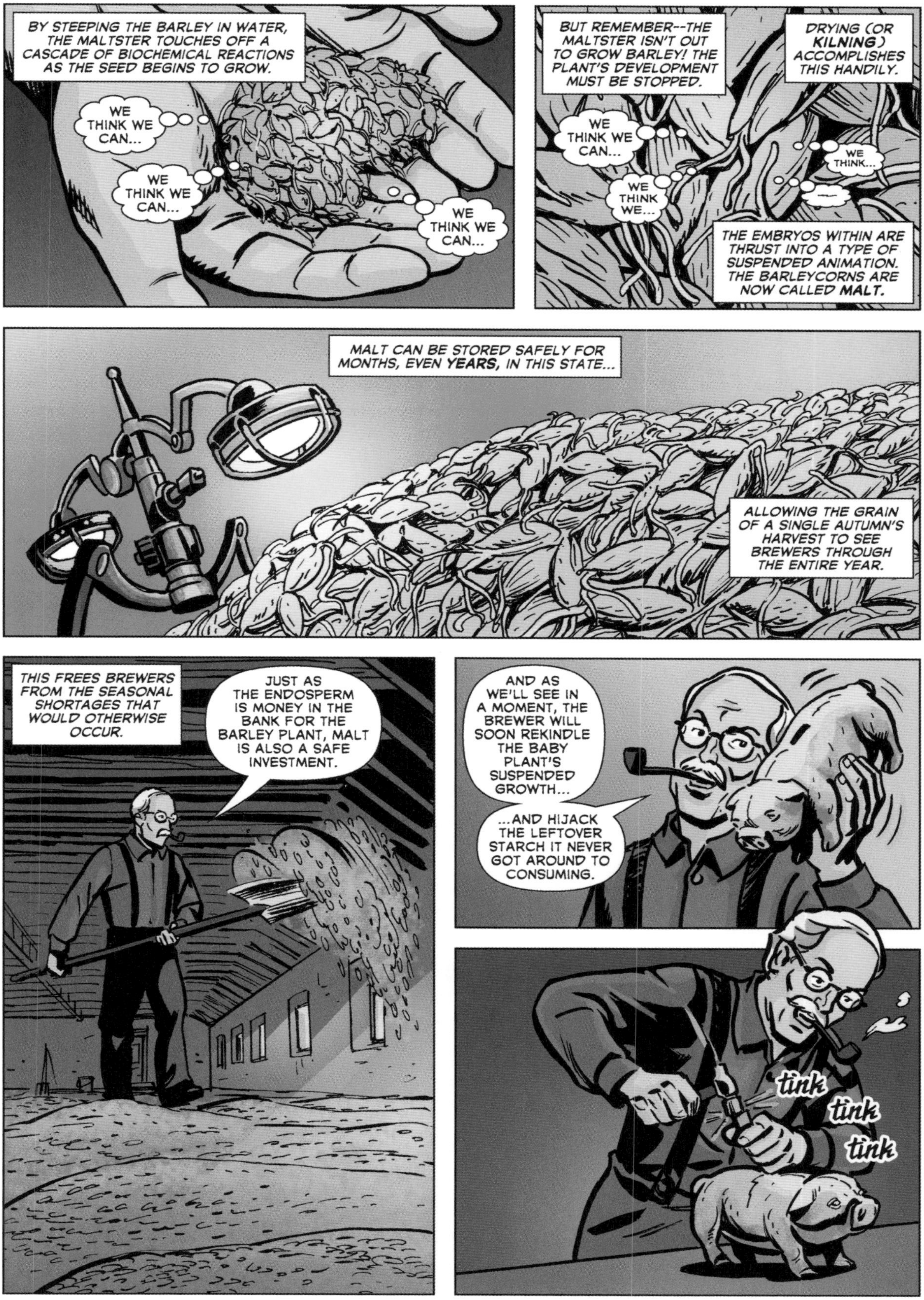
BY STEEPING THE BARLEY IN WATER, THE MALTSTER TOUCHES OFF A CASCADE OF BIOCHEMICAL REACTIONS AS THE SEED BEGINS TO GROW.
WE THINK WE CAN...
WE THINK WE CAN...
WE THINK WE CAN...
BUT REMEMBER--THE MALTSTER ISN'T OUT TO GROW BARLEY! THE PLANT'S DEVELOPMENT MUST BE STOPPED.
DRYING (OR KILNING) ACCOMPLISHES THIS HANDILY.
WE THINK WE CAN...
WE THINK WE...
WE THINK...
THE EMBRYOS WITHIN ARE THRUST INTO A TYPE OF SUSPENDED ANIMATION. THE BARLEYCORNS ARE NOW CALLED MALT.
MALT CAN BE STORED SAFELY FOR MONTHS, EVEN YEARS, IN THIS STATE...
ALLOWING THE GRAIN OF A SINGLE AUTUMN'S HARVEST TO SEE BREWERS THROUGH THE ENTIRE YEAR.
THIS FREES BREWERS FROM THE SEASONAL SHORTAGES THAT WOULD OTHERWISE OCCUR.
JUST AS THE ENDOSPERM IS MONEY IN THE BANK FOR THE BARLEY PLANT, MALT IS ALSO A SAFE INVESTMENT.
AND AS WE'LL SEE IN A MOMENT, THE BREWER WILL SOON REKINDLE THE BABY PLANT'S SUSPENDED GROWTH...
...AND HIJACK THE LEFTOVER STARCH IT NEVER GOT AROUND TO CONSUMING.
tink
tink
tink

THE AMOUNT OF TIME AND TEMPERATURE THAT THE MALTSTER USES TO DRY THE GRAIN DETERMINES THE COLOR AND AMOUNT OF **ROASTINESS** THAT WILL BE TRANSFERRED TO THE FINISHED BEER.

JOHN BARLEYCORN ROAST-A-RAMA

THE SPECTRUM GOES FROM PALE PILSNER MALT...

...TO BISCUITY MUNICH STYLE...

...TO AMBER AND CARAMELY CRYSTAL MALTS...

...TO DARK-ROASTED CHOCOLATE AND BLACK MALTS.

BREWERS, TO START THEIR CREATIONS, CAN PICK FROM A PANOPLY OF ROASTS.

BEER IS PRIMARILY MADE WITH THE LIGHTER COLORED, BASE, MALTS.

BUT BY JUDICIOUSLY MIXING AND MATCHING SMALL AMOUNTS OF CRYSTAL, ROASTED, OR OTHER "SPECIALTY MALTS," BREWERS CAN CREATE ANY TYPE OF BEER:

PALE, AMBER, OR INKY BLACK... ROASTY, TOASTY, OR MALTY SWEET.

BREWERS CAN ALSO MIX IN MALTED WHEAT OR UNMALTED CEREAL GRAINS, KNOWN AS **ADJUNCTS**, FOR OTHER STYLES OF BEER.

THE RESULTING COLOR OF THE BEER CAN BE MEASURED USING THE STANDARD REFERENCE METHOD, OR SRM, SCALE.

A STRAW-COLORED **LIGHT LAGER** CAN HAVE AN SRM AS LOW AS 2. AN **AMBER ALE** WOULD TYPICALLY BE ABOUT 10. AND A JET-BLACK **STOUT** COULD BE UP TO 40 SRM.

ONCE THE BREWER HAS DETERMINED WHAT MIX OF MALTS TO USE IN THE RECIPE, THE MALT NEEDS TO BE GROUND UP, OR **MILLED.**

MILLING CRACKS OPEN THE PROTECTIVE SEED COAT. THIS ALLOWS BEER'S NEXT KEY INGREDIENT TO PERMEATE THE MALT:

GRRRRRR

WATER.

SQUEAK!
SQUEAK!

THE MILLED MALT, NOW REFERRED TO AS **GRIST,** IS READY FOR THE NEXT PART OF THE SHOW.

THE GRIST IS MIXED WITH HOT WATER IN A STEP CALLED **MASHING IN.** THE RESULTING OATMEAL-LIKE MIXTURE IS KNOWN AS **MASH.**

HERE IN THE **MASH TUN,** THE BREWER REVIVES THE BIOCHEMICAL REACTIONS THAT WERE SUSPENDED WHEN THE MALT WAS DRIED.

REMEMBER, MALT IS FULL OF STARCH.

STARCHES ARE LONG CHAINS OF SUGAR MOLECULES, OR **GLUCOSE POLYMERS.**

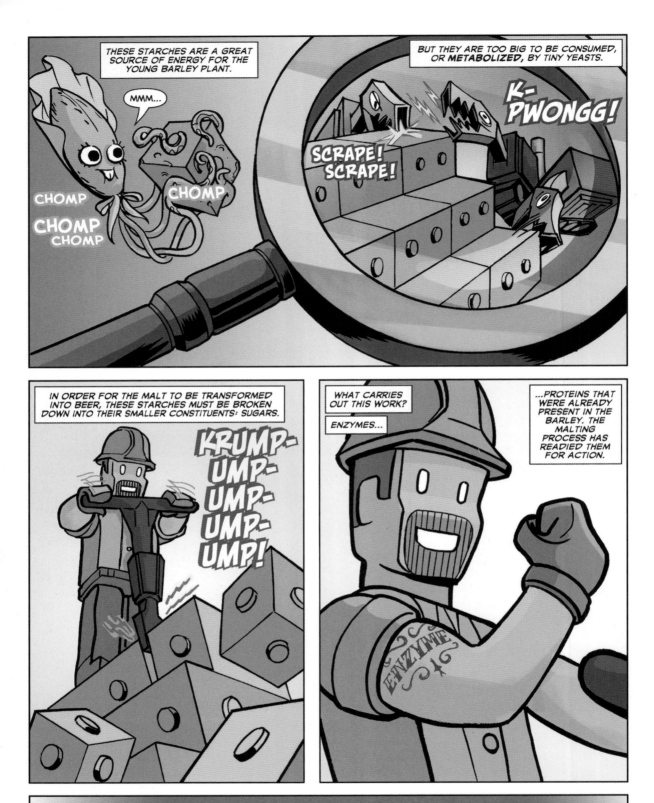

THERE ARE MANY TYPES OF THESE ENZYMES, KNOWN COLLECTIVELY AS **AMYLASES.**
SOME CHOP THE STARCHES INTO LONG CHUNKS. OTHERS BREAK THESE CHUNKS
INTO SMALLER PIECES. THE DIFFERENT ENZYMES FUNCTION BEST AT SLIGHTLY
DIFFERENT TEMPERATURES. BY SUBTLY ALTERING THE TEMPERATURE OF THE
MASH, THE BREWER CAN FAVOR CERTAIN ENZYMES OVER OTHERS. SMALLER
CHUNKS ARE EASIER TO FERMENT. THEY MAKE FOR A BEER THAT IS **DRY.**
ON THE OTHER HAND, LARGER CHUNKS RESULT IN GREATER **SWEETNESS.**

THERE ARE TWO DIFFERENT MASHING TECHNIQUES EMPLOYED BY BREWERS TO ACHIEVE THE REQUIRED TEMPERATURES FOR EFFICIENT MASHING AND STARCH CONVERSION.

THE ENGLISH TRADITION:
INFUSION MASHING

THE GERMAN OR CONTINENTAL TRADITION:
DECOCTION

THE INFUSION MASHING TECHNIQUE CONSISTS SIMPLY OF MIXING THE GRIST WITH A CERTAIN AMOUNT OF HOT WATER. IDEALLY, THE MASH SHOULD REACH A TEMPERATURE OF BETWEEN 145°F AND 155°F.

DECOCTION IS A BIT MORE COMPLICATED. IN THIS METHOD, THE MIX OF GRIST AND WATER HAPPENS AT A LOWER TEMPERATURE. THEN A PORTION OF THE MASH, USUALLY ABOUT ONE-THIRD, IS REMOVED.

THIS SMALLER AMOUNT GETS BOILED AND IS LATER REINTRODUCED TO THE MAIN MASH, DIALING UP THE OVERALL TEMPERATURE.

A CLASSIC TRIPLE DECOCTION BRINGS THE MASH THROUGH THREE TEMPERATURE STEPS, STARTING AT ABOUT 98.6°F. BECAUSE THIS IS THE SAME TEMPERATURE AS HUMAN BLOOD, GERMAN BREWERS OF YORE--IN THE DAYS BEFORE THERMOMETERS--MERELY NEEDED TO DIP THEIR ELBOWS IN THE MASH TO ENSURE THEY WERE ON THE RIGHT TRACK!

DECOCTION VS. INFUSION MASHING IS JUST ONE DIVERGENCE BETWEEN THE ENGLISH AND GERMAN BREWING TRADITIONS. WE WILL EXPLORE MORE AS THE STORY UNFOLDS.

THE MASHING IS DONE. ALL THE STARCHES HAVE BEEN BROKEN DOWN.

BUT WE'RE STILL A LONG WAY FROM THE FINISHED PRODUCT.

TUNK!

WE'RE NOW WORKING WITH A CHUNKY, RUNNY, OATMEAL-LIKE STEW OF SWEET LIQUID AND SOLID, GRAINY HUSKS.

IT'S TIME FOR LAUTERING: SEPARATING AND CLARIFYING THE SWEET LIQUID, OR WORT, FROM ALL THE UNDESIRABLE CEREAL DETRITUS.

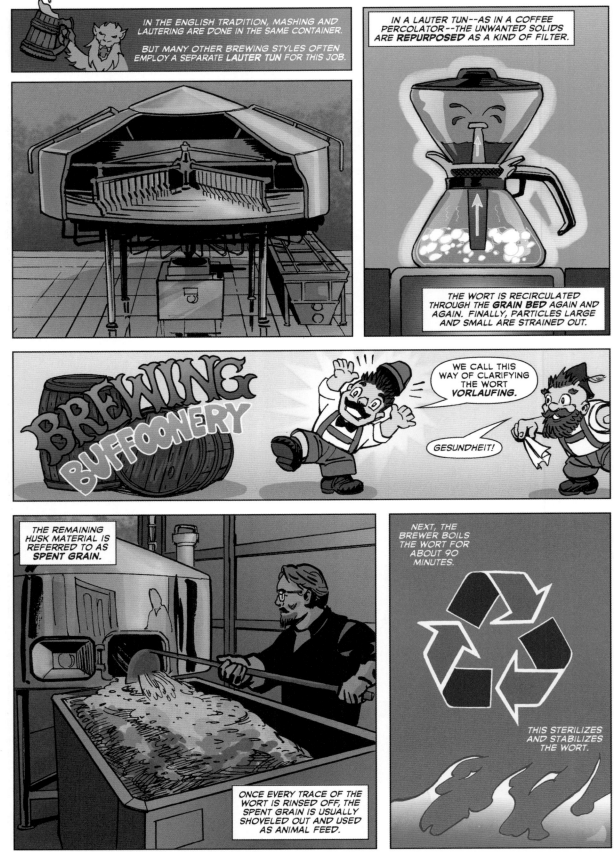

IN THE ENGLISH TRADITION, MASHING AND LAUTERING ARE DONE IN THE SAME CONTAINER.

BUT MANY OTHER BREWING STYLES OFTEN EMPLOY A SEPARATE *LAUTER TUN* FOR THIS JOB.

IN A LAUTER TUN--AS IN A COFFEE PERCOLATOR--THE UNWANTED SOLIDS ARE *REPURPOSED* AS A KIND OF FILTER.

THE WORT IS RECIRCULATED THROUGH THE *GRAIN BED* AGAIN AND AGAIN. FINALLY, PARTICLES LARGE AND SMALL ARE STRAINED OUT.

BREWING BUFFOONERY

WE CALL THIS WAY OF CLARIFYING THE WORT *VORLAUFING.*

GESUNDHEIT!

THE REMAINING HUSK MATERIAL IS REFERRED TO AS *SPENT GRAIN.*

ONCE EVERY TRACE OF THE WORT IS RINSED OFF, THE SPENT GRAIN IS USUALLY SHOVELED OUT AND USED AS ANIMAL FEED.

NEXT, THE BREWER BOILS THE WORT FOR ABOUT 90 MINUTES.

THIS STERILIZES AND STABILIZES THE WORT.

IN SOME NEW, STATE-OF-THE-ART BREWERIES, SPENT GRAIN IS EVEN USED IN BIOREACTORS TO CREATE ELECTRICITY TO POWER THE OPERATION!

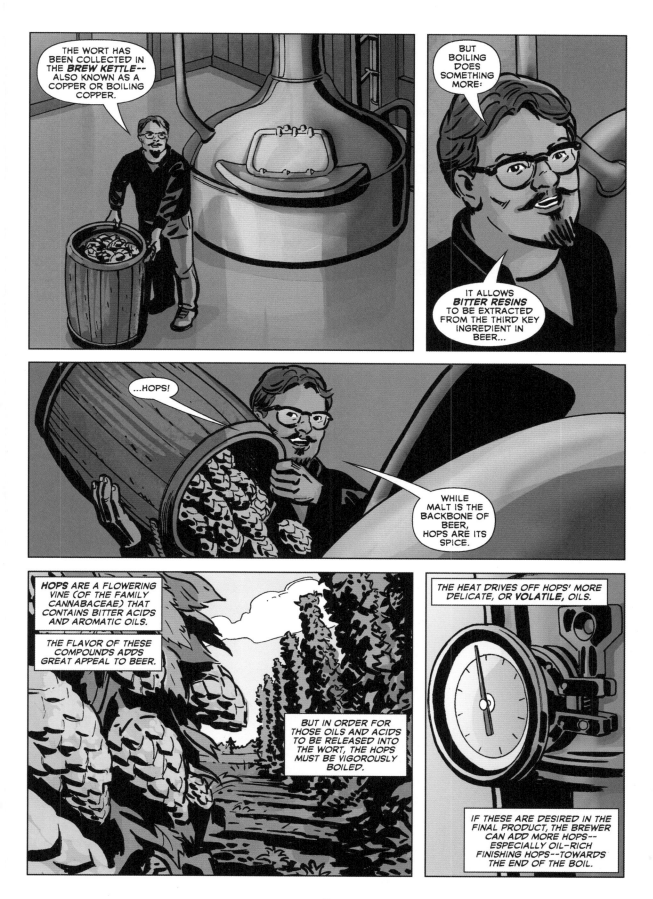

THE WORT HAS BEEN COLLECTED IN THE *BREW KETTLE*-- ALSO KNOWN AS A COPPER OR BOILING COPPER.

BUT BOILING DOES SOMETHING MORE:

IT ALLOWS *BITTER RESINS* TO BE EXTRACTED FROM THE THIRD KEY INGREDIENT IN BEER...

...HOPS!

WHILE MALT IS THE BACKBONE OF BEER, HOPS ARE ITS SPICE.

HOPS ARE A FLOWERING VINE (OF THE FAMILY *CANNABACEAE*) THAT CONTAINS BITTER ACIDS AND AROMATIC OILS.

THE FLAVOR OF THESE COMPOUNDS ADDS GREAT APPEAL TO BEER.

BUT IN ORDER FOR THOSE OILS AND ACIDS TO BE RELEASED INTO THE WORT, THE HOPS MUST BE VIGOROUSLY BOILED.

THE HEAT DRIVES OFF HOPS' MORE DELICATE, OR *VOLATILE*, OILS.

IF THESE ARE DESIRED IN THE FINAL PRODUCT, THE BREWER CAN ADD MORE HOPS-- ESPECIALLY OIL-RICH FINISHING HOPS--TOWARDS THE END OF THE BOIL.

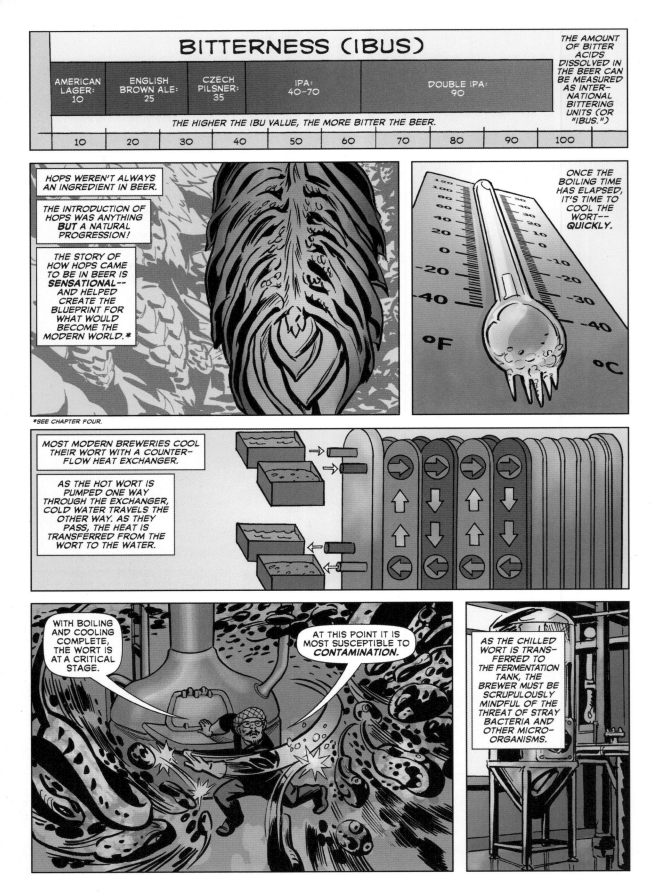

BITTERNESS (IBUS)

AMERICAN LAGER: 10	ENGLISH BROWN ALE: 25	CZECH PILSNER: 35	IPA: 40-70	DOUBLE IPA: 90	THE AMOUNT OF BITTER ACIDS DISSOLVED IN THE BEER CAN BE MEASURED AS INTER-NATIONAL BITTERING UNITS (OR "IBUS.")

THE HIGHER THE IBU VALUE, THE MORE BITTER THE BEER.

10	20	30	40	50	60	70	80	90	100

HOPS WEREN'T ALWAYS AN INGREDIENT IN BEER.

THE INTRODUCTION OF HOPS WAS ANYTHING *BUT* A NATURAL PROGRESSION!

THE STORY OF HOW HOPS CAME TO BE IN BEER IS *SENSATIONAL*-- AND HELPED CREATE THE BLUEPRINT FOR WHAT WOULD BECOME THE MODERN WORLD.*

*SEE CHAPTER FOUR.

ONCE THE BOILING TIME HAS ELAPSED, IT'S TIME TO COOL THE WORT-- *QUICKLY.*

MOST MODERN BREWERIES COOL THEIR WORT WITH A COUNTER-FLOW HEAT EXCHANGER.

AS THE HOT WORT IS PUMPED ONE WAY THROUGH THE EXCHANGER, COLD WATER TRAVELS THE OTHER WAY. AS THEY PASS, THE HEAT IS TRANSFERRED FROM THE WORT TO THE WATER.

WITH BOILING AND COOLING COMPLETE, THE WORT IS AT A CRITICAL STAGE.

AT THIS POINT IT IS MOST SUSCEPTIBLE TO *CONTAMINATION.*

AS THE CHILLED WORT IS TRANS-FERRED TO THE FERMENTATION TANK, THE BREWER MUST BE SCRUPULOUSLY MINDFUL OF THE THREAT OF STRAY BACTERIA AND OTHER MICRO-ORGANISMS.

AND HERE WE INTRODUCE THE ONE-- *AND ONLY*-- MICROORGANISM THAT WE *DO* WANT IN THE WORT: YEAST.

YEAST, BEER'S LAST KEY INGREDIENT, IS ITS LIFE FORCE.

BREWERS MAKE WORT. BUT *YEAST* MAKES BEER.

SKREE-EET!

MEMORIZE THIS, SO WE MAY GIVE OUR MICROSCOPIC FRIENDS THEIR PROPS.

YEAST CONSUMES THE SUGARS IN THE WORT AND CONVERTS THEM INTO ALCOHOL AND CARBON DIOXIDE.

AGAIN, THIS BIOCHEMICAL PROCESS IS CALLED FERMENTATION.

DEPENDING ON THE STRENGTH AND STYLE OF THE BEER, ACTIVE FERMENTATION CAN LAST FROM THREE DAYS TO A WEEK OR TWO.

AND WHAT A WEEK IT'S BEEN!

FROM THE FARMER'S FIELD, THE BARLEY HAS BEEN HARVESTED, MALTED, ROASTED, AND MILLED-- ONLY TO BE MASHED IN HOT WATER, LAUTERED, AND BOILED WITH BITTER HOPS.

AT EACH STEP IN THAT PROCESS, THE BREWER HAS MADE CHOICES THAT WILL AFFECT THE CHARACTER OF THE FINISHED BREW. NOW THE BREWER CAN ONLY WAIT, CONFIDENT THAT ALL THE VARIABLES HAVE BEEN ADEQUATELY CONTROLLED TO CREATE A MASTERPIECE. AND WAIT THE BREWER MUST...

ONCE THE YEAST HAVE CONSUMED ALL THE AVAILABLE SUGARS, THEY START TO GO INTO A TYPE OF HIBERNATION AND SETTLE TO THE BOTTOM OF THE FERMENTATION TANK.

SCIENTIFICALLY, THIS IS KNOWN AS FLOCCULATION.

AT THIS STAGE, THE YEAST CAN BE HARVESTED AND ADDED TO ANOTHER BATCH OF FRESH WORT.

OUR MICRO-SCOPIC FRIENDS WILL REAWAKEN AND START THE WHOLE PROCESS OVER AGAIN.

ONE BATCH OF BEER BEGETS THE NEXT!

IN THE MIDDLE AGES, THE YEAST-RICH SLURRY TAKEN FROM ONE BATCH TO INOCULATE THE NEXT WAS REFERRED TO AS "GODISGOOD:"

..."BICAUSE IT COMETH OF YE GRETE GRACE OF GOD."

SOME STRAINS OF YEAST HAVE BEEN CULTIVATED FOR GENERATIONS IF NOT CENTURIES.

THEY EVENTUALLY EVOLVED-- LITERALLY!--INTO DISTINCT CULTURES THAT IMPART A UNIQUE CHARACTER TO THE BEERS THEY CREATE.

ONCE THE YEAST HAS DONE THE WORK OF FERMENTA-TION, WE FINALLY, LEGITI-MATELY, HAVE BEER.

La Lorraine

La Lorraine

IT STAYS IN THE TANK A WHILE FOR CONDITIONING. ANY REMAINING YEAST SETTLES OUT. THE FLAVORS OF THE DRINK CONTINUE TO DEVELOP AND MELD.

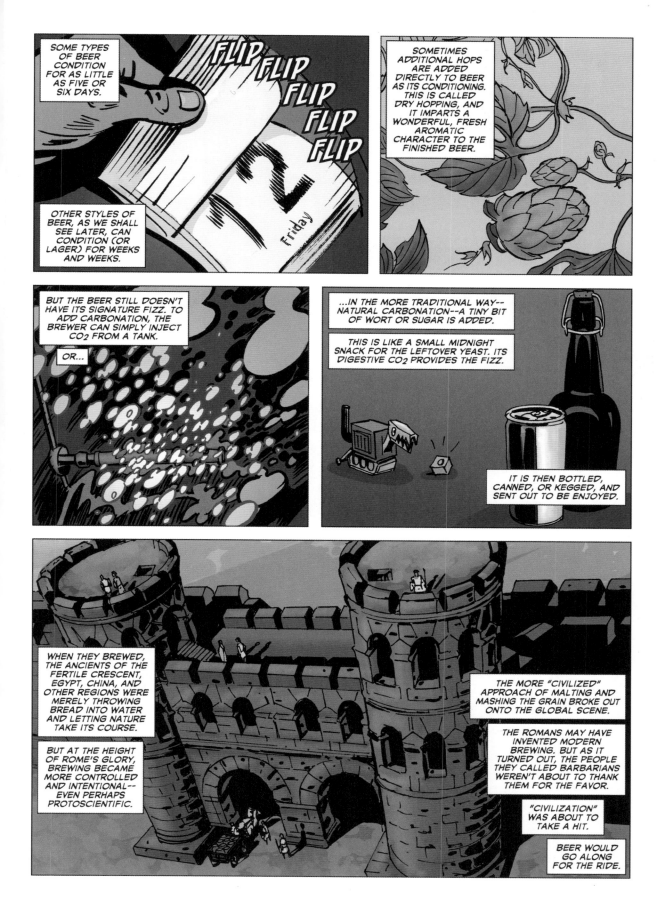

SOME TYPES OF BEER CONDITION FOR AS LITTLE AS FIVE OR SIX DAYS.

FLIP FLIP FLIP FLIP FLIP

12 Friday

OTHER STYLES OF BEER, AS WE SHALL SEE LATER, CAN CONDITION (OR LAGER) FOR WEEKS AND WEEKS.

SOMETIMES ADDITIONAL HOPS ARE ADDED DIRECTLY TO BEER AS ITS CONDITIONING. THIS IS CALLED DRY HOPPING, AND IT IMPARTS A WONDERFUL, FRESH AROMATIC CHARACTER TO THE FINISHED BEER.

BUT THE BEER STILL DOESN'T HAVE ITS SIGNATURE FIZZ. TO ADD CARBONATION, THE BREWER CAN SIMPLY INJECT CO_2 FROM A TANK.

OR...

...IN THE MORE TRADITIONAL WAY-- NATURAL CARBONATION--A TINY BIT OF WORT OR SUGAR IS ADDED.

THIS IS LIKE A SMALL MIDNIGHT SNACK FOR THE LEFTOVER YEAST. ITS DIGESTIVE CO_2 PROVIDES THE FIZZ.

IT IS THEN BOTTLED, CANNED, OR KEGGED, AND SENT OUT TO BE ENJOYED.

WHEN THEY BREWED, THE ANCIENTS OF THE FERTILE CRESCENT, EGYPT, CHINA, AND OTHER REGIONS WERE MERELY THROWING BREAD INTO WATER AND LETTING NATURE TAKE ITS COURSE.

BUT AT THE HEIGHT OF ROME'S GLORY, BREWING BECAME MORE CONTROLLED AND INTENTIONAL-- EVEN PERHAPS PROTOSCIENTIFIC.

THE MORE "CIVILIZED" APPROACH OF MALTING AND MASHING THE GRAIN BROKE OUT ONTO THE GLOBAL SCENE.

THE ROMANS MAY HAVE INVENTED MODERN BREWING. BUT AS IT TURNED OUT, THE PEOPLE THEY CALLED BARBARIANS WEREN'T ABOUT TO THANK THEM FOR THE FAVOR.

"CIVILIZATION" WAS ABOUT TO TAKE A HIT.

BEER WOULD GO ALONG FOR THE RIDE.

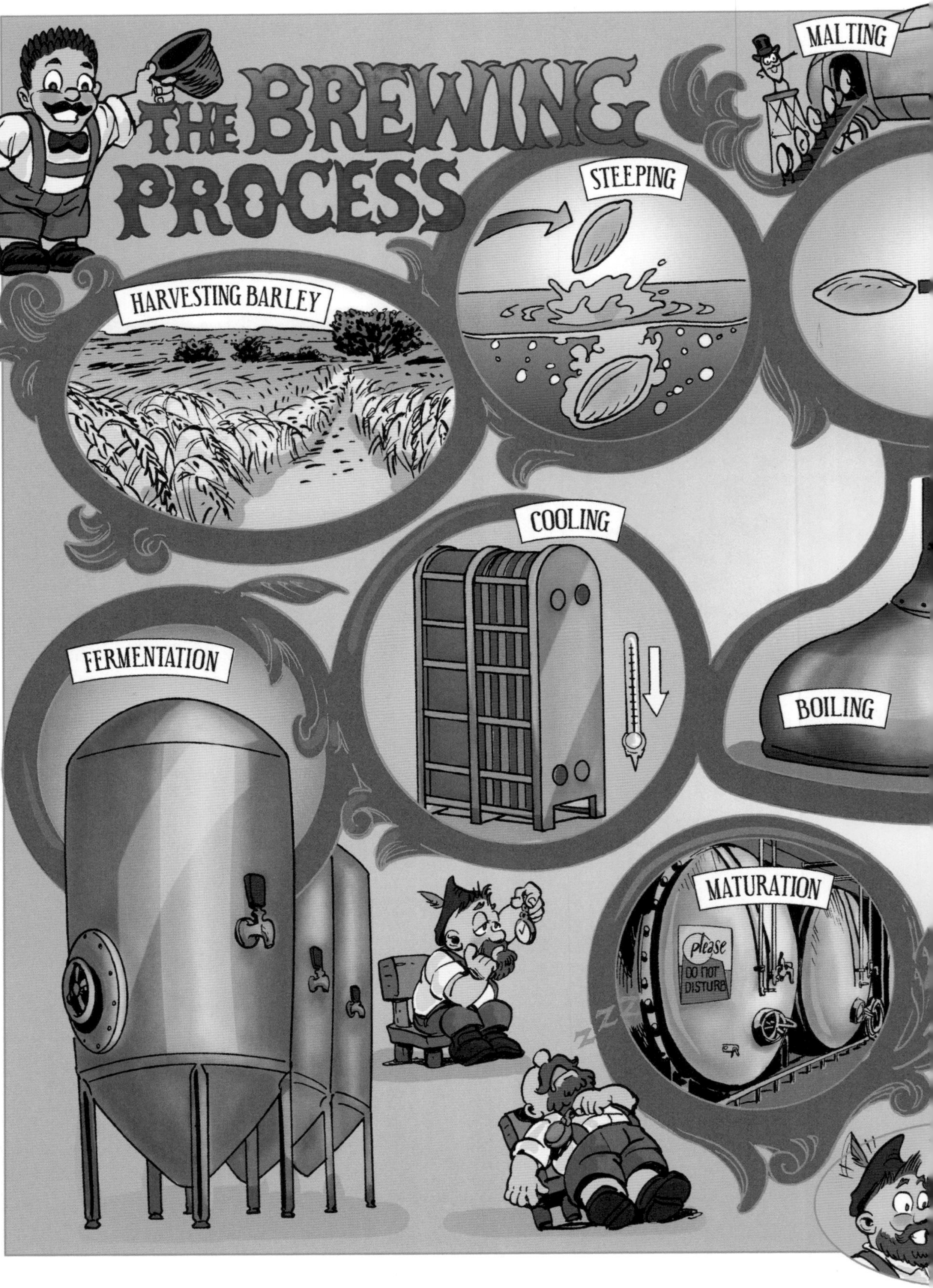
THE BREWING PROCESS
MALTING
STEEPING
HARVESTING BARLEY
COOLING
FERMENTATION
BOILING
MATURATION
please
DO NOT
DISTURB

GERMINATION

KILNING

MILLING

HOPS

LAUTER TUN

MASH TUN

FILTRATION

KEGGING

BOTTLING OR OTHER PACKAGING

End of Chapter Two

Dark Ages and Medieval Beer

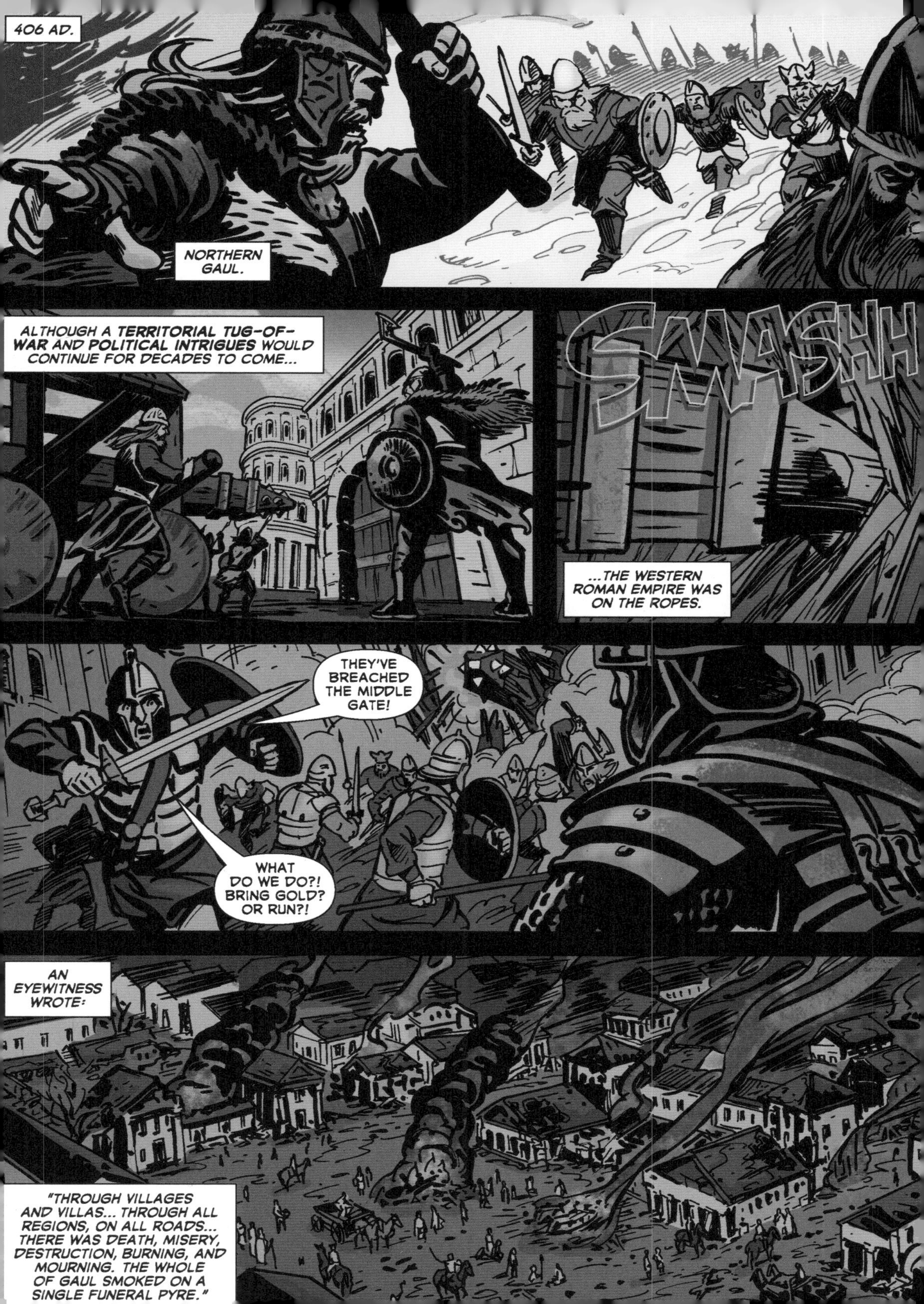
406 AD.
NORTHERN GAUL.
ALTHOUGH A TERRITORIAL TUG-OF-WAR AND POLITICAL INTRIGUES WOULD CONTINUE FOR DECADES TO COME...
SMASHH
...THE WESTERN ROMAN EMPIRE WAS ON THE ROPES.
THEY'VE BREACHED THE MIDDLE GATE!
WHAT DO WE DO?! BRING GOLD? OR RUN?!
AN EYEWITNESS WROTE:
"THROUGH VILLAGES AND VILLAS... THROUGH ALL REGIONS, ON ALL ROADS... THERE WAS DEATH, MISERY, DESTRUCTION, BURNING, AND MOURNING. THE WHOLE OF GAUL SMOKED ON A SINGLE FUNERAL PYRE."

EDWARD GIBBON, THE FOREMOST CHRONICLER OF ROME'S FINAL DAYS, BLAMED **RELIGION** FOR THE FALL OF THIS ANCIENT SUPERPOWER.

ONCE A POLYTHEISTIC GRAB BAG OF GODS AND CULTS...

ROME HAD UNDERGONE A SWEEPING TRANSFORMATION IN HOW IT WORSHIPPED.

IT WAS NO[W] A CHRISTIA[N] EMPIRE.

JESUS'S TEACHINGS-- RENOUNCING EARTHLY DELIGHTS, BEING KIND TO NEIGHBORS, TURNING THE OTHER CHEEK INSTEAD OF LASHING OUT IN VIOLENCE...

...WERE **ALIEN INDEED** TO THE VALUES OF THE ANCIENT ROMAN EMPERORS AND ITS SENATORIAL CLASS.

SPORADIC PERSECUTIONS GRUESOMELY MADE MARTYRS OF THE DISCIPLES OF THE HEBREW "KING OF KINGS."

JESUS NEVER MENTIONED BEER.

BUT, PURPORTEDLY, HE COULD TURN WATER INTO WINE. HE COULD MIRACULOUSLY **SERVE ENTIRE CONGREGATIONS** WITH JUST A SMALL AMOUNT OF IT.

SO JESUS MUST HAVE HAD A SPECIAL APPEAL TO OENOPHILES. PERHAPS THAT SMOOTHED THE WAY FOR THE EMPEROR THEODOSIUS, IN THE YEAR 380, TO PRONOUNCE ALL RELIGIONS **EXCEPT** CHRISTIANITY* ILLEGAL.

* AND JUDAISM

FOUNDERS OF THE CHRISTIAN CHURCH LIKEWISE HONORED WINE. BUT THEY HELD BEER IN DISDAIN.

Frigidus enim zythus. Est autem ægyptiorum quidam potus, sed frigidus & turbidus...sed inflammant potius & insuaues sunt bibentibus & ob vehementem frigiditatem morbos insanibiles pariunt.

TRANSLATION: "BEER IS A COLD AND CLOUDY DRINK OF THE EGYPTIANS THAT INFLAMES WITH ITS INTENSE COLD AND CAUSES INCURABLE DISEASES."

CHRISTIANS WENT WAY OUT OF THEIR WAY TO COMMINGLE THEIR NEW RELIGION WITH WINE.

BECAUSE JESUS HAD LIKENED HIS BLOOD TO THE STUFF, THEY MADE IT A CHRISTIAN'S **DUTY** TO DRINK WINE THROUGH THE SACRAMENT OR RITE OF THE EUCHARIST.

THIS FIRM PARTNERSHIP BETWEEN ALCOHOL AND SALVATION WOULD LATER PAY BIG DIVIDENDS FOR BEER DRINKING

SPREADING SALVA-TION WAS PART OF A CHRISTIAN'S JOB.

SO **MISSIONARIES** PENETRATED DEEP INTO FOREIGN LANDS, ESTABLISHING THE CHURCH WHEREVER THEY COULD.

GFCHKM

Der h. Bonifatius verläßt England, um den Deutschen den h. Glauben zu verkündigen.

WOULD THE HINTERLAND PAGANS ACCEPT THIS EXOTIC NEW THEOLOGY FROM A DISTANT AND FOREIGN DESERT?

BEER MIGHT JUST HAVE MADE THE DIFFERENCE IN THE HEARTS AND MINDS OF POTENTIAL CONVERTS.

IN ONE OF BEER'S CREATION MYTHS, A LEGENDARY GERMANIC CHIEFTAIN, KING GAMBRINUS, IS DESPERATELY THIRSTY.

WATER IS UNSATISFYING TO HIM.

GAMBRINUS CRIES FOR AID TO THE GODS. HE PITS PAGAN POLYTHEISM AND CHRISTIAN MONOTHEISM AGAINST EACH OTHER.

NOW LIST TO ME, YE HEATHEN GODS, AND EKE YE CHRISTIAN TOO...

BOTH ZERNEBOCK AND JUPITER, AND MARY CLAD IN BLUE!

AND MIGHTY THOR THE THUNDERER, AND ANY ELSE THAT BE, THE ONE WHO AIDS ME IN MY NEED HIS SERVANT I WILL BE!

AN ANGEL APPEARS TO GAMBRINUS. SHE TEACHES HIM HOW TO BREW BEER.

IN THE BARLEY WHERE THOU SLEEPEST THERE HIDES A NECTAR CLEAR...

...WHICH MEN SHALL KNOW IN LATER TIMES AS PORTER, ALE OR BEER.

GAMBRINUS PROCEEDS TO ORDER ALL HIS UNDERLINGS TO SMASH THEIR PAGAN IDOLS AT ONCE...

...OR FACE EXECUTION.

LEAVE ODIN, UNDER PAIN OF DEATH!

WHAMMM!

THE UNCOMPROMISING NATURE OF THE CHIEFTAIN'S ORDERS SHOULD COME AS NO SURPRISE IN SUCH A VIOLENT AGE AND IN SUCH A CULTURE OF HONOR, BOASTING, BLOODSPORT, AND STRICT MASCULINITY.

MANY BARBARIANS WORSHIPPED THE GOD ODIN-- ALSO KNOWN AS OTHIN, WOTAN, OR WODAN. *

ODIN REWARDED GLORIOUS BATTLEFIELD DEATHS WITH ENDLESS DRINKING AND CAROUSING IN THE AFTERLIFE.

FOR WHOM EACH WEEK'S "WEDNESDAY" IS STILL NAMED.

ON EARTH, WE KNOW THESE WARRIORS CENTERED THEIR LIVES AROUND DRINKING HALLS WHERE THEY PLIED THEMSELVES WITH HEROIC DOSES OF BEER AND OTHER ALCOHOL.

IN *BEOWULF*, A COURAGEOUS SWORDSMAN BATTLES THE VICIOUS DRAGON, GRENDEL, WHO DARED TO ENTER A BEER HALL AND ATTACK THE FIGHTERS GATHERED THERE.

HA!

YIIIIAAAHHH!

THE EPIC POEM *BEOWULF* ATTESTS TO THIS HARD-FIGHTING, HARD-PARTYING LIFESTYLE--AND MENTIONS BEER SEVERAL TIMES.

"THE CRASHES AND CRIES COMING FROM THE HALL FILLED THE DANES WITH DREAD, LIKE DRAUGHTS OF BITTER AND BALEFUL BEER."

CHRISTIAN MISSIONARIES' QUEST TO CONVERT SUCH BARBRARIANS TOOK THEM TO PLACES SO FIERCE AND FARAWAY THAT NOT EVEN ROME HAD CONQUERED THEM.

FOR INSTANCE: IRELAND.

IRELAND WAS CHRISTIANIZED, ACCORDING TO TRADITION...

...BY A FIGURE WHO HAS SINCE BECOME A LATTER-DAY *IDOL* OF BEER DRINKING.

ST PATRICK BLESS US

SAINT PATRICK WAS NOT IRISH AT ALL, BUT WAS INSTEAD A CHRISTIAN MISSIONARY FROM ENGLAND.

GIVEN THE RIGORS OF ITS CLIMATE, IRELAND WAS NOT EXACTLY FLUSH IN WINE GRAPES.

BUT BEER ABOUNDED.

AND IN THE STORIES OF LOCAL CHRISTIAN MIRACLES...

Dobhach Bride ST. BRIGID'S WELL

...THE WORLD'S FAVORITE DRINK TOOK THE SACRED PLACE THAT WINE TYPICALLY ENJOYED.

SAINT BRIGIT WAS CREDITED WITH THE POWER OF TURNING WATER--EVEN HER BATHWATER!-- INTO BEER.

ANOTHER PRIMARY IRISH SAINT, COLUMBA (543-615 AD), ONCE CAME UPON A CASK OF BEER MEANT TO BE SACRIFICED TO ODIN.

ACCORDING TO THE STORY, COLUMBA BREATHED ON IT.

HIS PIOUS PUFF OF EXHALATION MADE THE PAGAN CASK EXPLODE.

HAAHHH...

SHHACCK!

BEER'S FILLING IN FOR WINE AS A DEVOTIONAL DRINK WAS NOT THE ONLY THING THAT DISTINGUISHED EARLY IRISH CHRISTIANITY.

AS ELSEWHERE, SOME TOOK THE NEW RELIGION'S STRICTURES MORE SERIOUSLY THAN OTHERS.

THE MOST REVERENT TURNED SHARPLY AWAY FROM THE MATERIAL WORLD

THEY BECAME MONKS.

SOME CHOSE TO LIVE AS DESERT HERMITS. OTHERS JOINED INTO COMMUNITIES OF FELLOW FAITHFUL. SOME OF THESE DEVELOPED INTO MONASTERIES.

AFTER ITS ARRIVAL IN IRELAND, THIS TRADITION OF MONASTICISM GREW PARTICULARLY HARSH.

SOME IRISH MONKS PLEDGED THEMSELVES TO AN EXILE OF PERPETUAL WANDERING IN THE MOST DISTANT AND DANGEROUS PLACES.

THESE "WHITE MARTYRS" WOULD SPREAD THE WORD OF GOD OR DIE TRYING.

MAY THE WINDS CARRY ME WHERE THOU WILLEST ME TO BE, O FATHER.

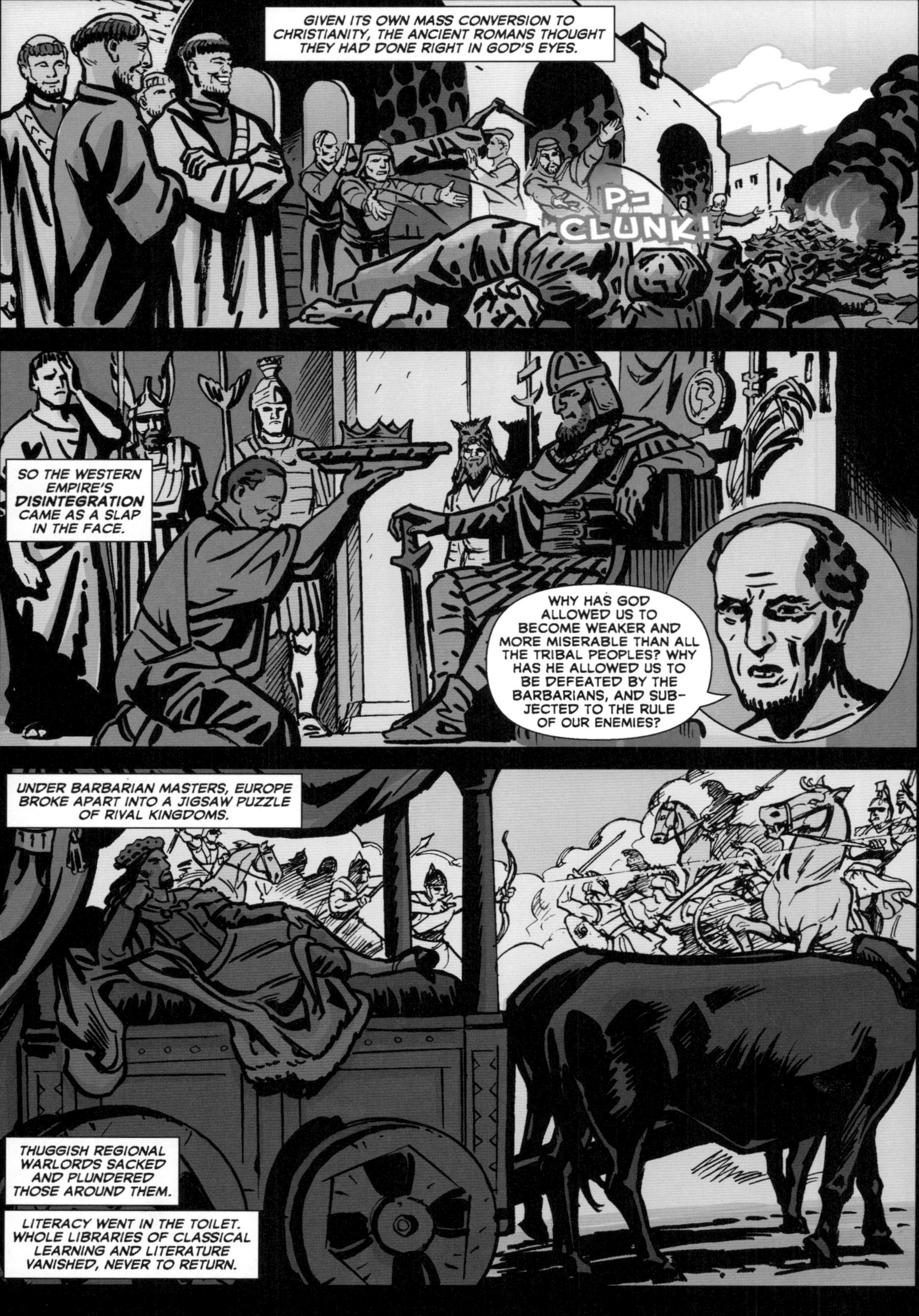
GIVEN ITS OWN MASS CONVERSION TO CHRISTIANITY, THE ANCIENT ROMANS THOUGHT THEY HAD DONE RIGHT IN GOD'S EYES.
P-CLUNK!
SO THE WESTERN EMPIRE'S **DISINTEGRATION** CAME AS A SLAP IN THE FACE.
WHY HAS GOD ALLOWED US TO BECOME WEAKER AND MORE MISERABLE THAN ALL THE TRIBAL PEOPLES? WHY HAS HE ALLOWED US TO BE DEFEATED BY THE BARBARIANS, AND SUBJECTED TO THE RULE OF OUR ENEMIES?
UNDER BARBARIAN MASTERS, EUROPE BROKE APART INTO A JIGSAW PUZZLE OF RIVAL KINGDOMS.
THUGGISH REGIONAL WARLORDS SACKED AND PLUNDERED THOSE AROUND THEM.
LITERACY WENT IN THE TOILET. WHOLE LIBRARIES OF CLASSICAL LEARNING AND LITERATURE VANISHED, NEVER TO RETURN.

THE ADVANCE OF TRADE AND TECHNOLOGY-- WHICH HAD FLOURISHED OVER BREATH-TAKING DISTANCES AND BROUGHT LUXURIES EVEN TO THE OUTERMOST FRINGES OF THE EMPIRE--BIT THE DUST.

WINE NO LONGER FLOWED FREELY FROM SOUTHERN EUROPE AND THE MEDITERRANEAN.

ACROSS MUCH OF THE WESTERN WORLD, BEER ONCE MORE REIGNED SUPREME.

DURING WHAT'S COMMONLY KNOWN AS "THE DARK AGES" EVERYONE NORTH OF THE ALPS DRANK BEER MORNING, NOON, AND NIGHT.

BEER WAS, PURELY AND SIMPLY, A STAPLE OF THE DAILY DIET.

EVEN FOR CHILDREN.

TODDLERS GRADUATED TO THE CUP OF BEER FRESH FROM THE MOTHER'S BREAST.

IT SEEMS OFTEN A LOWER-ALCOHOL "SMALL BEER," WRUNG OUT OF AN ALREADY USED MASH, WAS THE BREW FIT FOR TOTS.

IT SHOULD ALSO BE NOTED THAT THE PRACTICE OF OBTAINING MULTIPLE BREWS FROM A SINGLE MASH WAS AN EVERYDAY TECHNIQUE BEFORE THE ADVENT OF "SCIENTIFIC BREWING."

HARDLY CHANGING AT ALL SINCE THE ROMANS' INNOVATIONS, BEER WAS STUCK IN AN EVOLUTIONARY RUT.

BREWERS--TO CARRY OUT THEIR TASK-- STILL UNCONSCIOUSLY RELIED ON THE QUIRKS OF WILD, AIRBORNE YEAST.

Meet The Beer:
Lambic

Color:
Light:
3-7 SRM

Bitterness:
Low;
0-10 IBU

Strength:
Moderate;
5-7% ABV

HOPS

MALT

FOOD

MALT CHARACTER:
BREWED WITH AT
LEAST 30% UNMALTED
WHEAT, SOFT MALT
CHARACTER OFTEN
OVERSHADOWED BY
ACIDIC, TART FERMEN-
TATION CHARACTER
AND CAN BE INTENSELY
DRY. WILD YEASTS
CONTRIBUTE "BARN-
YARD" FUNKINESS.

HOP CHARACTER:
ALMOST NONEXISTENT
HOP BITTERNESS.
LAMBICS ARE TRADITIONALLY
BREWED WITH HOPS THAT
HAVE BEEN AGED FOR
YEARS TO REDUCE
BITTERNESS AND HOP
AROMATICS. HOPS
ARE USED PRIMARILY
FOR THEIR
PRESERVATIVE
PROPERTIES.

FOOD PAIRINGS:
TART LAMBICS MAKE
TERRIFIC APPERTIFS
AND ARE ALSO
TRADITIONALLY SERVED
WITH MUSSELS AND
OTHER SEAFOOD. FRUIT
LAMBICS ARE WONDERFUL
DESSERT BEERS.
THEIR FRUITY ACIDITY
PERFECTLY COMPLE-
MENTS THE RICHNESS
OF CHOCOLATE
CAKE.

CLASSIC EXAMPLES:
BOON OUDE GUEZE,
CANTILLON ROSE DE GAMBRINUS,
DRIE FONTEINEN KRIEK,
ALLAGASH RESURGAM

LAMBIC IS ONE OF THE WORLD'S OLDEST STYLES OF BEER.

IN THE ZENNE VALLEY OF BELGIUM, EVEN THE CONTEMPORARY TECHNIQUES OF BREWING LAMBIC HARKEN BACK TO THE MIDDLE AGES.

LAMBIC IS "SPONTANEOUSLY" FERMENTED. UNLIKE MOST OTHER BEERS, THE WORT OF A LAMBIC IS NOT INOCULATED WITH A PURE STRAIN OF YEAST PREPARED IN A SUPPLIER'S LABORATORY. INSTEAD, ONLY WILD YEAST AND BACTERIA-- THOSE NATURALLY OCCURRING IN THE ATMOSPHERE--COME INTO PLAY.

THESE MICROBES ARE ALLOWED TO SETTLE INTO LAMBIC WORT WHILE IT SLOWLY COOLS IN LARGE, OPEN "COOL-SHIPS." ONCE THE SUGARY LIQUID HAS ATTRACTED ALL THE AIRBORNE MICROORGANISMS IT NEEDS, BREWERS THEN TRANSFER IT TO WOODEN CASKS TO FERMENT. IT IS SOMETIMES AGED FOR YEARS.

LAMBIC'S WILD FERMENTATION PROCESS CREATES A TARTLY ACIDIC BEER WITH A PRONOUNCED EARTHY "FUNK."

THE UNIQUE MICROFLORA LIVING IN AND AROUND A LAMBIC BREWERY ARE LARGELY RESPONSIBLE FOR THE FLAVOR AND TEXTURE OF THE BREWS MADE WITHIN. SO LAMBIC BREWERS FIND THEMSELVES STRANGELY BEHOLDEN TO THE POPULATION OF INVISIBLE-TO-THE-NAKED-EYE BACTERIA AND YEAST FOUND IN THEIR LOCAL ENVIRONMENTS.

IN THEIR QUEST TO PRESERVE SIGNATURE TASTE AND QUALITY, LAMBIC BREWERS OFTEN GO SO FAR AS TO ALLOW COBWEBS TO BUILD UP INSIDE THEIR WALLS FOR GENERATIONS. SOME EVEN REFUSE TO REPLACE BROKEN TILES ON THEIR ROOFS!

THIS SPONTANEOUS SORT OF FERMENTATION TENDS TO BE UNPREDICTABLE AND SEASONAL. IT IS CHALLENGING TO ACHIEVE CONSISTENCY IN A LAMBIC YEAR IN AND YEAR OUT. SO THIS CONNOISSEUR STYLE IS OFTEN BLENDED. GUEUZE, FOR EXAMPLE, IS A BLEND OF OLD AND YOUNG LAMBIC. GUEUZE IS FURTHERMORE REFERMENTED IN THE BOTTLE, RESULTING IN A SPRITZY CARBONATION AKIN TO CHAMPAGNE.

LAMBICS ARE ALSO OFTEN BLENDED WITH FRUIT.

THIS NOTABLY INCLUDES SOUR CHERRIES ("KRIEK") OR RASPBERRIES ("FRAMBOISE").

LAMBIC WAS NOT ALWAYS ALONE IN REQUIRING FERAL YEASTS. FOR MILLENNIA, ALL BEER WAS SPONTANEOUSLY FERMENTED BY THIS SAME METHOD. AND UNTIL VERY RECENTLY, THE LAMBIC BREWERS OF BELGIUM WERE THE LAST HOLDOUT PRACTITIONERS OF THESE ANTIQUATED BREWING TRADITIONS.

YET BELGIAN SOUR BEERS SUCCEEDED IN ATTAINING A MYSTERIOUS CULT STATUS AMONG BEER AFICIONADOS.

WITH THE CRAFT BEER RENAISSANCE OF THE 1970s AND 1980s (SEE CHAPTER EIGHT), SOME INTREPID HOMEBREWERS BEGAN TO EXPLORE THE ARCHAIC TECHNIQUES OF BREWING SOUR BEER--INVESTIGATING HOW SPONTANEOUS FERMENTATION PLAYS OUT IN SUCH DIVERSE LOCATIONS AS MAINE, MICHIGAN, AND THE U.K.

ONCE EXOTIC RARITIES, THESE WILD BEERS-- SOME OF THE WORLD'S OLDEST--HAVE BEEN REDISCOVERED AS BEER'S NEWEST SENSATION!

IT SHOULD GO WITHOUT SAYING THAT THIS WAS A TIME UTTERLY WITHOUT BEER BRANDS.

Brunhilde & Fredegunda's Catfight Ale

CATOBLEPAS HEAVY-HEAD
The beer with foam on the bottom!

Χατοβλεπαο

DRIVES OFF IMPS AND FEVERS!

BALANCES THE HUMOURS!

IMMUREMENT IPA

X ILLITERACY LAGER

SAINT'S RELIC RED

UNIQUE DIVINE APPENDAGE IN EACH BOTTLE!

WE SAW THAT, UNDER ROMAN RULE, EUROPE MAY HAVE HAD SOME "PROFESSIONAL" BREWING.

BUT GIVEN THE TREND OF *RADICAL SIMPLIFICATION*-- TOOLS, POTTERY, AND HOUSES BECOMING SMALLER AND CRUDER-- SURELY THE LIFE'S WORK OF ANY *CERVASARIUS* WOULD ALSO HAVE BEEN DUST IN THE WIND.

INSTEAD, BEER WAS BREWED HOUSEHOLD BY HOUSEHOLD-- AND MOSTLY BY *HAUSFRAUS*, FEMALE SLAVES, OR OTHER FREEWOMEN.

SOME WOULD NATURALLY DISPLAY MORE OF A KNACK FOR BREWING THAN OTHERS.

THESE TALENTED WOMEN WOULD BECOME KNOWN AS *BREWSTERS* OR *ALEWIVES*.

THE DOMICILES OF THESE BREWSTERS BECAME PLACES FOR MEN TO MEET AND HANG OUT.

THESE BEERY HEARTHS WOULD GRADUALLY EVOLVE INTO TAVERNS AND INNS SERVING THE DRINKING PUBLIC--IN OTHER WORDS, THE FIRST PUBLIC-HOUSES OR *PUBS*.

WHY SO MUCH BEER?

WHY WASN'T THIRST SLAKED WITH, FOR EXAMPLE, WATER?

PEOPLE HAD AN "IT'S COMPLICATED" RELATIONSHIP WITH WATER IN THIS SUPERSTITIOUS AND PRESCIENTIFIC AGE.

PERSISTENT FOLK BELIEFS HELD THAT SPIRITS OR FAIRIES INHABITED WATER SOURCES.

"WATER ELVES" OR THE LIKE MIGHT DEMAND TRIBUTE OR SOME SPECIAL SHOW OF RESPECT.

OTHERWISE, SOMEONE IMPROPERLY DRAWING WATER COULD BE STRUCK WITH A DEADLY CURSE.

SINCE BREWERS STILL DID NOT UNDERSTAND HOW FERMENTA-TION WORKED OR EVEN WHY BEER SPOILED, THEY WERE ALSO TREMENDOUSLY SUPER-STITIOUS ABOUT THEIR CRAFT.

LIKEWISE, ESPECIALLY IN TOWNS, SANITATION STANDARDS WERE FIT TO SEND EVEN THE MOST MODERATE MODERN GERM-FREAKS INTO PANIC ATTACKS.

"EVIL MAGIC," "LITTLE PEOPLE," AND COSMIC FORCES LIKE THE POSITION OF THE SUN WERE THOUGHT TO AFFECT HOW BATCHES OF BEER TURNED OUT!

THE DRINKING SUPPLIES WERE A COCKTAIL OF HUMAN AND ANIMAL WASTE AND OTHER POLLUTANTS. CHOLERA AND OTHER DISEASES THRIVED IN WATER.

ALTHOUGH BREWERS WERE NOT PURIFYING THEIR BEER ON PURPOSE, THERE WAS THIS "HAPPY ACCIDENT":

JUST LIKE IN THE EVEN MURKIER PERIODS OF HISTORY, BEER IN THE 1st MILLENNIUM AD WAS OFTEN USED AS A MEDICINE.

WHEN SOMEONE IS "PIERCED BY A SWORD OR LANCE," A COLLECTION OF MEDIEVAL MEDICAL WRITING RECOMMENDED "TEPID BEER [MIXED] WITH SERPENT'S FAT."

THEY COULD NOT MAKE BEER WITHOUT BOILING THEIR WORT.

THE SUBJECTION TO HIGH TEMPERATURES OF THIS LIQUID HANDILY KILLED OFF PATHOGENS.

IT WAS A BLESSING THAT BEER WAS SO LIFE-AFFIRMING. LIFE ITSELF WAS NOT ALWAYS SO LIFE-AFFIRMING IN THOSE DAYS. MOST PEOPLE WERE ENJOINED EITHER TO THE DRUDGERY OF WORKING THE LAND OR THE BRUTISH BRAVADO OF THE WARRIOR'S LIFE.

AND SOON VIKING MARAUDERS WERE ADDING TO THEIR WOES.

BUT NOT ALL HAD GONE DARK.

THE CANDLE OF WESTERN CIVILIZATION WAS ALL BUT BEING BLOWN OUT.

THANKS IN PART TO THE AFOREMENTIONED WANDERING IRISH MONKS, PARTS OF EUROPE THAT HAD NEVER BEEN CHRISTIAN, OR WERE LAPSING BACK INTO PAGANISM, SOON SAW MONASTERIES DOTTING THE LANDSCAPE.

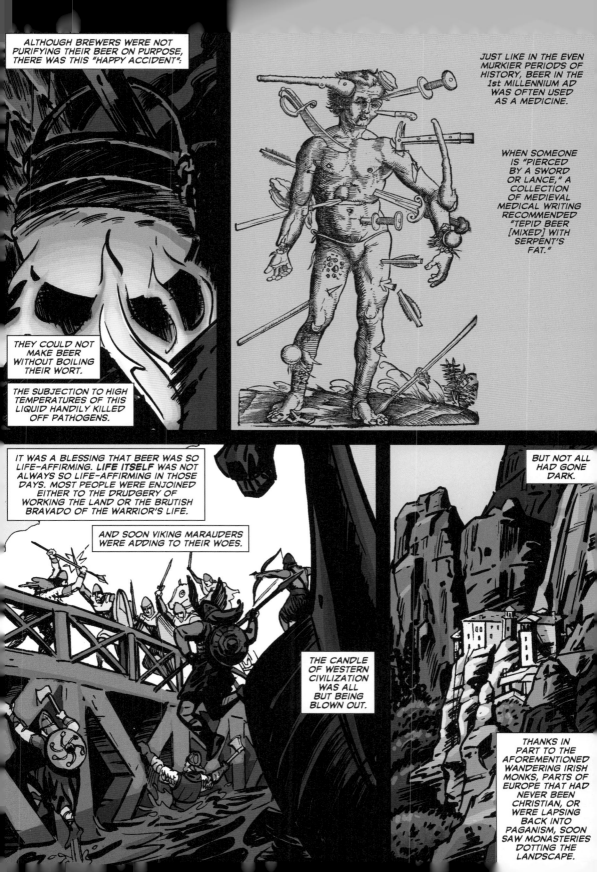

BECAUSE IT WAS THOUGHT THAT KNOWLEDGE HELPED THEM BETTER WORSHIP GOD, THESE MONASTERIES BECAME STRONGHOLDS OF LEARNING.

WARRIOR-KINGS BROODED OVER THE FACT THAT CAREERS OF PILLAGING AND MURDER WOULD DESTINE THEM TO BURN IN HELL.

SO TO SHORE UP THEIR OWN SALVATION, THEY OFTEN DONATED VAST STORES OF TREASURE AND WEALTH TO THE MONKS.

MANY MONASTERIES HAD BEEN ORGANIZED AROUND A SET OF RULES PUT DOWN BY THE ITALIAN SAINT BENEDICT OF NURSIA (C. 480-547).

THE RULE OF SAINT BENEDICT ORDERED MONKS TO A LIFE OF BOTH PRAYER AND WORK, LIKE TILLING FIELDS.

IDLENESS IS AN ENEMY OF THE SOUL. THEREFORE THE BRETHREN OUGHT TO BE EMPLOYED AT CERTAIN TIMES IN LABORING WITH THEIR HANDS...

...FOR THEN THEY ARE MONKS IN VERY DEED, WHEN THEY LIVE BY THE LABOR OF THEIR HANDS...

THE MONASTERIES HAD TO BE INDEPENDENT AND SELF-CONTAINED. THEY ALSO WERE OBLIGATED TO OFFER HOSPITALITY TO TRAVELERS.

ONE UPSHOT OF THESE STRICTURES WAS THAT THE MONKS HAD TO BREW THEIR OWN BEER.

BEER MIGHT SEEM TO US LIKE A LUXURY, HARDLY SOMETHING TO BE ENJOYED BY THOSE WHO HAVE TAKEN VOWS OF POVERTY. BUT AS WE HAVE NOTED, BEER HAS THE SAME ESSENTIAL INGREDIENTS AS BREAD. LOGICALLY, THEN, IT IS COMPATIBLE WITH A PAUPER'S DIET OF BREAD AND WATER! FURTHERMORE, BEER OFFERED NEEDED SUSTENANCE AT TIMES OF MANDATORY, RELIGIOUS FASTING.

MOREOVER, IF JESUS COULD DRINK ALCOHOL, SHOULDN'T HIS MOST STEADFAST ADHERENTS DO THE SAME?

Meet The Beer:

Trappist Dubbel

Color:
Deep Amber to Red;
10 - 17 SRM

Bitterness:
Low to Moderate;
15 - 24 IBU

Strength:
Moderate to Strong;
6.5 - 8% ABV

MALT

MALT CHARACTER:
RICH MALT CHARACTER WITH A WARMING RUM-LIKE ALCOHOL NOTE FROM THE USE OF CARAMELIZED CANDI SUGAR. FRUITY, ESTERY, SPICY AROMAS AND FLAVORS RESULTANT OF THE UNIQUE BELGIAN ALE YEAST STRAINS.

HOPS

HOP CHARACTER:
LOW TO MODERATE HOP BITTERNESS WITH SUBTLE, REFINED HOP AROMAS BALANCED WITH UNIQUE YEAST AROMATICS

FOOD

FOOD PAIRINGS:
HEARTY MEATS AND STEWS. WONDERFUL WITH GAME MEATS AND SHARP, CREAMY "ABBEY" CHEESES.

CLASSIC EXAMPLES:
WESTMALLE DUBBEL,
CHIMAY PREMIÈRE (RED LABEL),
LA TRAPPE DUBBEL,
OMMEGANG ABBEY ALE,
SIERRA NEVADA OVILA ABBEY DUBBEL

THE MONASTIC BREWING TRADITION CONTINUES MOST PROMINENTLY IN THE TRAPPIST ALES OF BELGUIM.

THE TRAPPIST MONASTERY-BREWERIES OF CHIMAY, ORVAL, WESTMALLE, ROCHEFORT, WESTVLETEREN, ACHEL, LA TRAPPE (IN THE NETHERLANDS) AND ENGELSZELL (IN AUSTRIA) WERE JOINED IN 2014 BY THE BROTHERS OF THE ST. JOSEPH ABBEY IN SPENCER, MASSACHUSETTS. THEY ARE THE ONLY ENTITIES ALLOWED TO INCLUDE "AUTHENTIC TRAPPIST PRODUCTS" ON THEIR LABELS.

MONASTERIES SUCH AS THESE BREW ROBUST ALES OF DISTINCTIVE CHARACTER.

ALTHOUGH THE MONKS MAY ENGAGE THE HELP OF LAY BREWERS (SECULAR PERSONS NOT ORDAINED INTO RELIGIOUS SERVICE), TRAPPIST ALES ARE ALWAYS PRODUCED WITHIN THE WALLS OF THE MONASTERY.

THE TRAPPISTS BEGAN TO MAKE THESE BEERS COMMERCIALLY AVAILABLE AT THE TURN OF THE 20th CENTURY--BOOSTED BY A 1919 LAW LIMITING THE SALE OF LIQUOR IN BELGIAN BARS.

THE GOAL OF SELLING THE BEERS WAS TO FINANCIALLY SUPPORT THE MONASTERIES AND FUND THEIR CHARITABLE WORKS.

MONASTERIES BREW AS MANY AS FOUR STYLES. MOST BREW A *DUBBEL* ALE (SEE ABOVE), WHICH IS TRADITIONALLY A MODERATELY STRONG MALTY AMBER ALE. ALSO COMMON IS A *TRIPEL*, WHICH IS USUALLY PALER IN COLOR, HOPPIER, AND OF INCREASED ALCOHOLIC STRENGTH (8-10 ABV). SOME ALSO MAKE A *PATERSBIER* (OR *FATHER'S BEER*) AT A MUCH LOWER ABV FOR CONSUMPTION BY THE MONKS AT THE ABBEY. LASTLY, A *QUADRUPEL* (OR *QUAD*) IS A MUCH STRONGER AND DARKER VERSION AT THE OTHER END OF THE SPECTRUM.

TRAPPIST ALES ARE ALMOST ALWAYS MADE WITH A SIZABLE ADDITION OF HIGHLY FERMENTABLE CANDI

THE *CANDI* SUGAR ALLOWS THESE BEERS OF IMPRESSIVE STRENGTH TO MAINTAIN A DELICATE LIGHTNESS OF BODY.

ANOTHER THING THESE BEERS HAVE IN COMMON IS THE MONKS' USE OF SPECIAL YEASTS THAT PRODUCE FRUITY ESTERS AND SPICY PHENOLICS IN ADDITION TO ETHANOL.

THIS LENDS ANOTHER LAYER TO THESE COMPLEX ALES.

WHILE OTHER BREWERIES MAKE SIMILAR STYLES (OFTEN IN CONJUNCTION WITH OTHER MONASTARIES) THEIR OFFERINGS CANNOT BE LABELED "TRAPPIST." THEY MUST INSTEAD BE CALLED "ABBEY ALES."

BECAUSE OF THE REQUIREMENT TO SERVE SO MANY PEOPLE, MONASTIC BREWING OFTEN HAD TO BE LARGE SCALE.

"HERE LET THE BROTHERS BREW"

THE HARD WORK OF THE MONKS (AS WELL AS FEMALE **NUNS** IN THEIR SEPARATE INSTITUTIONS) RAMPED UP BOTH THE AMOUNT AND QUALITY OF MEDIEVAL BEER.

THE SAINT GALL MONASTERY IN PRESENT-DAY SWITZERLAND WAS ORDERED BUILT WITH THREE BREWERIES: ONE FOR PILGRIMS AND THE POOR, ONE FOR THE MONKS THEMSELVES, AND ONE FOR GUESTS AND LOCAL NOBLEMEN.

THE WEIHENSTEPHAN ABBEY IN BAVARIA, GERMANY, BEGAN BREWING IN THE YEAR 1040...

AND STILL PRODUCES BEER TODAY!

BREWERS THROUGHOUT MEDIEVAL TIMES TINKERED WITH RECIPES FOR BEER.

SEEKING NEW FLAVORS, THEY ADDED TO THEIR BREWS ALL KINDS OF HERBS AND OTHER SUBSTANCES: TREE SAPS, LAUREL, CARAWAY, MINT, GINGER, EVEN ACORNS.

... ALONG WITH THE SAME HONEY, FRUIT, AND OTHER SWEETENERS USED SINCE PRIMEVAL TIME

WITH SOME OF THESE FIXINGS AVAILABLE ONLY AT CERTAIN TIMES OF THE YEAR, THERE WERE MANY SPECIAL, SEASONAL AND HOLIDAY RECIPES.

WEDDINGS WERE CELEBRATED WITH A DRINKING PARTY KNOWN AS A **BRIDE-ALE**.

BRIDAL

what's hot
FASHION
PREVIEW
Stylish New Gowns for
Every Bride's Budget

75
RECEPTION
IDEAS FROM
REAL COUPLES

FROM THIS WE GET THE MODERN TERM "BRIDAL"--TO INDICATE ANYTHING PERTAINING TO THE BRIDE AT A WEDDING.

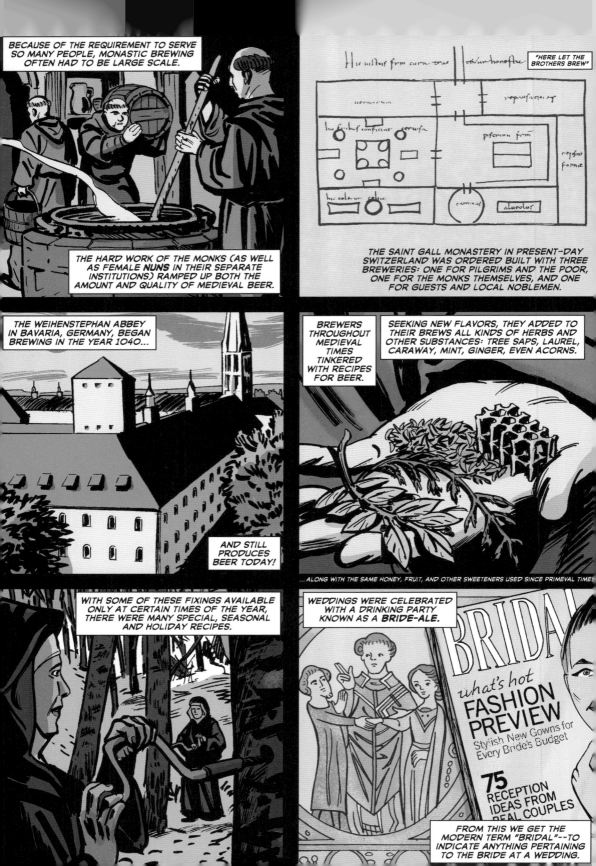

BUT AMONG ALL THE BEER FLAVORINGS IN THE DARK AGES PANTRY, THERE EXISTED ONE CURIOUS BEER ADDITIVE THAT STOOD HEAD AND SHOULDERS ABOVE THE REST:

GRUIT

GRUIT WAS OVERWHELMINGLY THE MOST COMMON SUBSTANCE USED TO FLAVOR BEER AND COUNTERBALANCE THE SWEETNESS OF THE MALT.

GRUIT WAS A MIXTURE OF CRUSHED AND COMPRESSED SPICES. IT COULD BE FOUND NEARLY EVERYWHERE BEER WAS MADE.

YET PARADOXICALLY, WHAT EXACTLY WAS IN IT IS, TODAY, A MYSTERY.

ONE REASON FOR THIS IS THAT (AT LEAST IN SOME PLACES) THE RECIPE WAS A CLOSELY-GUARDED SECRET.

BOG MYRTLE WAS LIKELY A PRINCIPAL INGREDIENT--

--ALONG WITH HEATHER AND YARROW.

THE MEDIEVAL AUTHORITY STRUCTURE-- POWER- AND MONEY-HUNGRY KINGS, NOBLES, AND CHURCH FIGURES--WERE NOT BLIND TO ALL THE BREWING AND DRINKING GOING ON. THEY SOUGHT TO CONTROL IT AND PROFIT FROM IT.

SO THEY ASSERTED THAT ONLY THEY POSSESSED THE SO-CALLED *GRUITRECHT:* THE RIGHT TO DISTRIBUTE GRUIT.

THEY ESTABLISHED AN **OFFICIAL GOVERNMENTAL MONOPOLY** TO SELL AND COLLECT TAXES ON GRUIT. SO ANYTIME ANYONE BREWED BEER, IT WOULD LINE THEIR POCKETS.

Gruithuis

GRUITRECHT

GRUITRECHT COULD, LIKE ANY OTHER POSSESSION, BE GRANTED OR TRANSMITTED TO SOMEONE ELSE: LIKE A BISHOP, A COUNT, OR A LOCAL WEALTHY BUSINESSMAN.

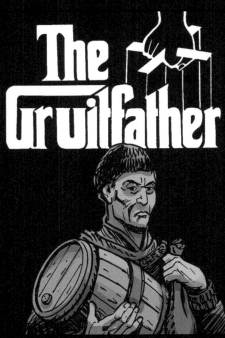

The Gruitfather

GROWING FAT AND RICH OFF OF GRUIT-GOLD, *GRUITRECHT* COULD TURN INTO AN EXTORTIONIST, MAFIA-LIKE **RACKET.**

BREWERS ABLE TO BUY **GRUIT** IN BULK MIGHT BE ABLE TO HAGGLE FOR A DISCOUNT. SO BREWING BEGAN TO BE NUDGED FROM A SMALL, HOME-CENTERED, RURAL ENTERPRISE TO A LARGE, COMMERCIAL, URBAN ONE.

THESE CYNICAL **GRUIT** PROFITEERS DID NOT SEE IT COMING...

...BUT ANOTHER BEER REVOLUTION WAS AFOOT.

THE POPULARITY OF A **WHOLE NEW BEER ADDITIVE** WAS **SWEEPING** THE LAND.

IT WAS POISED TO TRANSFORM BEER YET AGAIN. AND IT WOULD TRAMPLE THE LUCRATIVE **GRUITRECHT** UNDERFOOT.

End of Chapter Three

Chapter Four

The Hops Revolution: Beer Becomes a Commodity

BUT OCCASIONALLY WITHERING DISASTERS GIVE RISE TO THE MOST FRUITFUL ADVANCEMENTS.

HAMBURG HAD TO BE REBUILT FROM THE GROUND UP.

OPPORTUNITY CAME HAND IN HAND WITH THIS BACKBREAKING LABOR.

HAMBURG'S BREWERS HAD A ONCE IN A LIFETIME CHANCE TO **MODERNIZE** THEIR WORKSHOPS, REFASHIONING THEM WITH LARGER CELLARS, WIDER ENTRYWAYS, AND OTHER FEATURES TO BENEFIT THE MAKING AND SELLING OF BEER.

AND IN THE YEARS THAT FOLLOWED, THE WARES OF HAMBURG'S BREWERS SHOOK UP **EVERYTHING** THAT WAS KNOWN ABOUT BEER.

WHAT REINVIGORATED BREWING AS PEOPLE KNEW IT?

WE CAN SUM IT UP IN A SINGLE WORD...

...HOPS.

IN CHAPTER THREE, WE CREDITED HOPS WITH BEING THE "SPICE" OF BEER. TODAY, YOU WOULD BE HARD-PRESSED TO FIND A BEER MADE WITHOUT IT.

BUT FOR MOST OF BEER'S HISTORY, ADDING HOPS WOULD HAVE BEEN ABOUT AS COMMON AND ACCEPTABLE AS USING, SAY, ASPARAGUS, AS A FLAVORING.

AFTER ALL, EATING HOPS SHOOTS JUST LIKE ASPARAGUS WAS ONCE THE ONLY WAY PEOPLE WERE KNOWN TO CONSUME THE BITTER WILD PLANT.

BACK WHEN GRUIT WAS THE ALL-STAR BEER FLAVORING, HOPS HAD BARELY MANAGED TO MAKE IT INTO THE GAME.

IT WAS IN A FARM LEAGUE, SITTING IGNORED ON THE BENCH.

A FEW MONASTERIES AND CONVENTS HAD BEEN USING HOPS SINCE AT LEAST THE 820S.

RESINS AND OILS IN HOPS FLOWERS ARE POTENT ANTIMICROBIAL AGENTS.

THEY, THEREFORE, NOT ONLY GIVE BEER A SHARP, BITTER TASTE, BUT ALSO HUGELY IMPROVE ITS SHELF LIFE.

EVIDENTLY, EARLY MONKS OR NUNS HAD DISCOVERED THAT HOPPED BEERS LASTED LONGER. THE KNOWLEDGE AND USE OF HOPS SLOWLY SPREAD FROM THERE.

IN A WORLD WHERE GRUIT-FLAVORED BEER HAD TO BE DRUNK PRACTICALLY RIGHT WHEN AND WHERE IT WAS MADE, THIS TECHNOLOGICAL BREAKTHROUGH TURNED THE ENTIRE BEER ECONOMY ON ITS HEAD.

MVP
BEER
HOPS!

THE RICH AND POWERFUL--LIKE THE CATHOLIC CHURCH AND MONOPOLISTS WHO FARMED OUT THE COLLECTING OF TAXES AND LINED THEIR POCKETS WITH GRUIT MONEY--SAW THE WRITING ON THE WALL.

MVP
BEER

FLOOD THE MARKET WITH BEER THAT CAN LAST--AND BE STOCKPILED--AND SUDDENLY THE OUTLOOK FOR A STEADY TRADE IN GRUIT LOOKS PRETTY DIM.

Gruithuis

IN THE 1360S, THE BISHOP OF LIÈGE AND UTRECHT COMPLAINED ABOUT THE DENT IN HIS GRUIT INCOME TO EMPEROR CHARLES IV.

SIGH...

IN 1321, AN IRATE COUNT WILLIAM III OF HOLLAND WENT SO FAR AS TO BAN HOPPED BEER FROM ENTERING HIS DOMAIN.

SUCH LUMINARIES VIED TO SUPPRESS HOPS AT ALL COSTS.

SIGH...

SWOOOSH!

THIS IS HARDLY SURPRISING. IT WAS COMMON FOR THE AUTHORITIES TO ACT AS ECONOMIC BULLIES IN THE MIDDLE AGES.

ALL TOO OFTEN, WHEN WOULD-BE TRAVELERS OR PEDDLERS WISHED TO USE A ROAD, CROSS A BRIDGE, OR ENTER A TOWN, MARKET, OR FAIR, THEY HAD TO PAY RESTRICTIVE TOLLS THAT ULTIMATELY WENT TO A KING OR BISHOP.

BUT AROUND THE YEAR 1200, JUST AS HOPS WAS EMERGING FROM OBSCURITY, A NEW FORCE IN SOCIETY WAS COMING UP AS WELL...

...A FORCE UNWILLING TO REMAIN UNDER THE THUMB OF THE CHURCH OR MONARCHY.

A MERCHANT CLASS WAS ESPECIALLY ASCENDANT IN PLACES LIKE HAMBURG, LÜBECK, AND OTHER PORT TOWNS IN NORTHERN EUROPE.

PORT TOWNS COULD SIDESTEP THE TOLLS AND ABYSMAL DIRT ROADS THAT COMPLICATED OVERLAND SHIPPING.

HOPPED BEER COMBINED POWERFULLY WITH MARITIME MERCHANTS' BUSINESS SAVVY, MASTERY OF SHIPPING LANES, AND KNACK FOR PLAYING POLITICAL HEAVYWEIGHTS OFF EACH OTHER.

THESE CAPITALISTS ARRANGED AN EXCLUSIVE, MUTUAL "YOU SCRATCH MY BACK, I'LL SCRATCH YOURS" LEGAL ALLIANCE: THE HANSEATIC LEAGUE.

UPON THE HUMBLE REQUEST OF OUR FRIENDS, THE BURGOMASTER, COUNCILLORS, AND CITIZENS OF THE CITY OF LÜBECK...

...[I] GRACIOUSLY [DEEM] IT PROPER AND TO THE HONOR OF GOD...TO GRANT CERTAIN PRIVILEGES TO SUCH MERCHANTS OF GERMAN SPEECH AS COME...TO OUR KINGDOM WITH THEIR WARES.

KING MAGNUS VI OF NORWAY, 1278

THIS POINT IS WORTH REPEATING: BEFORE HOPS, BEER SOURED SO SPEEDILY THAT IT WAS NEXT TO IMPOSSIBLE TO SHIP (AND SELL) IT ANY SUBSTANTIAL DISTANCE FROM WHERE IT WAS PRODUCED. IT SIMPLY *DID NOT QUALIFY* AS AN ARTICLE FOR TRADE.

BUT WITH THE HELP OF HANSEATIC SHIPS AND TRADING POSTS....

...HAMBURG BEER WAS SOON FLOODING INTO NEIGHBORING LANDS, SUCH AS FLANDERS AND DENMARK.

AND PEOPLE WERE EMBRACING THE NOVEL, BITTER FLAVOR OF HOPS.

AMSTERDAM, JUST A PINT-SIZE SETTLEMENT IN THE EARLY DAYS OF THE HANSEATIC LEAGUE, BECAME A KEY PORT OF ENTRY FOR HAMBURG BEERS.

IN SHORT ORDER, THE DUTCH *REVERSE ENGINEERED* THE HOPPED BEER RECIPES. SOON, THEY WERE ABLE TO OUTDO THE LEAGUE AT ITS OWN GAME.

FOREIGN TRADE BUILT UP THE HAMLET OF AMSTERDAM INTO THE WORLD-CLASS, BEER-LOVING CITY IT IS TODAY.

The Gruitfather

THE PERPETRATORS OF THE *GRUIT SHAKEDOWN* HAD MET THEIR MATCH.

GRUIT FELL BY THE WAYSIDE, DESTINED TO DISAPPEAR ALTOGETHER.

THE TAX HUNGRY, NOT TO BE COMPLETELY OUTDONE, TOOK A DIFFERENT TACK.

BEREFT OF GRUIT MONEY, THEY TAXED HOPS OR SIMPLY CHARGED AN EXCISE TAX ON BEER.

BUT THE DAMAGE HAD BEEN DONE.

TOGETHER, BEER AND TRADE HAD ISSUED TYRANNY A BLACK EYE...

...THE FIRST OF SEVERAL.

TRADE'S PROGRESSION FROM PROVINCIAL VILLAGES TOWARD THE **GLOBAL** VILLAGE WASN'T ALL IT WAS CRACKED UP TO BE, HOWEVER.

COMMERCE HAD PAID OFF BIG. BUT SUCCESS CAME AT A PRICE.

1348.

ALL WAS NOT WELL ON A TRADE SHIP RETURNING FROM THE CRIMEA TO THE ITALIAN PORT OF MESSINA.

THE SAILORS SUFFERED FROM HIGH FEVER AND STRANGE, DARK, PUS-FILLED SWELLINGS.

IT SEEMS RATS, FLEAS ON THE RATS, OR BOTH WERE CARRYING **YERSINIA PESTIS**--THE AGENT OF THE CATASTROPHIC PLAGUE THAT WOULD BECOME KNOWN AS **THE BLACK DEATH.**

THE BLACK DEATH WAS FEARSOMELY CONTAGIOUS. IT WIPED OUT AT LEAST ONE-THIRD OF THE POPULATION OF EUROPE, THE MIDDLE EAST, AND NORTH AFRICA.

MANY LANDS AND CITIES WERE MADE DESOLATE.

GIOVANNI VILLANI, 1340S.

SOME FLED TO THE COUNTRY-SIDE. BUT NOT ALL TOOK THE APOCALYPSE SO SERIOUSLY.

OTHERS... AFFIRMED THAT DRINKING BEER, ENJOYING ONE-SELF, AND GOING AROUND SINGING AND RUCKUS-RAISING... AND LAUGHING AT THE WHOLE BLOODY THING WAS THE BEST MEDICINE...

...AND THESE PEOPLE PUT INTO PRACTICE WHAT THEY HEARTILY ADVISED TO OTHERS: DAY AND NIGHT, GOING FROM TAVERN TO TAVERN, DRINKING WITHOUT MODERATION OR MEASURE.

THE INVENTION OF THE COVERED BEER STEIN SEEMS TO HAVE BEEN ONE RESULT OF THE BLACK PLAGUE.

THE MASSES OF DEAD CREATED SWARMS OF FLIES, WHICH SOME FEARED MIGHT SPREAD THE DISEASE.

TO KEEP FLIES OUT OF BEER, NEW LAWS MADE COVERED DRINKING CONTAINERS MANDATORY. THUS THE CLASSIC HINGED LID DESIGN WAS BORN.

TINK!

AT THAT TIME, THE BIOLOGICAL NUTS AND BOLTS OF FERMENTATION AND SPOILAGE WERE BEYOND THE GRASP OF BREWERS.

LIKEWISE, THOSE SEARCHING FOR CLUES ABOUT HOW TO TREAT THE PLAGUE COULD LOOK ONLY TO SUPERSTITION OR, AT BEST, TO PSEUDOSCIENTIFIC GUESSWORK.

MANY BELIEVED THE PLAGUE WAS GOD'S REVENGE FOR LIVES OF SIN.

FLAGELLANTS WANDERED FROM TOWN TO TOWN, WHIPPING THEMSELVES WITH LEATHER STRAPS AND SPIKES.

CRACK!

CRACK!

CRACK!

REPENT! REPENT!

TO STOP THE BLACK DEATH, THE CHURCH OFFERED THIS SAGE AND MEDICALLY SOUND ADVICE:

AVOID INDECENT CLOTHING, PRAY TO THE VIRGIN MARY, AND MAKE DONATIONS TO THE CLERGY.

THE LOSS OF LIFE BROUGHT ON BY THE PLAGUE WAS SO ENORMOUS THAT THE BOTTOM DROPPED OUT OF THE GRAIN MARKET. PRICES FOR FOOD -- AND BEER -- PLUMMETED.

THOSE WHO SURVIVED THE EPIDEMIC SUDDENLY FOUND THEMSELVES WITH DRASTICALLY REDUCED COMPETITION FOR WORK.

SERVING GIRLS AND UNSKILLED WOMEN... AND STABLE BOYS WANT AT LEAST 12 FLORINS PER YEAR, AND THE MOST ARROGANT AMONG THEM 18 OR 24 FLORINS PER YEAR[!]

MATTEO VILLANI, 1363.

PARADOXICALLY, THE GRIEF AND HORROR OF THE PLAGUE IMPROVED LIVING AND WORKING CONDITIONS FOR THE SURVIVORS.

CIVILIZATION WAS LEFT TO GRAPPLE WITH THIS NEW PARADIGM OF A SMALLER POPULATION AND EMPOWERED WORKERS.

ONE STRATEGY WAS TECHNOLOGICAL INNOVATION.

THE PLAGUE HAD DECIMATED THE RANKS OF MONKS AND PROFESSIONAL SCRIBES.

THE PERPETUATION AND DISSEMINATION OF KNOWLEDGE-- CARRIED OUT BY LABORIOUSLY HAND COPYING BOOKS-- SEEMED TO FACE AN INSURMOUNTABLE THREAT.

BUT THE INVENTION OF THE PRINTING PRESS SECURED THE ADVANCE OF LEARNING.

THIS WORLD-ALTERING DEVELOPMENT WAS ARGUABLY A LEGACY OF LABOR CONDITIONS IN THE WAKE OF THE BLACK DEATH.

THE FIRST COMPREHENSIVE BOOKS ON BEER WERE PUBLISHED.

THE ART AND SCIENCE OF BREWING COULD NOW LEAVE THE CONFINES OF THE WORKSHOP AND OUTLIVE THE EXPERTS WHO HAD MASTERED IT.

AFTER THE PLAGUE, BREWERS REINVESTED IN EQUIPMENT AND INNOVATED TO MAKE UP FOR LABOR SHORTAGES.

BY THE TIME THE BLACK DEATH PETERED OUT, ITS SURVIVORS LOOKED WITH HINDSIGHT ON THE CHURCH'S (QUESTIONABLE) PUBLIC HEALTH RECOMMENDA- TIONS. MANY FOUND THEM SORELY LACKING.

THE PRIESTHOOD LOST ESTEEM IN THE BARGAIN.

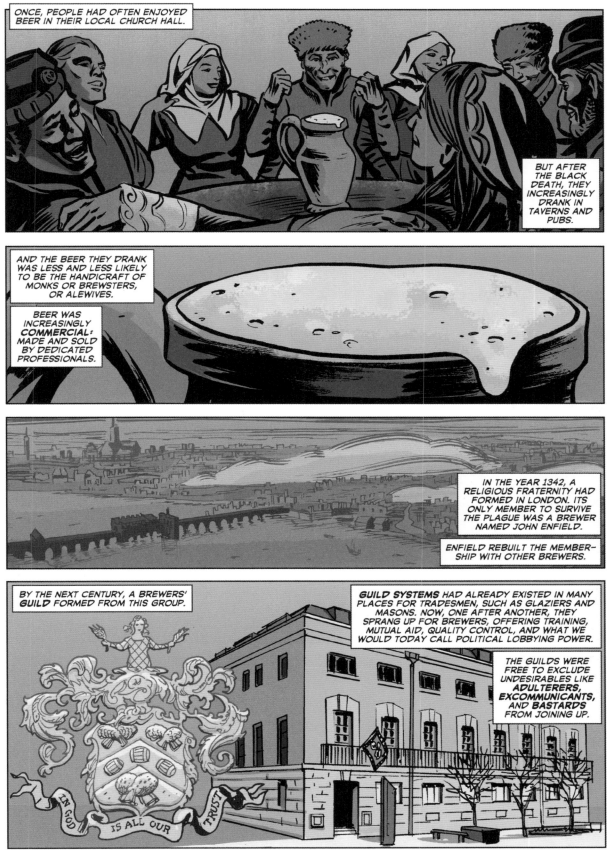

ONCE, PEOPLE HAD OFTEN ENJOYED BEER IN THEIR LOCAL CHURCH HALL.

BUT AFTER THE BLACK DEATH, THEY INCREASINGLY DRANK IN TAVERNS AND PUBS.

AND THE BEER THEY DRANK WAS LESS AND LESS LIKELY TO BE THE HANDICRAFT OF MONKS OR BREWSTERS, OR ALEWIVES.

BEER WAS INCREASINGLY **COMMERCIAL:** MADE AND SOLD BY DEDICATED PROFESSIONALS.

IN THE YEAR 1342, A RELIGIOUS FRATERNITY HAD FORMED IN LONDON. ITS ONLY MEMBER TO SURVIVE THE PLAGUE WAS A BREWER NAMED JOHN ENFIELD.

ENFIELD REBUILT THE MEMBERSHIP WITH OTHER BREWERS.

BY THE NEXT CENTURY, A BREWERS' **GUILD** FORMED FROM THIS GROUP.

GUILD SYSTEMS HAD ALREADY EXISTED IN MANY PLACES FOR TRADESMEN, SUCH AS GLAZIERS AND MASONS. NOW, ONE AFTER ANOTHER, THEY SPRANG UP FOR BREWERS, OFFERING TRAINING, MUTUAL AID, QUALITY CONTROL, AND WHAT WE WOULD TODAY CALL POLITICAL LOBBYING POWER.

THE GUILDS WERE FREE TO EXCLUDE UNDESIRABLES LIKE **ADULTERERS, EXCOMMUNICANTS,** AND **BASTARDS** FROM JOINING UP.

IN GOD IS ALL OUR TRUST

THE MODERN BREWERS HALL IN LONDON. EARLIER VERSIONS OF THE GUILD, OR LIVERY COMPANY, OF BEER PRODUCERS EXISTED ON THIS SAME SITE SINCE AT LEAST 1403.

GUILD OFFICERS IN PARIS TASTED EVERY BREW BEFORE ALLOWING IT TO GO UP FOR SALE.

BEER MADE A DECIDED EMERGENCE FROM THE KITCHEN. BREWING BECAME A MALE BUSINESS THAT GENERATED MANLY PROFITS.

IN LARGE PART, WOMEN WERE SQUEEZED OUT.

DON'T CALL US, WE'LL CALL YOU!

SLAM!

NINKASI WOULD HAVE WEPT. THE DEATH KNELL HAD SOUNDED FOR THE MILLENNIA-OLD TRADITION OF ALEWIVES AND BREWSTERS.

THOSE WHO COULD AFFORD IT DRANK WHATEVER FOREIGN, IMPORTED BREWS WERE IN VOGUE AT ANY GIVEN MOMENT.

A NOTABLE EXCEPTION WAS ANNA JANSSENS, A BREWER'S WIDOW WHO LIVED IN ANTWERP IN THE 1500s AND AT ONE POINT RAN FOUR BREWERIES.

POPULAR BREWERS' POCKETBOOKS DEPENDED ON THEIR ABILITY TO CHURN OUT SUCH QUALITY PRODUCTS.

AND BECAUSE LOCAL GOVERNMENTS ACCRUED SO MUCH TAX REVENUE FROM BREWING, THEY ALSO DEPENDED ON BREWERS REMAINING REPUTABLE.

A BEER PURITY LAW CALLED THE **REINHEITSGEBOT** (ORIGINALLY THE **SURROGATVERBOT**) ORIGINATED IN MUNICH IN 1447. ITS AIM WAS TO ENSURE A COPIOUS AND DEPENDABLE BEER SUPPLY-- AND WITH IT THE BRISK FLOW OF MONEY INTO CHURCH AND GOVERNMENT COFFERS.

THE **REINHEITSGEBOT** SPREAD TO COVER ALL OF BAVARIA.

THE LAW FORBADE ALL CORNER-CUTTING ADDITIVES FROM BEER.

ITS LANGUAGE WAS EXPLICIT: BEER COULD BE MADE WITH ONLY THREE INGREDIENTS: HOPS, WATER, AND BARLEY.

MÜNCHNER
REINHEITSGEBOT
30. November Anno Domini 1487
Albrecht IV. Herzog von Bayern

BEER'S FOURTH INGREDIENT, YEAST, HAD YET TO BE DISCOVERED.

THESE SPECIFICATIONS WERE A MOVE DECIDEDLY IN FAVOR OF BARLEY. PREVIOUSLY, BEER HAD OFTEN BEEN MADE WITH A MIX OF GRAINS.

AS PRICE AND AVAILABILITY FLUCTUATED, OTHER CEREALS HAD OFTEN FOUND THEIR WAY INTO THE WORT.

THE **REINHEITSGEBOT**--WITH ITS CONCURRENT AIM TO RESERVE WHEAT AND RYE FOR BREAD MAKING-- WAS A BIG STEP TOWARD MODERN BEER. TODAY BARLEY HAS A MONOLITHIC PRESENCE IN OUR SUDS.

ELSEWHERE, HOWEVER, BREWING TINKERERS WERE ADDING A LAUNDRY LIST OF EXPERIMENTAL INGREDIENTS.

LINSEED OIL, BUCKWHEAT, EGGS, OYSTER SHELLS, THE SKINNED FEET OF OXEN OR CALVES, AND ASHES WERE ALL USED TO COUNTER SPOILAGE OR IMPART CERTAIN QUALITIES TO BEER.

WHATEVER ELSE MAY HAVE BEEN SLIPPED INTO THEIR BREWS...

... ENGLISHMEN INITIALLY FOUND THE TASTE OF HOPS REPUGNANT.

IN THE PARLANCE OF THE DAY, ENGLISHMEN DRANK UNHOPPED ALE. HOPPED BEER WAS FOR FOREIGNERS: FLEMISH, DUTCH, GERMAN, AND OTHER IMMIGRANTS. *

* THIS ALE/BEER DISTINCTION FROM THE 15th AND 16th CENTURIES IS NOW INVALID. FOR A MORE TIMELY DISCUSSION OF WHAT DISTINGUISHES ALE FROM BEER, SEE CHAPTER SIX.

PERHAPS INEVITABLY, TIMES AND TASTES CHANGED. BEER, ESPECIALLY IN THE BIG CITIES OF THE BRITISH ISLES, LARGELY TOOK THE PLACE OF ALE.

BUT BEFORE THAT SHIFT IN ATTITUDES...

...ONE PROPER ANGLOPHILE, WILLIAM SHAKESPEARE, MADE CERTAIN HIS CHARACTERS PRAISED **ALE** RATHER THAN **BEER**.

FOR A QUART OF ALE IS A DISH FIT FOR A KING.

A WINTER'S TALE

WOULD I WERE IN AN ALEHOUSE IN LONDON!

I WOULD GIVE ALL MY FAME FOR A POT OF ALE AND SAFETY.

KING HENRY V

THE PLACES WHERE SHAKESPEARE AND OTHERS OF THE INTELLECTUAL CASTE WENT TO DRINK WERE SOMEWHAT REMOVED FROM THE SUSPICIOUS EYES AND EARS OF THE AUTHORITIES.

THE ANCHOR

SOME OF THESE SO-CALLED PUBLIC HOUSES BECAME CITADELS OF FREE SPEECH.

ALES IN HAND, RACONTEURS COULD TACKLE ALL CONTROVERSIES-- WITH NARY A WORRY OF ARREST FOR BEING A TRAITOR OR HERETIC.

GEORGE FOX, ANTIESTABLISHMENT AGITATOR AND A FOUNDER OF QUAKERISM, ABOUT 1650.

FOR INSTANCE, DRINKERS COULD ONCE GET IN SERIOUS JEOPARDY FOR ENDORSING MARTIN LUTHER.

HIS "PROTESTS" AGAINST CORRUPT ROMAN CATHOLIC CHURCH PRACTICES HELPED GIVE RISE TO PROTESTANT CHRISTIANITY.

POCK POCK POCK!

SHATTERING THE CATHOLIC POWER STRUCTURE'S THOUSAND-YEAR GRIP ON EUROPE MUST HAVE BEEN THIRSTY WORK.

MARTIN LUTHER ZESTFULLY PARTOOK OF BEER.

IN 1521, HIGH CHURCH AUTHORITIES SUMMONED HIM TO ANSWER FOR THE TURMOIL HE CAUSED. HE REFUSED TO RETRACT HIS VIEWS.

LUTHER DID, HOWEVER, PRAISE A MUG OF BOCK BEER AS...

...THE BEST DRINK KNOWN TO MAN.

82

Meet The Beer:

Bock

Color: Copper to Light Garnet; 14 - 25 SRM

Bitterness: Low to Medium; 20 - 30 IBU

Strength: Moderate to Stong; 6 - 8% ABV

MALT

HOPS

FOOD

MALT CHARACTER: ROBUST MALT FLAVORS AND AROMAS SIMILAR TO THE CRUST OF A HEARTY LOAF.

HOP CHARACTER: STRONG MALT CHARACTER OVERSHADOWS HOP BITTERNESS. PERCEIVED BITTERNESS TENDS TO BE LESS THAN THE IBU VALUE WOULD INDICATE.

FOOD PAIRINGS: HEARTY ROAST PORK, GERMAN SAUSAGES.

CLASSIC EXAMPLES: EINBECKER UR-BOCK DUNKEL, SPATEN OPTIMATOR, EKU 28, TOMMYKNOCKER BUTT HEAD BOCK

BOCK HAILS FROM THE CITY OF EINBECK, WHICH JOINED THE HANSEATIC LEAGUE IN THE YEAR 1368.

THE BREWS OF EINBECK (NOW PART OF MODERN GERMANY) BECAME FAMOUS THROUGHOUT NORTHERN EUROPE AS SOME OF THE FINEST (AS WELL AS SOME OF THE STRONGEST) AVAILABLE.

CITIZENS OF EINBECK WERE GRANTED THE RIGHT TO BREW THEIR OWN BEER. BUT THE CITY COUNCIL VIGOROUSLY OVER-SAW PRODUCTION, QUALITY, MARKETING, AND EXPORTATION.

THE CITY EVEN PROVIDED A LARGE, COMMUNAL BREW KETTLE THAT WAS TRANSPORTED FROM HOUSE TO HOUSE.

BREWING AND FERMENTATION TOOK PLACE IN THAT BREW KETTLE, WHICH IS EVIDENCED TODAY BY THE HIGH ARCHES OF THE DOORWAYS ON MANY OF THE HOMES. THESE HIGH ARCHES WERE NECESSARY TO ALLOW PASSAGE OF THE KETTLE. ROOF VENTS WERE ALSO REQUIRED TO FACILITATE AIR CIRCULATION SO THAT MALT COULD BE DRIED.

A LOTTERY WAS HELD AT THE BEGINNING OF MAY (THE END OF THE BREWING SEASON) TO DETERMINE THE ORDER OF THE NEXT YEAR'S BREWING. THIS OCCASION WAS ALSO OBSERVED WITH A FESTIVAL IN WHICH A SPECIAL BEER STYLE, *MAIBOCK*, WAS SERVED, TO HELP HERALD THE TRANSITION FROM SPRING TO SUMMER.

EINBECK'S RICH, MALTY BEER WAS SO POPULAR IN MUNICH THAT, IN 1612, EINBECK BREWMASTER ELIAS PICHLER WAS BROUGHT TO THAT CITY'S HOFBRÄUHAUS TO REPLICATE IT.

THE ACCENT OF SOUTHERN GERMANY CORRUPTED THE WORD "EINBECK" TO "BOCK," RESULTING IN THIS BEER STYLE'S ENDURING NAME.

BOCK ALSO MEANS "GOAT." THIS ACCOUNTS FOR THE FACT THAT IMAGES OF GOATS TEND TO BE PROMINENTLY FEATURED ON THE LABELS OF BOCK BEERS.

THE DEVELOPMENT OF BOCK BEER CONTINUED IN MUNICH (MOST NOTABLY WITH THE USE OF LAGER YEAST—SEE CHAPTER SIX). MONKS OF THE PAULANER ORDER CREATED AN EXTRA-STRONG VERSION FOR CONSUMPTION DURING LENT: A *DOPPELBOCK* THAT THEY NAMED *SALVATOR* ("SAVIOR").

OTHERS COPIED THE STYLE AND ESTABLISHED A CONVENTION OF USING THE SUFFIX "-ATOR" FOR THIS "LIQUID BREAD."

BACK IN EINBECK, INDIVIDUAL BREWING RIGHTS WERE MERGED AND THE CITY CREATED AN URBAN BREWERY IN 1794. THIS FACILITY MAKES BOCK TO THIS DAY, AND ITS FACADE PROUDLY PROCLAIMS:

"WITHOUT EINBECK, THERE WOULD BE NO BOCK BEER."

THE GENERATIONS THAT FOLLOWED MARTIN LUTHER FEUDED BITTERLY OVER FREEDOM OF RELIGION.

CRUNCH THE NUMBERS ON THE **EIGHTY YEARS' WAR** (1568–1648) AND THE **THIRTY YEARS' WAR** (1618–1648), AND YOU'LL COME UP WITH CATHOLIC VS. PROTESTANT BLOODSHED ON A BLISTERING SCALE.

THESE WARS WERE, IN PART, FINANCED BY THE TAX MONEY THAT WARRING GOVERNMENTS EXTRACTED FROM BEER DRINKERS.

ONE RELIGIOUS SEPARATIST GROUP WAS ESPECIALLY SICK OF INTOLERANCE.

AT LEAST, THEY WERE SICK OF INTOLERANCE DIRECTED AT THEM.

THEY EXILED THEMSELVES FROM ENGLAND TO THE NETHERLANDS. BUT EVEN THAT FAMOUSLY PROGRESSIVE COUNTRY DIDN'T AFFORD THEM THE FREEDOM TO LIVE AND WORSHIP AS THEY WISHED.

SO THESE GODLY MEN AND WOMEN SET THEIR SIGHTS ON A PLACE THAT JUST MIGHT BE FAR ENOUGH AWAY...

...THE NEW WORLD.

AND THEY BROUGHT BEER WITH THEM.

End of Chapter Four

Chapter Five

EMPIRE AND INDUSTRY: BEER GOES BIG

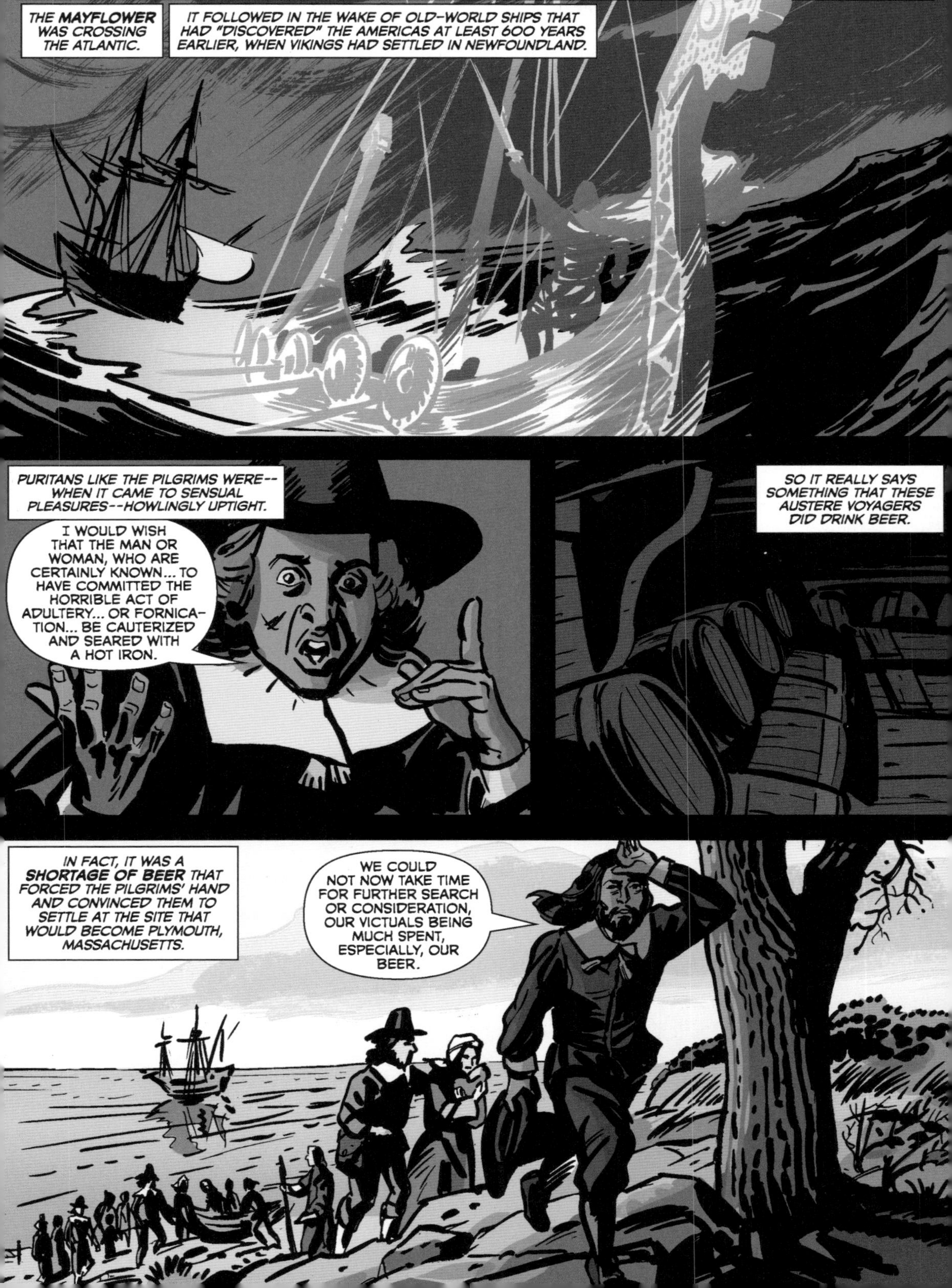
THE MAYFLOWER WAS CROSSING THE ATLANTIC.
IT FOLLOWED IN THE WAKE OF OLD-WORLD SHIPS THAT HAD "DISCOVERED" THE AMERICAS AT LEAST 600 YEARS EARLIER, WHEN VIKINGS HAD SETTLED IN NEWFOUNDLAND.
PURITANS LIKE THE PILGRIMS WERE--WHEN IT CAME TO SENSUAL PLEASURES--HOWLINGLY UPTIGHT.
I WOULD WISH THAT THE MAN OR WOMAN, WHO ARE CERTAINLY KNOWN... TO HAVE COMMITTED THE HORRIBLE ACT OF ADULTERY... OR FORNICATION... BE CAUTERIZED AND SEARED WITH A HOT IRON.
SO IT REALLY SAYS SOMETHING THAT THESE AUSTERE VOYAGERS DID DRINK BEER.
IN FACT, IT WAS A SHORTAGE OF BEER THAT FORCED THE PILGRIMS' HAND AND CONVINCED THEM TO SETTLE AT THE SITE THAT WOULD BECOME PLYMOUTH, MASSACHUSETTS.
WE COULD NOT NOW TAKE TIME FOR FURTHER SEARCH OR CONSIDERATION, OUR VICTUALS BEING MUCH SPENT, ESPECIALLY, OUR BEER.

SHIPS COULD BE **THOUSANDS** OF MILES FROM THE NEAREST FRESHWATER.

WITH ITS DISINFECTANT ALCOHOL AND HOPS (AND DUE TO THE FACT THAT IT WAS MADE WITH BOILED WATER IN THE FIRST PLACE), BEER WAS PIVOTAL TO THE SURVIVAL OF THOSE WHO PLIED THE SEAS.

IN 1588, EUROPE'S RELIGIOUS WARS WERE IN FULL SWING.

AND IT SEEMS THAT **SPOILED OR TAINTED BEER** CAME QUITE CLOSE TO CHANGING THE COURSE OF HISTORY.

[I] THINK FOUL SCORN THAT PARMA OR SPAIN, OR ANY PRINCE OF EUROPE, SHOULD DARE TO INVADE THE BORDERS OF MY REALMS!

QUEEN ELIZABETH I, 1588.

"POISONOUS" BEER WAS THOUGHT TO HAVE UNLEASHED A DEADLY EPIDEMIC AMONG ENGLAND'S SAILORS...

...AS THEY STRUGGLED TO FIGHT OFF THE VAST (CATHOLIC) SPANISH ARMADA'S BID TO INVADE ENGLAND AND DEPOSE ITS (PROTESTANT) QUEEN ELIZABETH I.

DESPITE THE BAD BEER, THE ARMADA WAS ROUTED.

BUT THE NUMBER OF ENGLISHMEN WHO DIED OF STARVATION AND DISEASE IN THE PROCESS WAS CONSIDERED A NATIONAL DISGRACE.

CRUNK!

THOOM!

IN 1621, THE EARLY SETTLERS OF MASSACHUSETTS MET AN INDIAN NAMED SAMOSET.

HAIL, ENGLISH-MEN!

⸘GASP!⸘

SAMOSET HAD ENCOUNTERED WHITE FISHERMEN IN MAINE AND HAD PICKED UP SOME ENGLISH WORDS AND WAYS FROM THESE PREVIOUS ENCOUNTERS.

THE NATIVE AMERICAN ASKED THE PILGRIMS IF THEY HAD ANY BEER.

IT'S NO WONDER THAT SAMOSET SHOWED SUCH ARDOR FOR A DRINK HE COULD HAVE SAMPLED ONLY A FEW TIMES BEFORE.

THERE IS NO EVIDENCE THAT, PRIOR TO THE ARRIVAL OF EUROPEANS, ANY ALCOHOLIC BEVERAGES-- LET ALONE BEER--HAD BEEN PRODUCED NORTH OF PRESENT-DAY ARIZONA AND NEW MEXICO.

IN THE AMERICAN SOUTHWEST AND POINTS SOUTH, HOWEVER, THERE HAD BEEN A VARIETY OF FERMENTED DRINKS, INCLUDING SOME WE WOULD HAVE TO CLASS AS BEERS.

INDIGENOUS CULTURES OF SOUTH AMERICA'S ANDES MOUNTAINS CONTINUE TO MAKE CHICHA BEER IN A PROCESS THAT INVOLVES WORKING BALLS OF CORN FLOUR IN PEOPLE'S MOUTHS.

WHAT WAS PROBABLY THE FIRST BEER EVER MADE IN THE NEW WORLD BY EUROPEANS WAS ALSO CORN BASED.

IN THE 1580S, ENGLISH COLONISTS AT ROANOKE ISLAND (MODERN NORTH CAROLINA) REPORTED MAKING A HOMEBREWED ALE WITH MAIZE.

IN NEW ENGLAND, PURITANICAL ATTITUDES PROMPTED THE CREATION OF A CORPS OF TITHINGMEN.

THE TITHINGMEN ARE REQUIRED DILIGENTLY TO INSPECT THE MANNER OF ALL DISORDERLY PERSONS [INCLUDING] NIGHT-WALKERS, TIPPLERS, [AND] SABBATH BREAKERS.

THESE MORAL POLICE WERE EMPOWERED TO PREVENT DRINKERS FROM ACTUALLY GETTING DRUNK.

DESIST YE, NEIGHBOR!

METHINKS THIS DRAUGHT ONE TOO MANY.

THE BEER-DRINKING DUTCH ALSO MADE INROADS IN WHAT WOULD BECOME THE NORTHEASTERN UNITED STATES.

CREDIT FOR THE FIRST PROPER BREWERY IN AMERICA WOULD SEEM TO GO TO HENDRICK JANSZ, WHO HAD A BREWERY IN MANHATTAN AS EARLY AS 1642.

NEW YORK CITY'S OLDEST REMAINING BUILDING IS FRAUNCES TAVERN, WHERE MANY A CASK OF BEER HAS BEEN DRAINED TO THE DREGS.

FRAUNCE'S TAVERN RESTAURANT.
on First Floor
Moderate Prices
Furnished Rooms by the Week
GEO. EHRET'S
EXTRA LAGER BEER

SOUTHWEST A BIT, WILLIAM PENN-- THE FOUNDER OF PENNSYLVANIA-- PROUDLY REPORTED:

OUR DRINK... HAS BEEN BEER... MOSTLY MADE OF MOLASSES, WHICH WELL BOYLED, WITH SASSAFRAS OR PINE INFUSED INTO IT, MAKES A VERY TOLERABLE DRINK.

IN [PHILADELPHIA] THERE IS AN ABLE MAN THAT HAS SET UP A LARGE BREW HOUSE, IN ORDER TO FURNISH THE PEOPLE WITH GOOD DRINK.

THE NEW, OPEN COUNTRY WAS A BREEDING GROUND FOR INNOVATION.

BENJAMIN FRANKLIN PICKED AWAY AT NATURE'S SECRETS, FURTHERING GROWING FIELDS OF "PHILOSOPHICAL" INQUIRY--LIKE PHYSICS.

BEER MUCH SOONER WARMS IN A BLACK MUG SET BEFORE THE FIRE, THAN IN A WHITE ONE, OR IN A BRIGHT SILVER TANKARD.

IN COLONIAL AMERICA, SCIENCE WASN'T THE ONLY HOT-BUTTON ISSUE MAKING TEETH GNASH.

AS THEY HAD BEEN IN ENGLAND, AMERICAN BEER-DRINKING GATHERINGS WERE HAVENS OF FREE SPEECH.

SWING, TORY VERMIN! WE'LL HAVE LIBERTY OR DEATH!

And gladly pay, in antient fashion,
the ceremonies of libation;
while briskly to each patriotic lip
Walks eager round the inspiring flip:
delicious draught! Whose powers inherit
The quintessence of public spirit;
which whoso tastes, perceives his mind
To nobler politics refined.
—John Trumbull

MALTSTER AND BREWER SAMUEL ADAMS BELIEVED BRITAIN WAS INFRINGING ON AMERICANS'...

...ESSENTIAL, UNALTERABLE RIGHT[S] IN NATURE...

...BY LAYING UNFAIR TAXES AND DUTIES.

ONE OF THESE WAS PROVIDING THE BRITISH SOLDIERS WHO OCCUPIED BOSTON WITH FIVE PINTS OF "SMALL BEER OR CYDER" PER DAY, FREE.

THE NERVE!

VIRGINIAN GENERAL GEORGE WASHINGTON, KNOWN TO ENJOY A GOOD ENGLISH IMPORTED BEER, WAS PERSUADED TO REBEL AGAINST THE SAME CROWN HE HAD FOUGHT FOR NEARLY ALL OF HIS ADULT LIFE.

THOMAS JEFFERSON LIKELY WORKED ON THE DECLARATION OF INDEPENDENCE AMONG BEER DRINKERS IN PHILADELPHIA'S CITY TAVERN.

THE AMERICAN REVOLUTION WAS UNDERWAY.

THE BATTLE OF MONMOUTH COURTHOUSE, NEW JERSEY, 1778.

THE AMERICANS' VICTORY BOLDLY PROVED TO THE WORLD THAT, YES, THE MASSES **COULD** TURN BACK THE RISING TIDE OF MONARCHAL ABSOLUTE POWER...

THE HOUR OF HVMILIATION

...THEN BEING EXERCISED IN FRANCE, PRUSSIA, AND SWEDEN.

ANOTHER SOVEREIGN WIELDING ABSOLUTE POWER WAS CZAR PETER I OF RUSSIA--A MAN WITH AMBITIONS TO TRANSFORM HIS UNDERDEVELOPED HOMELAND INTO A POWER PLAYER.

WHILE IN ENGLAND, PETER DEVELOPED A TASTE FOR ITS BEERS.

IN PARTICULAR, THE CZAR WAS PARTIAL TO THE BREWS OF THE PROVINCIAL TOWN OF BURTON-ON-TRENT.

WHEN IT CAME TO THE BEER GAME, BURTON HAD AN ACE IN THE HOLE: CALCIUM-RICH LOCAL WATER. THIS WATER COAXED THE SWEET, DARK STYLES OF BEER THEN BREWED IN BURTON TO THEIR FULLEST AND MOST DELICIOUS EXPRESSION.

THE BURTON BREWERS SOON FOUND AN EXPLOSIVELY LUCRATIVE MARKET AND BEGAN SHIPPING THEIR WARES ACROSS THE BALTIC TO SAINT PETERSBURG.

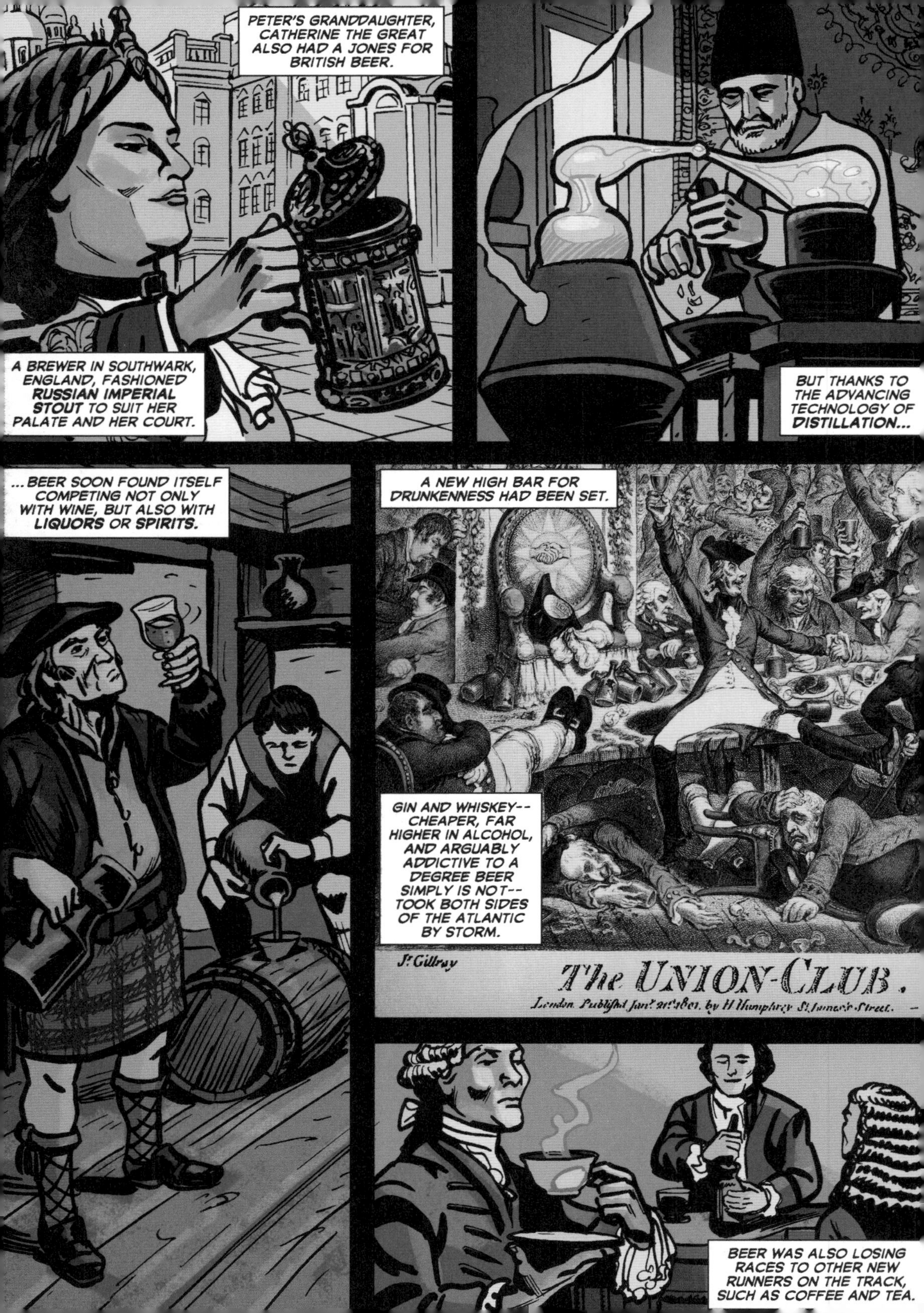

PETER'S GRANDDAUGHTER, CATHERINE THE GREAT ALSO HAD A JONES FOR BRITISH BEER.
A BREWER IN SOUTHWARK, ENGLAND, FASHIONED **RUSSIAN IMPERIAL STOUT** TO SUIT HER PALATE AND HER COURT.
BUT THANKS TO THE ADVANCING TECHNOLOGY OF **DISTILLATION...**
...BEER SOON FOUND ITSELF COMPETING NOT ONLY WITH WINE, BUT ALSO WITH **LIQUORS** OR **SPIRITS.**
A NEW HIGH BAR FOR DRUNKENNESS HAD BEEN SET.
GIN AND WHISKEY--CHEAPER, FAR HIGHER IN ALCOHOL, AND ARGUABLY ADDICTIVE TO A DEGREE BEER SIMPLY IS NOT--TOOK BOTH SIDES OF THE ATLANTIC BY STORM.
Js Gillray
The UNION-CLUB.
London. Publish'd Jany 21st 1801, by H Humphrey St James's Street.
BEER WAS ALSO LOSING RACES TO OTHER NEW RUNNERS ON THE TRACK, SUCH AS COFFEE AND TEA.

LUCKILY, A NEW BEER STYLE WAS WAITING IN THE WINGS TO PLUCK BREWING FROM STAGNATION.

THE INDUSTRIAL REVOLUTION WAS INTENSIFYING.

WORKERS WERE SWELLING FACTORIES IN LONDON, MANCHESTER, SHEFFIELD, AND BEYOND.

BREWERIES WERE EXPANDING TO FACTORY PROPORTIONS TOO.

A STEAM ENGINE WAS FIRST USED IN A BREWERY IN 1784, AT HENRY GOODWIN AND SAMUEL WHITBREAD'S SHOP.

CITY DWELLERS GREW MORE NUMEROUS BY THE DAY--AND THEY WERE THIRSTY.

AND WHAT BEER WERE PEOPLE ASKING FOR?

PORTER, A SLIGHTLY NEW TAKE ON ENGLISH STANDARD BROWN BEER.

THIS NEW/OLD PRODUCT WAS NAMED FOR THE MOST COMMON WORKING-CLASS PROFESSION IN LONDON: THAT OF PORTERS, WHO CARTED HEAVY THINGS AROUND TOWN.

Meet The Beer:
PORTER

Color:
Dark Brown to Near Black;
20 - 35 SRM

Bitterness:
Moderate to Hoppy;
20 - 40 IBU

Strength:
Moderate:
4.5 - 6% ABV

MALT

HOPS

FOOD

MALT CHARACTER: ROASTED MALT PREDOMINATES. PORTER MAY HAVE A SLIGHT CARAMEL SWEETNESS.

HOP CHARACTER: SHARP BITTERNESS BALANCED WITH ROASTY MALT. MILD HOP AROMATICS.

FOOD PAIRINGS: BARBECUED CHICKEN, CHOCOLATE COOKIES. WONDERFUL AS A BASE FOR BEEF STEW.

CLASSIC EXAMPLES: FULLER'S LONDON PORTER, SAMUEL SMITH'S TADDY PORTER, GREAT LAKES EDMUND FITZGERALD PORTER, ANCHOR PORTER

THE PREVAILING STORY OF PORTER'S ORIGINS IS TOO GOOD TO BE TRUE.

"THREE-THREADS" (A PUTATIVE BLEND OF CHEAP "TWOPENNY" BREW, BEER, AND ALE) WAS ONCE POPULAR IN LONDON. AND THERE IS A RIPPING GOOD YARN OUT THERE ABOUT A PLUCKY BREWER WHO CRACKED A METHOD OF CAPTURING ALL THE APPEAL OF THREE-THREADS IN A SINGLE RECIPE. BUT EVIDENCE TO SUPPORT THIS ACCOUNT OF THE FIRST PORTER IS SCANTY.

THREE-THREADS WAS JUST ONE OF A WELL-ESTABLISHED MULTI-TUDE OF BEER MIXES—FORMULATED BY DRINKERS SEEKING NEW FLAVORS AND BY BEER PURVEY-ORS TRYING TO PULL A FAST ONE ON CUSTOMERS AND TAXMEN. ONE COMMON PUBLICAN PRACTICE WAS TO MIX "MILD" (NEW) BEER WITH "STALE" (AGED) BROWN BEER.

EVIDENTLY BREWERS SAW OPPORTUNITY IN SIMULATING THESE BLENDS. THEY INTRODUCED NEW BREWS MADE WITH "BROWN MALT" KILNED IN DRUMS OVER OPEN FIRES. THIS MALTING METHOD LENT A DARK COLOR AND ROASTY FLAVOR TO THE BREW. THE HOPPING RATE WAS ALSO STEPPED UP.

THIS REVITALIZED LONDON BROWN BEER CAME TO BE KNOWN AS "ENTIRE BUTT."

"ENTIRE" BECAUSE ALL THE WORT OBTAINED FROM A SINGLE MASH WOULD BE COMBINED INTO ONE. (NORMALLY A SINGLE MASH WOULD YIELD SEVERAL SEPARATE WORTS OF VARYING STRENGTH. THESE WOULD THEN BE FERMENTED INTO MULTIPLE PRODUCTS OF DIFFERING QUALITY). AND "BUTT" BECAUSE THESE BREWS WERE AGED IN WOODEN VESSELS IN-HOUSE AT THE BREWERY. THIS GAVE THEM THE CHANCE TO MELLOW AND STABILIZE BEFORE BEING RELEASED TO THE TRADE. ("BUTT" WAS A COMMON PRE-20th CENTURY TERM FOR "BARREL" OR "CASK").

THE FORMULA FOR PORTER CHANGED AS TIME WENT ON. MALTING TECHNIQUES GREW MORE VARIED AND SOPHISTICATED. INCREASING TAX RATES ON MALT COERCED BREWERS TO TAKE ACTION. SO PORTER PRODUCERS BEGAN TO MAKE THE BEER PREDOMINANTLY WITH LIGHTER PALE MALT. THEY USED A PORTION OF ROAST "PATENT" MALT TO DARKEN THE RESULTING BREW. THIS

MORE EFFICIENT (AND PROFITABLE) USE OF RAW MATERIALS REMAINS HOW MOST MODERN PORTERS ARE BREWED TODAY.

AS THE STYLE PROLIFERATED, PORTERS OF MANY CALIBERS CAME ON THE MARKET. THE STRONGER ONES WERE DUBBED "STOUT PORTERS" OR "BROWN STOUTS." THIS WAS EVENTUALLY SHORTENED SIMPLY TO "STOUT." WHILE THE EXACT DIFFERENCES BETWEEN STOUTS AND PORTERS ARE DEBATABLE, STOUTS ARE GENERALLY THE STRONGER AND DRIER OF THE TWO.

WITH THE ASCENDANCE OF PALE ALES AND THEN PILSNER, THE POPULARITY OF PORTER WANED. BUT STOUT SURVIVED AS ONE OF THE MORE POPULAR STYLES OF BEER IN THE WORLD—AND A MAINSTAY OF CONTEMPORARY CRAFT BREWERS.

GUINNESS, THE IRISH BREWER SYNONYMOUS WITH STOUT, MADE A PORTER (KNOWN VERNACULARLY AS "PLAIN") UNTIL IT WAS PHASED OUT IN THE EARLY 1970s. THIS MIGHT HAVE BEEN THE DEATH KNELL FOR PORTER IF NOT FOR THE PIONEERING SAN FRANCISCO-BASED BREWER WHO REKINDLED THE STYLE (SEE CHAPTER EIGHT).

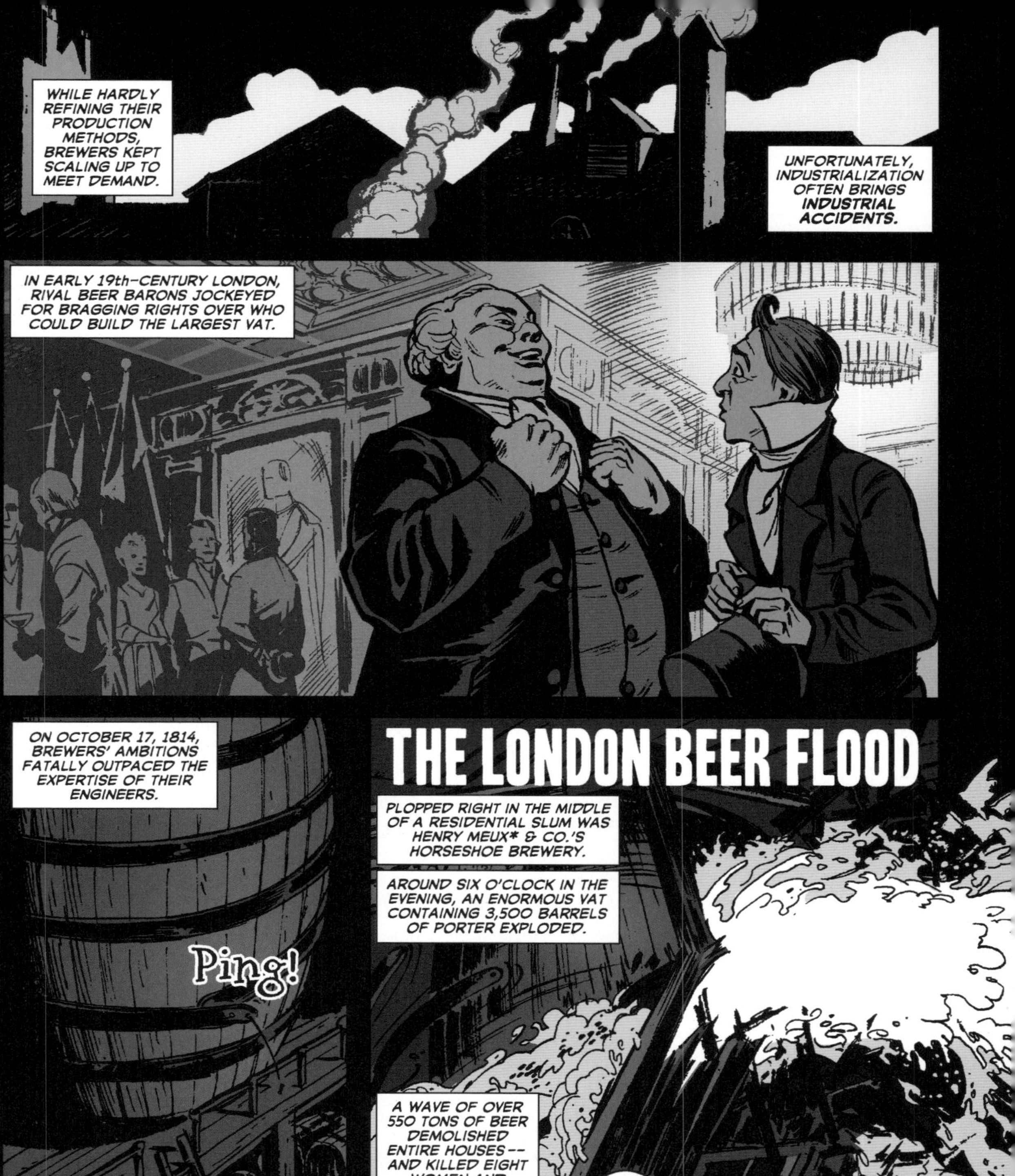
WHILE HARDLY REFINING THEIR PRODUCTION METHODS, BREWERS KEPT SCALING UP TO MEET DEMAND.
UNFORTUNATELY, INDUSTRIALIZATION OFTEN BRINGS INDUSTRIAL ACCIDENTS.
IN EARLY 19th-CENTURY LONDON, RIVAL BEER BARONS JOCKEYED FOR BRAGGING RIGHTS OVER WHO COULD BUILD THE LARGEST VAT.
ON OCTOBER 17, 1814, BREWERS' AMBITIONS FATALLY OUTPACED THE EXPERTISE OF THEIR ENGINEERS.
Ping!
OH DEAR...
THE LONDON BEER FLOOD
PLOPPED RIGHT IN THE MIDDLE OF A RESIDENTIAL SLUM WAS HENRY MEUX* & CO.'S HORSESHOE BREWERY.
AROUND SIX O'CLOCK IN THE EVENING, AN ENORMOUS VAT CONTAINING 3,500 BARRELS OF PORTER EXPLODED.
A WAVE OF OVER 550 TONS OF BEER DEMOLISHED ENTIRE HOUSES-- AND KILLED EIGHT WOMEN AND CHILDREN LIVING NEARBY.
!

*(PRONOUNCED **MEWKS.**)

THANKS TO PORTER, INDUSTRIAL-SCALE BREWING BECAME A WAY OF LIFE IN IRELAND AS WELL.

IRISH BREWS WERE HELD TO BE A BIT LOW-END AT THE TIME. "SCARCELY DRINKABLE" OPINED THE BRITISH HOME OFFICE.

BUT APPARENTLY ARTHUR GUINNESS WAS SURE HIS BEVERAGES WOULD BE A HIT. SO IN 1759 HE SIGNED A 9,000-YEAR LEASE ON A BREWERY IN DUBLIN.

HIS BREWERY'S REPUTATION FOR QUALITY ROCKETED ITS EXTRA STOUT PORTER TO LASTING INTERNATIONAL FAME.

FOR DECADES, EUROPEAN POWERS HAD FOUGHT OVER INDIA, ONE OF THE MOST RESOURCE-RICH PLACES ON EARTH.

ENGLAND'S EAST INDIA COMPANY-- A HUGE CORPORATION WITH AN ENTIRE ARMY OF ITS OWN-- WANTED CONTROL.

THE ENGLISH FOUGHT RUTHLESSLY UNTIL THEY HAD ESTABLISHED A VAST DOMINION OVER MODERN-DAY INDIA, BANGLADESH, AND PAKISTAN.

AND BRITISH OCCUPIERS IN THOSE DISTANT TROPICS CRAVED BEER. THEY PROVIDED THE BURTON BREWERS WITH AN EXPORT MARKET AS HOT AS VINDALOO.

WHAT THE WORLD WOULD SOON KNOW AS INDIA PALE ALE FLOODED INTO THE GULLETS OF BRITISH EXPATS.

Meet The Beer:
INDIA PALE ALE

Color:
Light Amber to
Deep Copper;
6 -14 SRM

Bitterness:
Very Bitter;
40 - 70 IBU

Strength:
Moderate to High;
5 - 7.5% ABV

MALT

HOPS

FOOD

MALT CHARACTER: CRISP MALT CHARACTER, WITH SOME SLIGHT CARAMEL OVERTONES AND A DRY FINISH.

HOP CHARACTER: EXPLOSIVE HOP CHARACTER. VERY BITTER AND BURSTING WITH RESINY AND FLORAL HOP AROMATICS.

FOOD PAIRINGS: SPICY THAI DISHES, INDIAN CURRIES, MEXICAN FOOD, BLUE CHEESE BURGERS.

CLASSIC EXAMPLES: MEANTIME INDIA PALE ALE, BELL'S TWO HEARTED ALE, STONE IPA, BEAR REPUBLIC RACER 5 INDIA PALE ALE

INDIA PALE ALE (IPA) SEEMS TO HAVE EVOLVED FROM AGED, OR **STOCK,** ALES BREWED ON COUNTRY ESTATES AND POPULAR WITH THE 18th–CENTURY ENGLISH GENTRY.

BREWED TO A HIGH STRENGTH FROM LIGHTLY KILNED PALE MALT AND AGGRESSIVELY HOPPED, THESE BEERS WERE WELL SUITED FOR EXPORT. THEY MATURED IN THE CASK ON THE LONG VOYAGE TO INDIA. THERE THEY WERE ENTHUSIASTICALLY ENJOYED--CHILLED--BY UPPER CLASS MERCHANTS AND CIVIL SERVANTS.

BRITONS LIVING ON THE INDIAN SUBCONTINENT FOUND IPA QUITE "SUITABLE FOR WARM CLIMATES."

INDIA PALE ALE WAS FIRST POPULARIZED BY LONDON BREWER GEORGE HODGSON IN THE 1790s. HOWEVER, IT WASN'T REFERRED TO AS INDIA PALE ALE UNTIL THE 1830S.

IN ADDITION TO BEING KNOWN FOR BREWING HOPPY PALE ALE OF HIGH QUALITY, HODGSON ALSO ESTABLISHED CONTACTS AT THE EAST INDIA COMPANY. THESE GAVE HIS BEER A LUCRATIVE ADVANTAGE. HODGSON'S PALE ALE BECAME FAMOUS.

IN THE 1820s, HODGSON'S SUCCESSORS RAN AFOUL OF THE EAST INDIA COMPANY. HIS SWEETHEART DEAL DRIED UP. THIS OPENED THE INDIAN MARKET TO COMPETITION. BURTON BREWERS SUCH AS ALLSOPP AND BASS FILLED THE VACUUM. THE BURTON BREWERS (BLESSED WITH THAT CALCIUM-RICH WATER THAT MADE FOR A CLEARER, MORE REFRESHING IPA) GREW TO BE GLOBAL POWERHOUSES.

THE BURTON IPAS BECAME TRENDY IN BRITAIN PROPER WHEN EXPATRIATES WHO HAD GROWN TO FANCY THEM RETURNED FROM INDIA.

THE GREAT EXHIBITION OF 1851 (WHICH FEATURED BURTON IPAS) SPARKED A TORRENT OF NATIONAL PRIDE IN BRITAIN. THE BURTON BREWERS REVELED AND CASHED IN ON IPA'S NEW DOMESTIC POPULARITY.

BUT IN THE LATE 1800s, THE EXPORT MARKET WANED. IN INDIA, TEA, GIN, AND LAGER BEERS MADE DOMESTICALLY OR IN EUROPE ECLIPSED IPA. AT HOME, NEW TAXES PRESSURED BRITISH BREWERS TO LOWER BEER STRENGTH. THEY SWITCHED TO PRODUCING "RUNNING BEERS." THESE BECAME TODAY'S ENGLISH PALE ALES AND BITTERS.

MODERN AMERICAN CRAFT BREWERS, INTRIGUED BY THE ROMANCE OF IPA, RESURRECTED THE STYLE.

THE BRASH, RESINY HOPS AVAILABLE IN THE U.S. COMPLEMENTED THE HOP-FORWARD STYLE. AFTER A CENTURY IN OBSCURITY, IPA BECAME THE MOST POPULAR CRAFT BREW.

THE ADVENTUROUS, AMERICAN SPIRIT CONTINUES. THE TREND IS TO EVER RATCHET UP HOPPING LEVELS, CREATING NEW INTERPRETATIONS SUCH AS **DOUBLE,** OR **IMPERIAL,** IPA. NOW BREWERS AROUND THE GLOBE ARE MAKING "AMERICAN-STYLE" IPAS.

BY THE EARLY 19th CENTURY, BEER HAD LITERALLY AND FIGURATIVELY COME A LONG WAY.

BUT BREWERS STILL **DIDN'T TRULY UNDERSTAND** EXACTLY WHAT THEY WERE DOING...

...EVEN AMIDST THE MODERN MIRACLES OF TRAINS, TELEGRAPHY, PHOTOGRAPHY, AND EARLY ELECTRICITY.

SUPERSTITIOUS NOTIONS OF HOW GOOD BEER WAS CREATED (THROUGH FERMENTATION) OR DESTROYED (THROUGH SPOILAGE) WERE STILL THE RULE OF THE DAY.

WILLIAM BLACK'S *PRACTICAL TREATISE ON BREWING*, PUBLISHED IN 1835, BLAMED BREWING MISHAPS ON "ATMOSPHERIC ELECTRICITY" AND "EARTH CURRENTS."

IT ALSO SAID, "NEITHER THE RAYS OF THE SUN OR MOON SHOULD EVER BE PERMITTED TO SHINE UPON THE WORT."

MOST BREWERS WERE SKEPTICAL-- IF NOT OUT-AND-OUT PARANOID-- ABOUT HARD SCIENCE.

NO...

NO!

THEY HONORED AGE-OLD "IF IT AIN'T BROKE, DON'T FIX IT" BREWING METHODS. THEY FEARED THAT EVEN THE SIGHT OF A SINGLE PIECE OF LABORATORY EQUIPMENT MIGHT LEAD THEIR CUSTOMERS TO CONCLUDE THAT THE BEER WAS BEING DOCTORED WITH CHEMICALS.

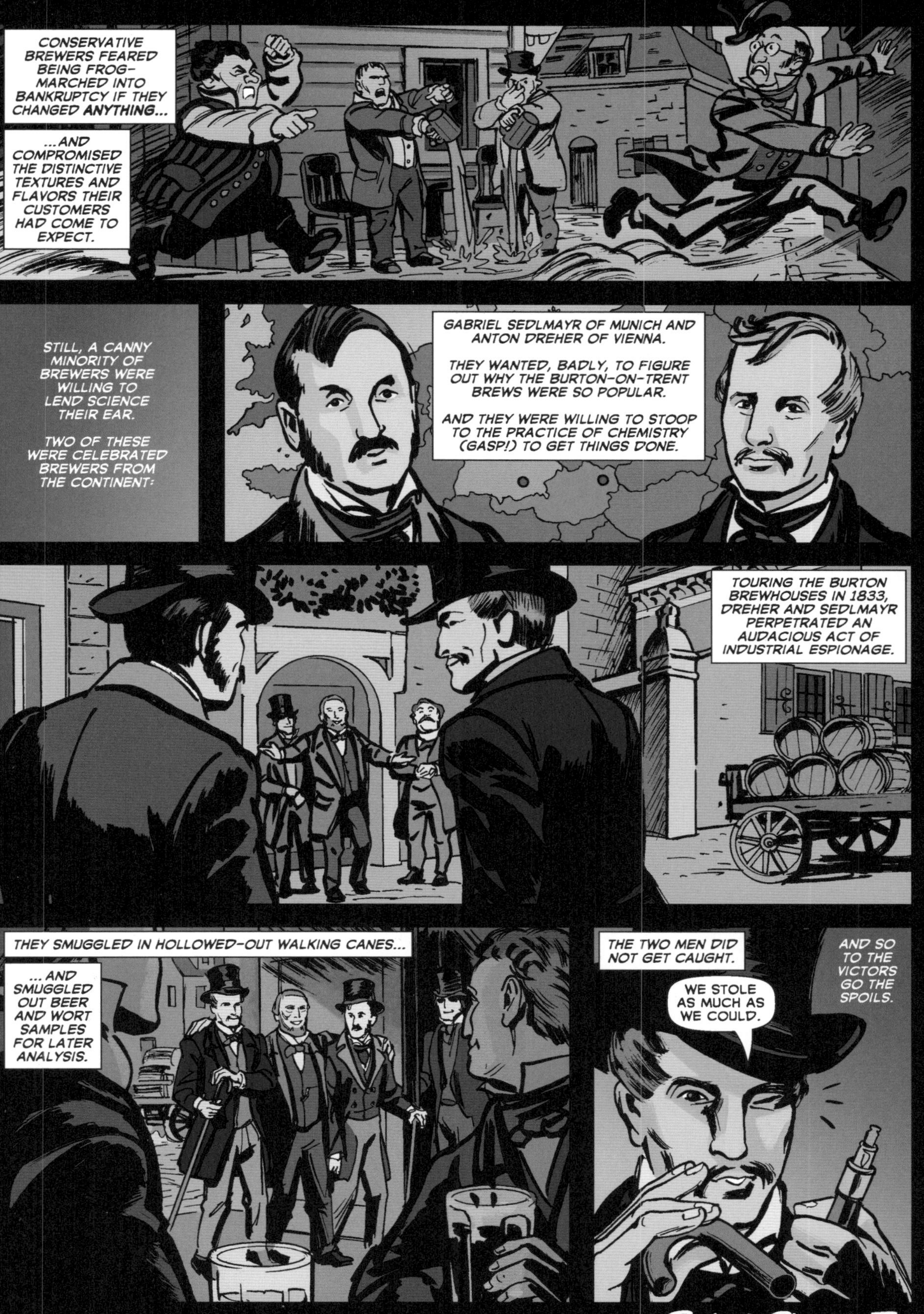

CONSERVATIVE BREWERS FEARED BEING FROG-MARCHED INTO BANKRUPTCY IF THEY CHANGED **ANYTHING**...
...AND COMPROMISED THE DISTINCTIVE TEXTURES AND FLAVORS THEIR CUSTOMERS HAD COME TO EXPECT.
STILL, A CANNY MINORITY OF BREWERS WERE WILLING TO LEND SCIENCE THEIR EAR.
TWO OF THESE WERE CELEBRATED BREWERS FROM THE CONTINENT:
GABRIEL SEDLMAYR OF MUNICH AND ANTON DREHER OF VIENNA.
THEY WANTED, BADLY, TO FIGURE OUT WHY THE BURTON-ON-TRENT BREWS WERE SO POPULAR.
AND THEY WERE WILLING TO STOOP TO THE PRACTICE OF CHEMISTRY (GASP!) TO GET THINGS DONE.
TOURING THE BURTON BREWHOUSES IN 1833, DREHER AND SEDLMAYR PERPETRATED AN AUDACIOUS ACT OF INDUSTRIAL ESPIONAGE.
THEY SMUGGLED IN HOLLOWED-OUT WALKING CANES...
... AND SMUGGLED OUT BEER AND WORT SAMPLES FOR LATER ANALYSIS.
THE TWO MEN DID NOT GET CAUGHT.
WE STOLE AS MUCH AS WE COULD.
AND SO TO THE VICTORS GO THE SPOILS.

End of Chapter Five

SCIENCE AND POLITICS TRANSFORM BEER— BUT FOR THE BETTER?

DETERMINED TO PLUMB THE SECRETS OF THEIR PURLOINED SAMPLES OF BURTON-ON-TRENT BEER...

...SEDLMAYR AND DREHER DECAMPED FOR THEIR BREWERIES BACK HOME.

ONE TAKEAWAY FROM THEIR FOREIGN ADVENTURE WAS THE ADOPTION OF AN INNOVATIVE ENGLISH MALTING METHOD.

PREVIOUSLY, BREWERS HAD DIRECTLY HEATED THE MALT...

...WHICH MINGLED THE GRAIN WITH SMOKE.

THIS IS WHY, UP TO THAT POINT, MOST BEERS HAD BEEN DARK BROWN, WITH A SMOKY FLAVOR.

BUT THANKS TO NEW TECHNOLOGIES, THE ENGLISH HAD LEARNED TO MAKE **WHITE MALT** BY SUBJECTING THE GRAIN TO **INDIRECT** HEAT...

...AT A FINELY TUNED AND **SIGNIFICANTLY LOWER** TEMPERATURE.

THIS PROCESS HELPED YIELD THE FASHIONABLE LIGHTER "PALE ALE" BREWS PRODUCED IN BURTON-ON-TRENT.

SEDLMAYR AND DREHER ULTIMATELY BROKE NEW GROUND BY COMBINING THE USE OF LIGHT MALTS...

...WITH A FERMENTATION TECHNIQUE THAT WAS **COMPLETELY ALIEN** TO THE ENGLISH SCHOOL OF BREWING.

NAMELY, THIS IS THE TECHNIQUE OF PRODUCING **LAGERS.**

AND LAGERS ARE--FOR BREWING PROFESSIONALS AND BEER GEEKS ANYWAY--WORLDS **APART** FROM BRITISH **ALES.**

LAGER BIER

A FRIENDLY DRINK

BACK IN THE DAYS OF WIDESPREAD BREWING BY CHRISTIAN BRETHREN, MANY MONASTERIES WERE SITUATED ON RECLUSIVE MOUNTAINTOPS.

IN FACT, THE NAME MUNICH ACTUALLY MEANS "MONKS," AND THEY DWELLED APLENTY IN THE ALPINE HIGHLANDS SOUTH OF THIS BREWING CENTER.

THERE WERE CAVES IN THOSE HIGHLANDS, AND MONKS REALIZED THEY COULD STUFF THE CAVES WITH ICE...

...EFFECTIVELY TURNING EACH DARK HOLLOW INTO A GRAND MAKESHIFT REFRIGERATOR...

...WHERE BEER COULD BE STORED ALL SUMMER WITHOUT SPOILING.

WHAT THE MONKS DIDN'T KNOW, HOWEVER...

...WAS THAT SOMETHING WAS HAPPENING TO THE YEAST INSIDE THESE COLD-PACKED BEERS.

ADHERENTS TO THE HEAVENLY FATHER WERE INADVERTENTLY **PLAYING GOD** WITH THE EVOLUTIONARY DESTINY OF YEAST MICROORGANISMS.

IN A TEXTBOOK "SURVIVAL OF THE FITTEST" SCENARIO, YEASTS THAT COULDN'T STAND THE PLUNGING TEMPERATURES DIED.

I ONLY REGRET THAT I HAVE BUT ONE LIFE TO GIVE FOR MY LAGER.

BUT OTHER YEASTS SURVIVED. AND THESE TENDED TO SETTLE TO THE **BOTTOM** OF FERMENTING BEER RATHER THAN FORMING A FOAMY HEAD ON **TOP**.

COME FALL, WHEN THESE "REFRIGERATED" BEERS WERE CONSUMED, THE COLD-TOLERANT YEASTS WERE SCOOPED OUT AND REUSED TO MAKE A FRESH BATCH. IN THIS WAY, ONLY THE HEARTIEST ORGANISMS WERE ALLOWED TO REPRODUCE.

OVER HUNDREDS OF YEARS THEY **MUTATED** INTO A NEW SPECIES: **SACCHAROMYCES PASTORIANUS.**

THE STRANGEST SUPER-HEROES OF ALL!

X-YEAST

UNLIKE *S. CEREVISIAE,* THE TOP-FERMENTING YEAST USED IN ALES, LAGER YEAST WORKS AT A SLOWER RATE. ALTHOUGH THIS LENGTHENS THE BREWING PROCESS, **S. PASTORIANUS** ACHIEVES A "CLEANER" FERMENTATION. FEWER BY-PRODUCTS, SUCH AS ESTERS AND KETONES, ARE LEFT OVER. THIS RESULTS IN A SMOOTHER, MORE CRISPLY FLAVORED BEER.

LAGERING MEANS MORE, HOWEVER, THAN JUST USING BOTTOM-FERMENTING YEAST.

IT ALSO MEANS STORING THE BEER IN A COOL OR REFRIGERATED CELLAR AND LETTING IT MATURE.

32.95   47.37

IN FACT, THE WORD *LAGER* COMES FROM THE GERMAN *LAGERN*, MEANING "TO STORE."

WHEN DREHER COMMINGLED LAGER YEAST WITH PALE MALTS, THE CRISP AND TASTY RESULT--*VIENNA LAGER*--WAS PRIZED BY CONNOISSEURS.

SEDLMAYR LIKEWISE SAW GREAT SUCCESS BY REINVIGORATING TRADITIONAL *MÄRZEN* BEER...

...BREWED IN MARCH AND STORED FOR FESTIVALS IN THE AUTUMN.

NOW, IN ITS MODERN INCARNATION, SEDLMAYR'S SPATEN BREWERY IS ONE OF JUST A HANDFUL OF MUNICH BREWERIES DULY AUTHORIZED TO BREW FOR THE MASSIVE BAVARIAN *OKTOBERFEST*.

FIRST CELEBRATED IN 1810 TO FETE THE MARRIAGE OF CROWN PRINCE LUDWIG TO PRINCESS THERESE OF SAXE-HILDBURGHAUSEN, THE MUNICH OKTOBERFEST IS NOW THE WORLD'S LARGEST BEER FESTIVAL.

THE SPATEN BREWERY FUNDED THE RESEARCH OF ENGINEER CARL VON LINDE.

THANKS TO LINDE'S BREAKTHROUGH-- MECHANICAL REFRIGERATION-- NEVER AGAIN WOULD BREWERS REQUIRE ICE CAVES OR CELLARS TO LAGER BEER.

AND BREWERS, AT LONG LAST, NO LONGER FACED SHUTDOWNS EVERY SUMMER.

klink!

BUT ANOTHER BEER INNOVATION WAS ABOUT TO ECLIPSE THE NEW AMBER LAGERS.

PILSNER IS THE BEHEMOTH OF BEERS. THIS STYLE IS SUCH A RUNAWAY HIT THAT IT MAKES UP 95% OF ALL BEER CONSUMED IN THE WORLD TODAY.

BUT THIS WASN'T ALWAYS SO.

IN 1838, THERE WAS NO JOY AMONG THE PEOPLE OF PLZEŇ, BOHEMIA (NOW THE CZECH REPUBLIC).

BEER MEANT THE WORLD TO THEM. BUT THE LOCAL BREWERS' LATEST WARES WERE VILE.

MOREOVER, BAVARIAN-STYLE BREWS FROM OUTSIDE SOURCES HAD SWAMPED THE MARKETPLACE, BRUISING CIVIC PRIDE.

IN A DISPLAY OF MASS DISAPPROVAL, THE CITIZENRY UPENDED DOZENS OF BEER BARRELS INTO THE GUTTER.

BUT WHAT WERE BEER MAKERS TO DO?

THE PLZEŇ BREWERS RESOLVED TO START FROM SCRATCH WITH A BRAND-NEW BREWERY AND MALT HOUSE.

THEY TURNED TO JOSEF GROLL...

... A MAN AS NOTORIOUS FOR HIS BAD MANNERS AS FOR HIS PROVERBIAL BLACK BELT IN BREWING.

BY 1842, A HIGH-PERFORMANCE BAVARIAN LAGER YEAST HAD MADE ITS WAY TO PLZEŇ.

BOHEMIA YEAST GRAND PRIX 1842

GROLL MERGED THIS YEAST WITH MILD BOHEMIAN HOPS, SWEET MORAVIAN BARLEY...

...AND PLZEŇ'S SOFT WATER, WHICH IS EXCEPTIONALLY LOW IN MINERALS.

THE RESULTS WERE UNEXPECTED.

THIS WAS NOT BAVARIAN BEER.

IT WAS SOMETHING THAT HAD NEVER EXISTED.

Meet The Beer:
Pilsner

Color: Straw Colored to Deep Gold; Creamy White Head; 2 - 6 SRM

Bitterness: Moderate to Hoppy; 25 - 45 IBU

Strength: Moderate; 4.5 - 5.5% ABV

MALT

MALT CHARACTER: PRIMARILY BREWED WITH PALE MALT. STRONG YET ROUNDED MALT FLAVOR. NO CARAMEL OVERTONES. DRY.

HOPS

HOP CHARACTER: SOLID HOP BITTERNESS, WELL-BALANCED WITH THE MALT. SPICY, FLORAL, "NOBLE" HOP AROMATICS, OFTEN SHOWCASING CZECH SAAZ HOPS. AGGRESSIVE YET REFINED.

FOOD

FOOD PAIRINGS: LIGHTER FOODS, SUCH AS CHICKEN, SEAFOOD, BRAT-WURST, AND OTHER MILD SAUSAGES. ALSO PAIRS WELL WITH SPICY FOOD, INCLUDING CHILI CON CARNE AND THAI CUISINE.

CLASSIC EXAMPLES: PILSNER URQUELL, BUDWEISER BUDVAR (CZECHVAR IN THE U.S.), VICTORY PRIMA PILS, BITBURGER PILS, BROOKLYN PILSNER

JOSEF GROLL'S INTERMINGLING OF BOHEMIAN BARLEY, SAAZ HOPS, SOFT PLZEŇ WATER, AND BAVARIAN LAGER YEAST CREATED A SENSATION WHEN IT WAS RELEASED TO THE DRINKING PUBLIC ON NOVEMBER 11, 1842.

A TYPE OF LAGER, PILSNER'S POPULARITY SWEPT AROUND THE WORLD.

THIS BRIGHT, CRISP, BLONDE QUAFF SUPPLANTED OTHER STYLES (SUCH AS IPA, PORTER, AND THE DARK LAGERS OF GERMANY) AND TRAVELED TO FAR-OFF LANDS (SUCH AS AMERICA AND THE FAR EAST).

PILSNER BECAME THE ARCHETYPAL MODEL OF WHAT WE THINK OF AS BEER.

PILSNER HAS A LIGHT BUT FULL MALT CHARACTER AND A SMOOTH FLAVOR. THESE AGREEABLE CHARACTERISTICS ARE THE RESULT OF ENGLISH-STYLE KILNING OF THE MALT AT LOWER TEMPERATURES AS WELL AS THE CONTINENTAL STYLE OF DECOCTION MASHING.

TOGETHER, THESE METHODS HELP DRAW OUT THE RICH FLAVORS OF THE BARLEY WITHOUT ADDING SWEETNESS.

THE HOPS USED IN PILSNER ARE TRADITIONALLY OF THE "NOBLE" TYPE.

THESE HOPS ARE HERITAGE VARIETIES KNOWN FOR THEIR PLEASANTLY REFINED, DELICATE AROMAS. NOBLE HOPS ARE DESIGNATED BY THEIR AREA OF ORIGIN. THESE INCLUDE THE HALLERTAU, TETTNANG, AND SPALT REGIONS OF GERMANY AND THE SAAZ (ŽATEC) AREA OF BOHEMIA (NOW THE CZECH REPUBLIC).

PILSNER (OR PILS) WAS QUICKLY ADOPTED IN GERMANY AND BROUGHT TO THE NEW WORLD AND BEYOND BY EMIGRANT BREWERS.

GERMAN INTERPRETATIONS OF PILSNER TEND TO BE A TOUCH LIGHTER IN COLOR, CRISPER, AND SLIGHTLY HOPPIER THAN THE CZECH EXAMPLES.

ON THE OTHER HAND, DUTCH VERSIONS, SUCH AS HEINEKEN AND GROLSCH, ARE A BIT SWEETER.

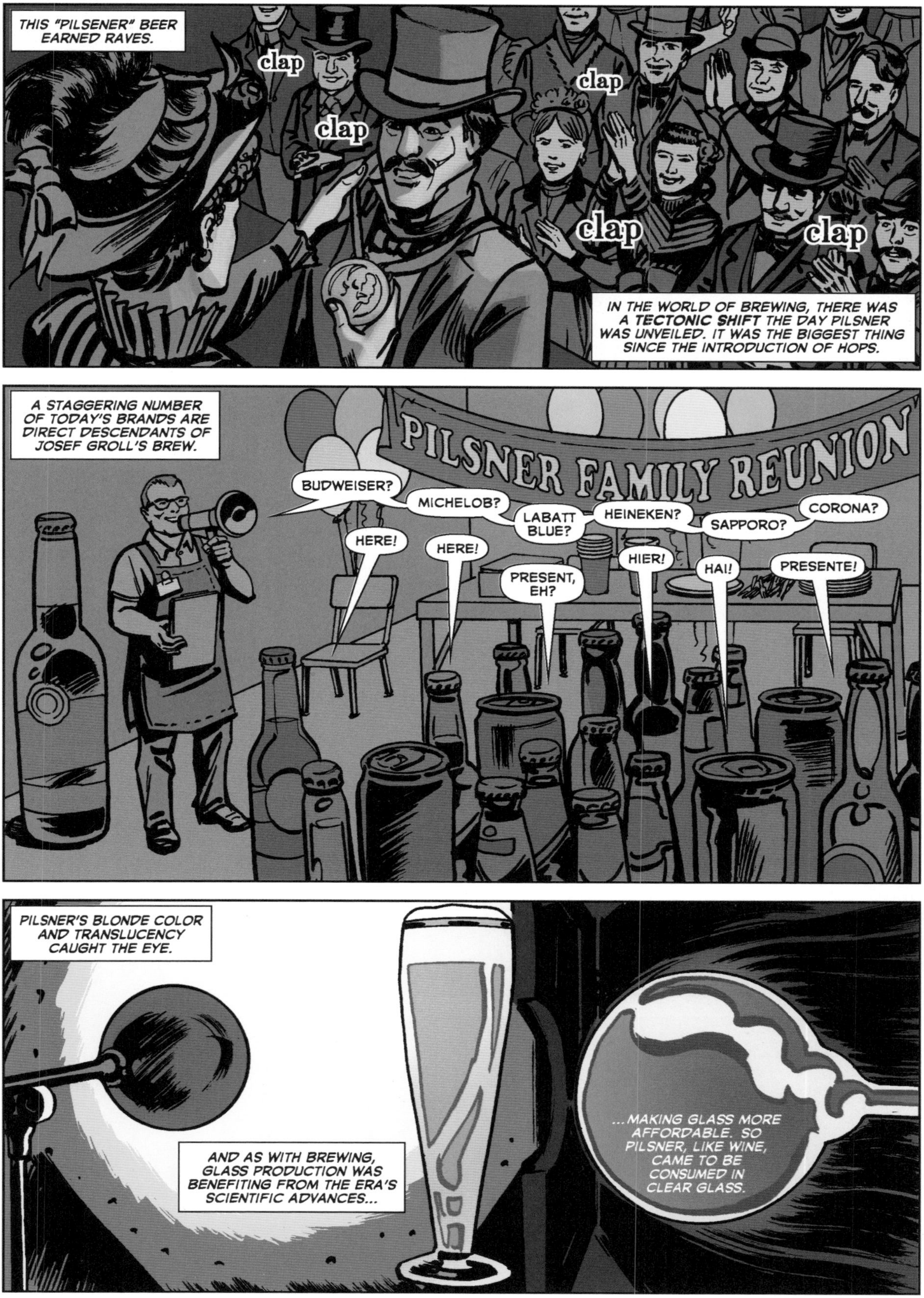
THIS "PILSENER" BEER EARNED RAVES.
clap
clap
clap
clap
clap
IN THE WORLD OF BREWING, THERE WAS A **TECTONIC SHIFT** THE DAY PILSNER WAS UNVEILED. IT WAS THE BIGGEST THING SINCE THE INTRODUCTION OF HOPS.
A STAGGERING NUMBER OF TODAY'S BRANDS ARE DIRECT DESCENDANTS OF JOSEF GROLL'S BREW.
PILSNER FAMILY REUNION
BUDWEISER?
MICHELOB?
LABATT BLUE?
HEINEKEN?
SAPPORO?
CORONA?
HERE!
HERE!
PRESENT, EH?
HIER!
HAI!
PRESENTE!
PILSNER'S BLONDE COLOR AND TRANSLUCENCY CAUGHT THE EYE.
AND AS WITH BREWING, GLASS PRODUCTION WAS BENEFITING FROM THE ERA'S SCIENTIFIC ADVANCES...
...MAKING GLASS MORE AFFORDABLE. SO PILSNER, LIKE WINE, CAME TO BE CONSUMED IN CLEAR GLASS.

ACROSS WESTERN CIVILIZATION AT THIS TIME, PEOPLE YEARNED FOR FREEDOM FROM THE HEAVY HAND OF HEREDITARY RULERS.

A LONG PERIOD OF THE MOST PROFOUND DEGRADATION WEIGHS HEAVILY ON GERMANY. IT MAY BE CHARACTERIZED BY THE WORDS: SUBJUGATION, STULTIFICATION, AND BLEEDING DRY OF THE PEOPLE!

PEOPLE MARCHED, HELD ELECTIONS, SIGNED PETITIONS, AND PRINTED PROGRESSIVE NEWSPAPERS AND CONSTITUTIONS.

BUT IN THE END, THE GENERALS AND NOBLES WHO RULED THEM CLIPPED THEIR WINGS.

VERY WELL, IF THEY DO NOT WANT TO HEAR ABOUT THE GRACE OF GOD...

...THEY WILL HAVE TO HEAR BY THE GRACE OF CANNON.

BULLETS STARTED TO FLY.

THE REVOLUTIONS OF 1848 WERE A FAILURE FOR THOSE WHO OPPOSED THE ESTABLISHMENT.

HUGE NUMBERS OF WORKING-CLASS AND MIDDLE-CLASS GERMANS PULLED UP STAKES AND WENT TO AMERICA.

FOUNDERS OF MIGHTY AMERICAN BEER EMPIRES EMERGED FROM THIS STOCK OF GERMAN IMMIGRANTS.

Frederick Miller, Frederick Pabst, Bernhard Stroh, Joseph Schlitz, Valentin Blatz, Frederick Schaefer, and Adolphus Busch

ADOLPHUS BUSCH SOLD BREWING SUPPLIES TO THE 40 PLUS BREWERIES IN SAINT LOUIS.

HE MARRIED INTO THE BREWING FAMILY OF EBERHARD ANHEUSER.

ANHEUSER'S BUSINESS WAS FAILING. HIS BEER WAS BOTTOM OF THE BARREL.

"ST. LOUIS ROWDIES WERE KNOWN TO PROJECT MOUTH-FULS OF IT BACK OVER THE BAR," REPORTED A BUSCH FAMILY CHRONICLER IN 1929.

BUSCH TURNED HIS FATHER-IN-LAW'S BREWERY'S PROSPECTS AROUND...

...THANKS TO A LAGER RECIPE A BUSINESS PARTNER BROUGHT BACK TO THE STATES AFTER LUNCHING AT A MONASTERY IN BUDWEIS, BOHEMIA.

WITH THE LAUNCH OF BUDWEISER, AN ICONIC AMERICAN BRAND WAS BORN.

THIS WAS NO BACKWARD-LOOKING BREWERY.

IT EXPLOITED EVERY AVAILABLE SCIENTIFIC AND TECHNOLOGICAL IMPROVEMENT.

BUSCH PIONEERED THE USE OF RAILROADS FOR DISTRIBUTION OF HIS PRODUCT.*

HE ALSO CONSTRUCTED A NETWORK OF ICEHOUSES TO HELP PRESERVE HIS BEER AT PEAK QUALITY.

*THIS INCLUDED A LAVISH PRIVATE RAILCAR, WHICH HE NAMED AFTER HIMSELF.

GERMAN-AMERICAN BREWERS BANDED TOGETHER INTO A FORMAL LEAGUE TO FACE PECULIAR ISSUES THEY FOUND IN THEIR ADOPTED COUNTRY.

ONE SUCH CONCERN?

AMERICAN SIX-ROW BARLEY WAS HIGHER IN PROTEIN AND HAD THICKER HUSKS THAN ITS OLD-WORLD FOREBEAR. THIS MADE THE BUDWEISER RECIPE--AND THOSE FOR SIMILAR LIGHT LAGERS--YIELD A HAZIER AND HARSHER FINAL PRODUCT.

TWO-ROWED HORDEUM DISTICHUM

SIX-ROWED HORDEUM VULGARE

BUSCH AND HIS RESEARCHERS FOUND THAT CORN AND RICE--OF WHICH AMERICA HAD NO SHORTAGE--WERE VALUABLE ADDITIONS THAT SOLVED THIS PROBLEM.

COUNTY

THESE ADJUNCTS ALSO MADE BEER CHEAPER TO PRODUCE.

MILLER, SCHAEFER, PABST, AND THE REST REACHED DIZZYING SUMMITS OF SUCCESS IN THE "LAND OF OPPORTUNITY." BUT BEER SCIENCE TRAILBLAZERS A HEMISPHERE AWAY HAD HELPED CLEAR THEIR PATHS.

EXPERTS HAD LONG BELIEVED FERMENTATION AND SPOILAGE TO BE CHEMICAL RATHER THAN BIOLOGICAL PROCESSES.

BUT ADVANCED MICRO-SCOPES, SUCH AS THOSE DEVELOPED BY ITALIAN GIOVANNI BATTISTA AMICI BEGINNING IN THE 1820S, ALLOWED RESEARCHERS TO BETTER OBSERVE THE WORLD AT THE CELLULAR LEVEL.

THUS ARMED, SCIENTISTS CHARLES CAGNIARD DE LA TOUR, FRIEDRICH KÜTZING, AND THEODOR SCHWANN--WORKING INDEPENDENTLY IN 1837--PROVED TO THE WORLD THAT YEAST IS A LIVING ORGANISM!

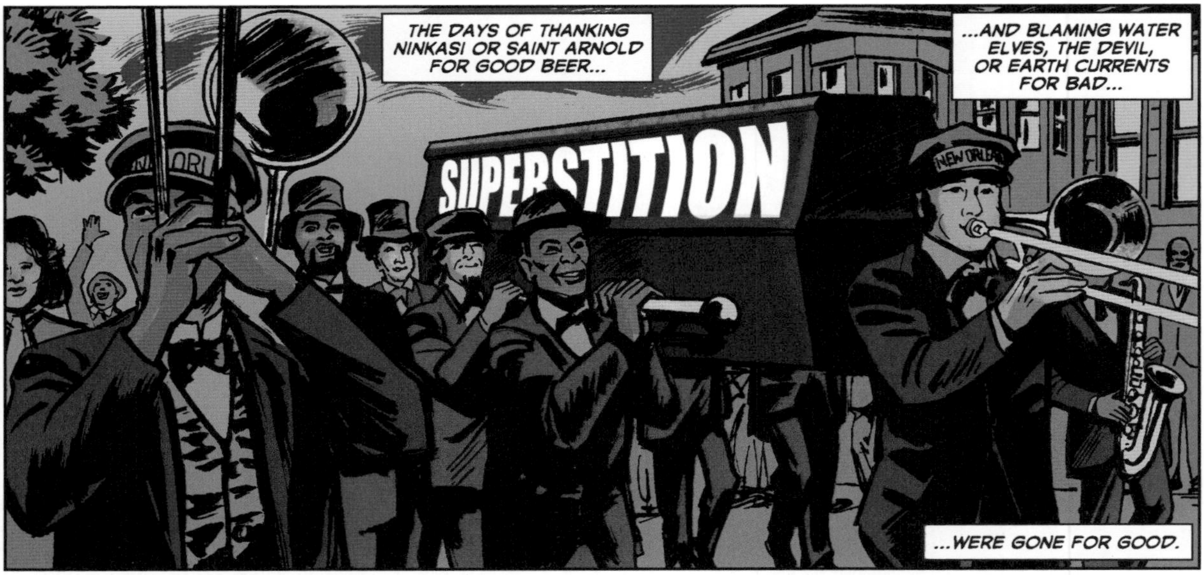
THE DAYS OF THANKING NINKASI OR SAINT ARNOLD FOR GOOD BEER...
...AND BLAMING WATER ELVES, THE DEVIL, OR EARTH CURRENTS FOR BAD...
SUPERSTITION
...WERE GONE FOR GOOD.

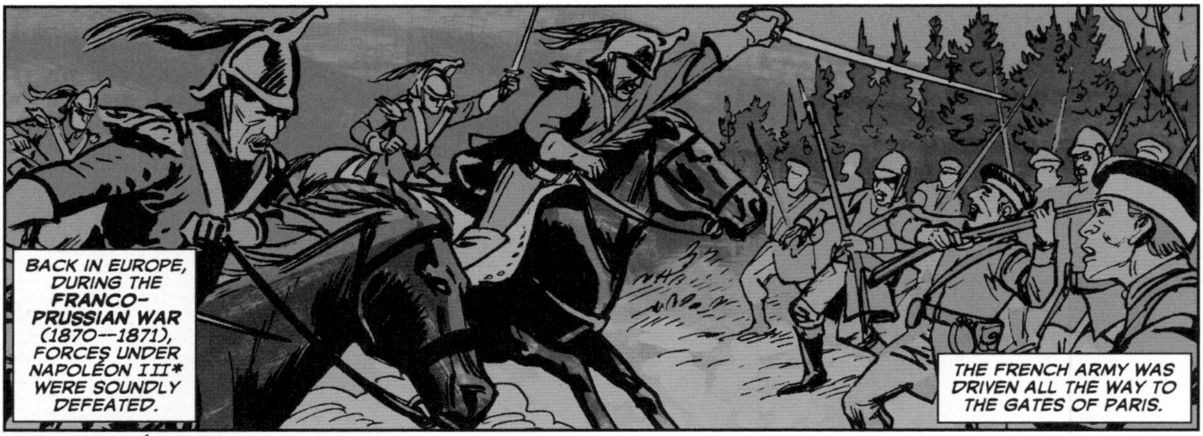
BACK IN EUROPE, DURING THE **FRANCO-PRUSSIAN WAR** (1870--1871), FORCES UNDER NAPOLÉON III* WERE SOUNDLY DEFEATED.
THE FRENCH ARMY WAS DRIVEN ALL THE WAY TO THE GATES OF PARIS.

*THE LATE NAPOLÉON BONAPARTE'S NEPHEW.

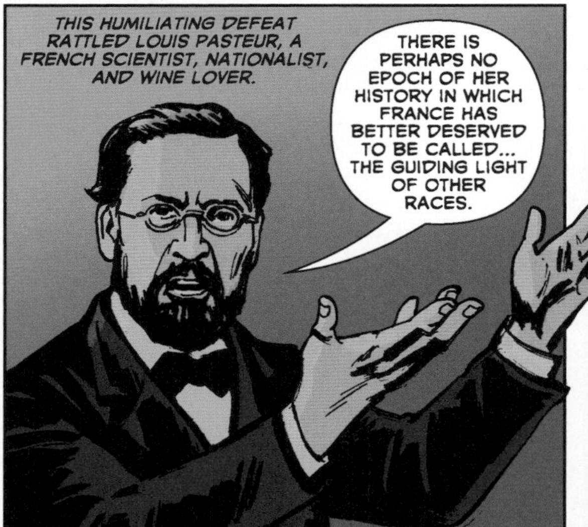
THIS HUMILIATING DEFEAT RATTLED LOUIS PASTEUR, A FRENCH SCIENTIST, NATIONALIST, AND WINE LOVER.
THERE IS PERHAPS NO EPOCH OF HER HISTORY IN WHICH FRANCE HAS BETTER DESERVED TO BE CALLED... THE GUIDING LIGHT OF OTHER RACES.

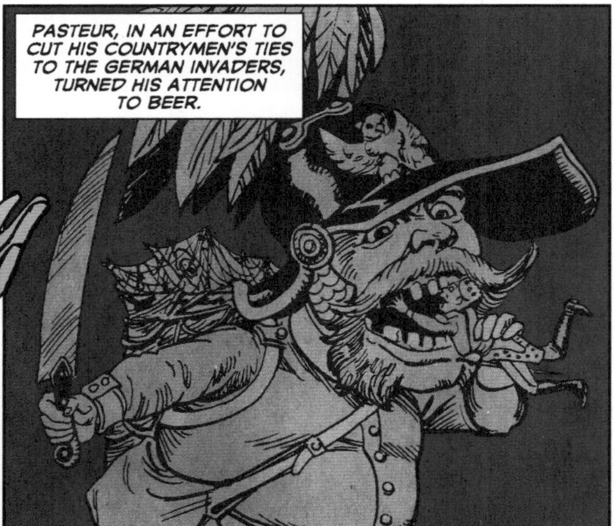
PASTEUR, IN AN EFFORT TO CUT HIS COUNTRYMEN'S TIES TO THE GERMAN INVADERS, TURNED HIS ATTENTION TO BEER.

PASTEUR HIT ON A PROCESS OF **TEMPORARILY HEATING BREWED BEER** TO KILL ANY LINGERING MICROORGANISMS.

L. PASTEUR.
Brewing Beer and Ale.

No. 135,245.

Patented Jan. 28, 1873.

LIKE REFRIGERATION, **PASTEURIZATION** PROVIDED A SHOT IN THE ARM TO BEER'S SHELF LIFE.

NHEUSER-BUSCH
BREWING ASS'N
The First Brewery to Introduce
PASTEURIZED BOTTLED BEER IN AMERICA.
BREWERS OF FINE BEER EXCLUSIVELY

SCIENTIST EMIL CHRISTIAN HANSEN HAD BEEN TAUGHT BREWING BY GABRIEL SEDLMAYR.

HE LATER FOUND WORK IN HIS HOME COUNTRY'S CARLSBERG BREWERY, IN COPENHAGEN, DENMARK.

HANSEN BUILT ON PASTEUR'S WORK AND DEVELOPED A LABORATORY METHOD TO CULTURE **GENETICALLY PURE** STRAINS OF YEAST.

BEFORE THIS, BREWERS HAD INADVERTENTLY BEEN USING A **MIXTURE** OF YEAST TYPES.

HANSEN'S GROUNDBREAKING WORK ENSURED THAT IN THE FUTURE, BREWER'S YEAST WOULD BE OPTIMIZED FOR ITS JOB.

ANTICIPATING TODAY'S OPEN SOURCE MOVEMENT, THE CARLSBERG BREWERY-- WHICH MIGHT HAVE PATENTED THIS TECHNOLOGY-- INSTEAD FREELY SHARED IT WITH THE BREWING WORLD.

PASTEUR MADE BEER KEEP LONGER.

HANSEN MADE IT TASTE BETTER.

BUT BREWERS AND BEER DRINKERS WOULD SOON LEARN THAT ALL THIS SCIENCE COULD CUT BOTH WAYS.

HARD AS THIS MAY BE TO BELIEVE, THE INNOCENT MASSES STILL DIDN'T KNOW THAT THERE WAS ACTUALLY ALCOHOL IN BEER!

MANY THOUGHT THE "EXCITEMENT" THEY FELT AFTER DOWNING A FEW BEERS CAME FROM AN INVIGORATING BOOST OF PURE NUTRITION.

IN OTHER WORDS, THEY BELIEVED THE HEALTHY WHOLE-GRAIN MALT INFUSED THEM WITH STRENGTH AND GUSTO.

GUINNESS FOR STRENGTH

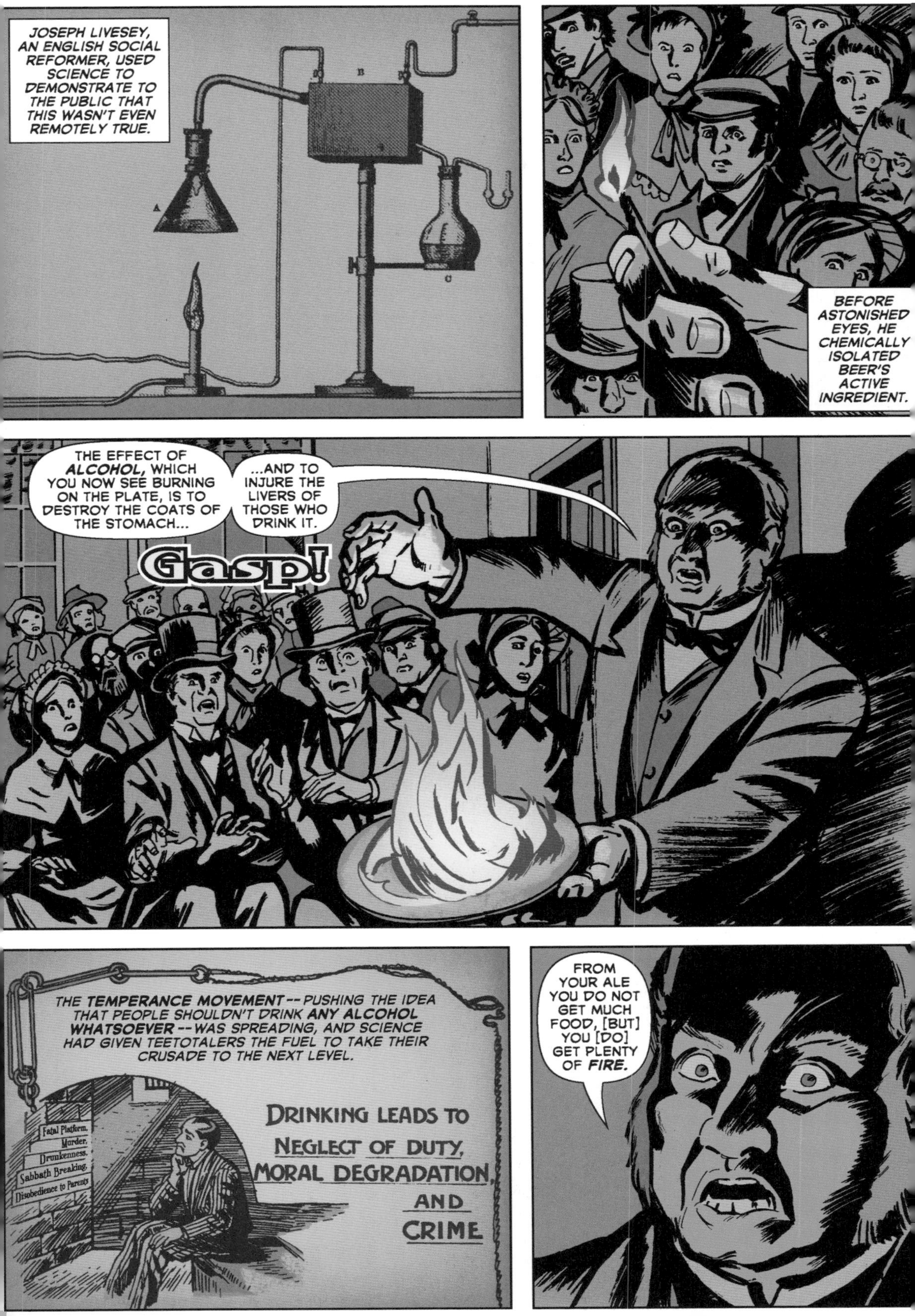
JOSEPH LIVESEY, AN ENGLISH SOCIAL REFORMER, USED SCIENCE TO DEMONSTRATE TO THE PUBLIC THAT THIS WASN'T EVEN REMOTELY TRUE.
B
A
C
BEFORE ASTONISHED EYES, HE CHEMICALLY ISOLATED BEER'S ACTIVE INGREDIENT.
THE EFFECT OF ALCOHOL, WHICH YOU NOW SEE BURNING ON THE PLATE, IS TO DESTROY THE COATS OF THE STOMACH...
...AND TO INJURE THE LIVERS OF THOSE WHO DRINK IT.
Gasp!
THE TEMPERANCE MOVEMENT--PUSHING THE IDEA THAT PEOPLE SHOULDN'T DRINK ANY ALCOHOL WHATSOEVER--WAS SPREADING, AND SCIENCE HAD GIVEN TEETOTALERS THE FUEL TO TAKE THEIR CRUSADE TO THE NEXT LEVEL.
Fatal Platform.
Murder.
Drunkenness.
Sabbath Breaking.
Disobedience to Parents
DRINKING LEADS TO NEGLECT OF DUTY, MORAL DEGRADATION, AND CRIME
FROM YOUR ALE YOU DO NOT GET MUCH FOOD, [BUT] YOU [DO] GET PLENTY OF FIRE.

REMEMBER THAT THE UNITED STATES WAS, IN A VERY REAL WAY, FOUNDED BY TRUE BELIEVERS IN AN UNFORGIVING GOD.

METHODISTS, QUAKERS, BAPTISTS, AND OTHERS VIEWED DRINKING AS A GATEWAY TO A CORNUCOPIA OF ANTISOCIAL TENDENCIES.

BUT IN BOTH THE OLD WORLD AND THE NEW, "DRINKING" PRIMARILY REFERRED TO BOOZY LIBATIONS LIKE RUM, GIN, AND WHISKEY.

Idiocy

Poverty

Insanity

Misery

The Alms House

Loss of Reason

Idleness

The Wrath of God

Disease

IQUORS &

ALCHOHOL

BRANDY

GIN

RUM

WHISKEY

THE TREE OF INTEMPERANCE.

BEER WAS NEARLY ALWAYS UPHELD AS A VIABLE AND ESSENTIALLY HARMLESS ALTERNATIVE.

I wish to see [beer] become common instead of the whiskey which kills one-third of our citizens and ruins their families.

THOMAS JEFFERSON, 1816.

BUT JOSEPH LIVESEY HELPED CLOSE THE BEER LOOPHOLE.

AS WITH THEIR RELIGION, AMERICANS HAVE LONG BEEN KNOWN TO PURSUE THINGS...

LIPS THAT TOUCH LIQUOR SHALL NOT TOUCH OURS

TOBACCO
THE USE OF TOBACCO, IN ANY FORM, IS A DIRTY, FILTHY, DISGUSTING, DEGRADING HABIT. NO GENTLEMAN WILL USE TOBACCO IN THIS CITY

YOU HAVE NO MORE RIGHT TO POLLUTE WITH TOBACCO SMOKE, THE ATMOSPHERE WHICH CLEAN PEOPLE HAVE TO BREATHE, THAN YOU HAVE TO SPIT IN THE WATER WHICH THEY HAVE TO DRINK

...WITH A KIND OF DOGGED, MANICHAEAN, BLUNT-FORCE MANIA.

MANY MEMBERS OF THE TEMPERANCE MOVEMENT WERE NO EXCEPTION.

CUT IT OUT, YOU FOOLS!

YOU WILL REAP NOTHING BUT SMOKER'S CANCER OR PARALYSIS FROM THIS NASTY, STINKING STUFF!

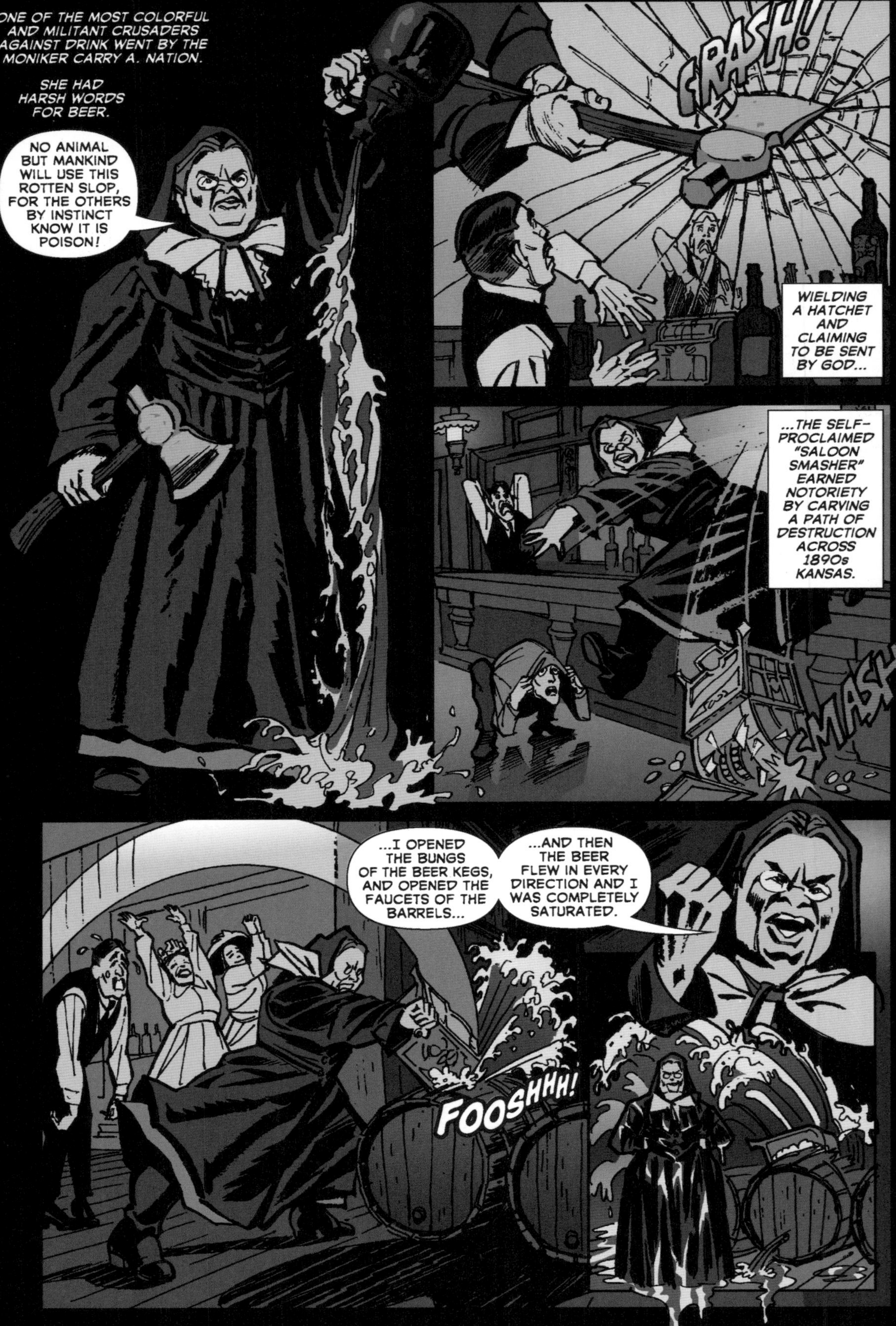
ONE OF THE MOST COLORFUL AND MILITANT CRUSADERS AGAINST DRINK WENT BY THE MONIKER CARRY A. NATION.
SHE HAD HARSH WORDS FOR BEER.
NO ANIMAL BUT MANKIND WILL USE THIS ROTTEN SLOP, FOR THE OTHERS BY INSTINCT KNOW IT IS POISON!
CRASH!
WIELDING A HATCHET AND CLAIMING TO BE SENT BY GOD...
...THE SELF-PROCLAIMED "SALOON SMASHER" EARNED NOTORIETY BY CARVING A PATH OF DESTRUCTION ACROSS 1890s KANSAS.
SMASH!
...I OPENED THE BUNGS OF THE BEER KEGS, AND OPENED THE FAUCETS OF THE BARRELS...
...AND THEN THE BEER FLEW IN EVERY DIRECTION AND I WAS COMPLETELY SATURATED.
FOOSHHH!

AT ITS BEGINNINGS, THE TEMPERANCE MOVEMENT-- AND THE "DRY" POLITICIANS WITHIN ITS RANKS-- SIMPLY TRIED TO PERSUADE PEOPLE NOT TO DRINK.

Behold the trade that ruins men, the beer saloon-- the robber's den, Good men declare with flashing eye, This murder trade is soon to die.

The saloons must go!

BUT MERE APPEALS TO MORALITY WEREN'T GETTING THE JOB DONE.

THE DRYS CRAVED THE POWER OF COERCIVE FORCE.

ELSEWHERE, BRITAIN, FRANCE, AUSTRIA-HUNGARY, RUSSIA, AND THE GERMAN EMPIRE HAD CRAVINGS OF THEIR OWN--AND PLENTY OF MUSCLE BEHIND THEIR STRONG-ARM TACTICS.

THESE NATION-STATES HAD BEEN DEVOURING NATURAL RESOURCES IN EVERY FOREIGN COUNTRY THEY COULD SINK THEIR TEETH INTO.

THE AGGRESSIVELY EXPANDING EUROPEAN POWERS CAUGHT THEMSELVES UP IN A WIDE NET OF ALLIANCES WITH, AND AGAINST, EACH OTHER.

Africa

India

Indochina

Bosnia and Herzegovina

THINGS CAME TO A HEAD IN 1914.

ARCHDUKE FRANZ FERDINAND, A FRIEND OF GERMANY'S KAISER WILHELM II, WAS SHOT IN SARAJEVO.

POP! POP!

THE ASSASSINATION RIPPLED OUT INTO THE PERILOUS CROSSCURRENTS OF THE DIPLOMATIC ENTANGLEMENTS OF THE EUROPEAN POWERS.

RUSSIA MOBILIZED ITS ARMY AGAINST GERMANY AND AUSTRIA-HUNGARY.

GERMANY LAUNCHED AN INVASION OF FRANCE.

BRITAIN CAME TO FRANCE'S AID.

THE HARROWING BARBARITIES OF WORLD WAR I HAD BEGUN.

AT FIRST, THE U.S. WAS DETERMINED TO STAY OUT OF THE CONFLICT.

BUT IN 1915, A GERMAN SUBMARINE SUNK A BRITISH PASSENGER SHIP.

WHEN THE RMS LUSITANIA PLUNGED BENEATH THE WAVES, 128 AMERICANS DIED.

U.S. NEUTRALITY WAS ANOTHER CASUALTY OF THAT GERMAN TORPEDO.

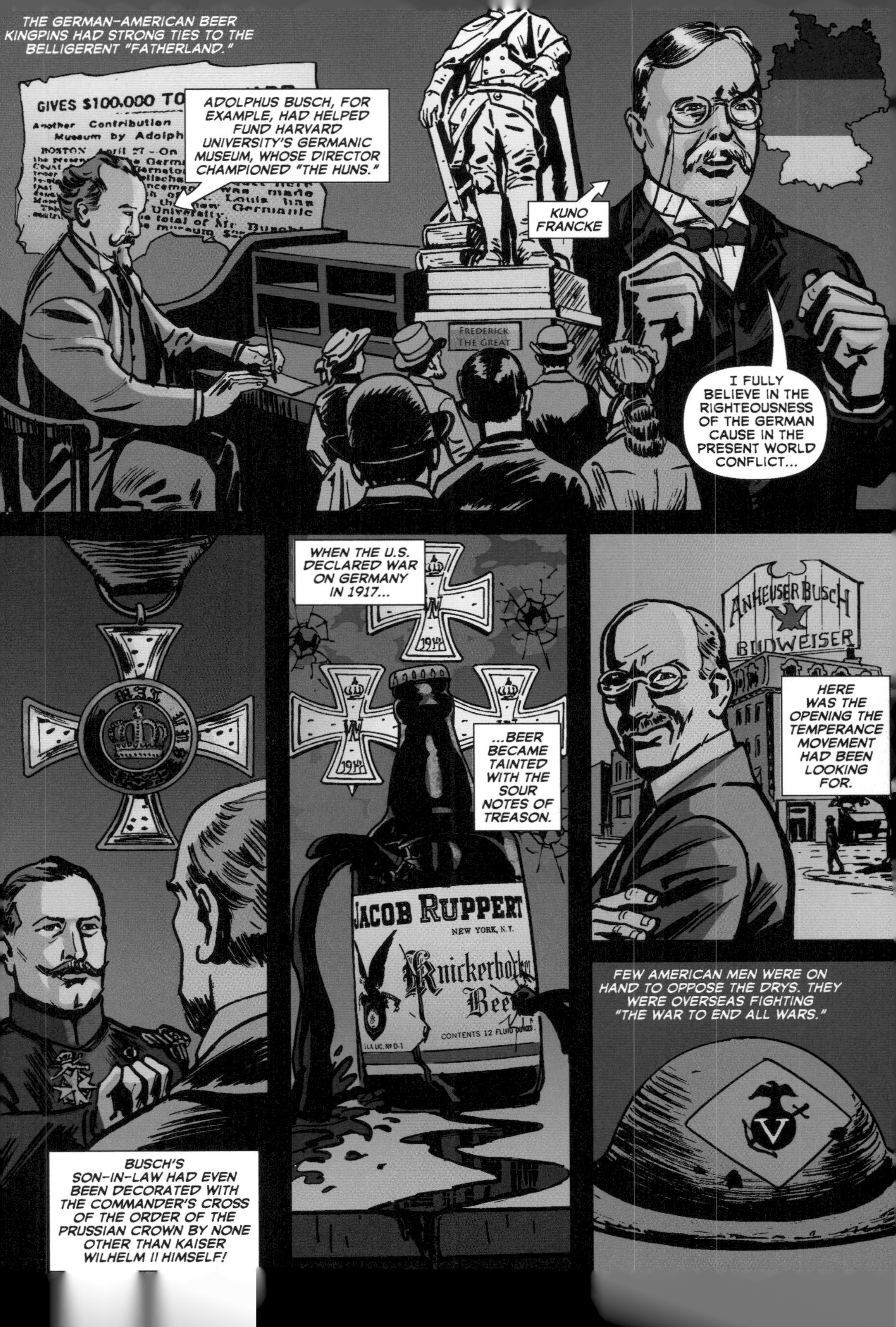
THE GERMAN-AMERICAN BEER KINGPINS HAD STRONG TIES TO THE BELLIGERENT "FATHERLAND."
GIVES $100,000 TO
Another Contribution
Museum by Adolph
ADOLPHUS BUSCH, FOR EXAMPLE, HAD HELPED FUND HARVARD UNIVERSITY'S GERMANIC MUSEUM, WHOSE DIRECTOR CHAMPIONED "THE HUNS."
FREDERICK THE GREAT
KUNO FRANCKE
I FULLY BELIEVE IN THE RIGHTEOUSNESS OF THE GERMAN CAUSE IN THE PRESENT WORLD CONFLICT...
BUSCH'S SON-IN-LAW HAD EVEN BEEN DECORATED WITH THE COMMANDER'S CROSS OF THE ORDER OF THE PRUSSIAN CROWN BY NONE OTHER THAN KAISER WILHELM II HIMSELF!
WHEN THE U.S. DECLARED WAR ON GERMANY IN 1917...
...BEER BECAME TAINTED WITH THE SOUR NOTES OF TREASON.
JACOB RUPPERT
NEW YORK, N.Y.
ANHEUSER BUSCH
BUDWEISER
HERE WAS THE OPENING THE TEMPERANCE MOVEMENT HAD BEEN LOOKING FOR.
FEW AMERICAN MEN WERE ON HAND TO OPPOSE THE DRYS. THEY WERE OVERSEAS FIGHTING "THE WAR TO END ALL WARS."

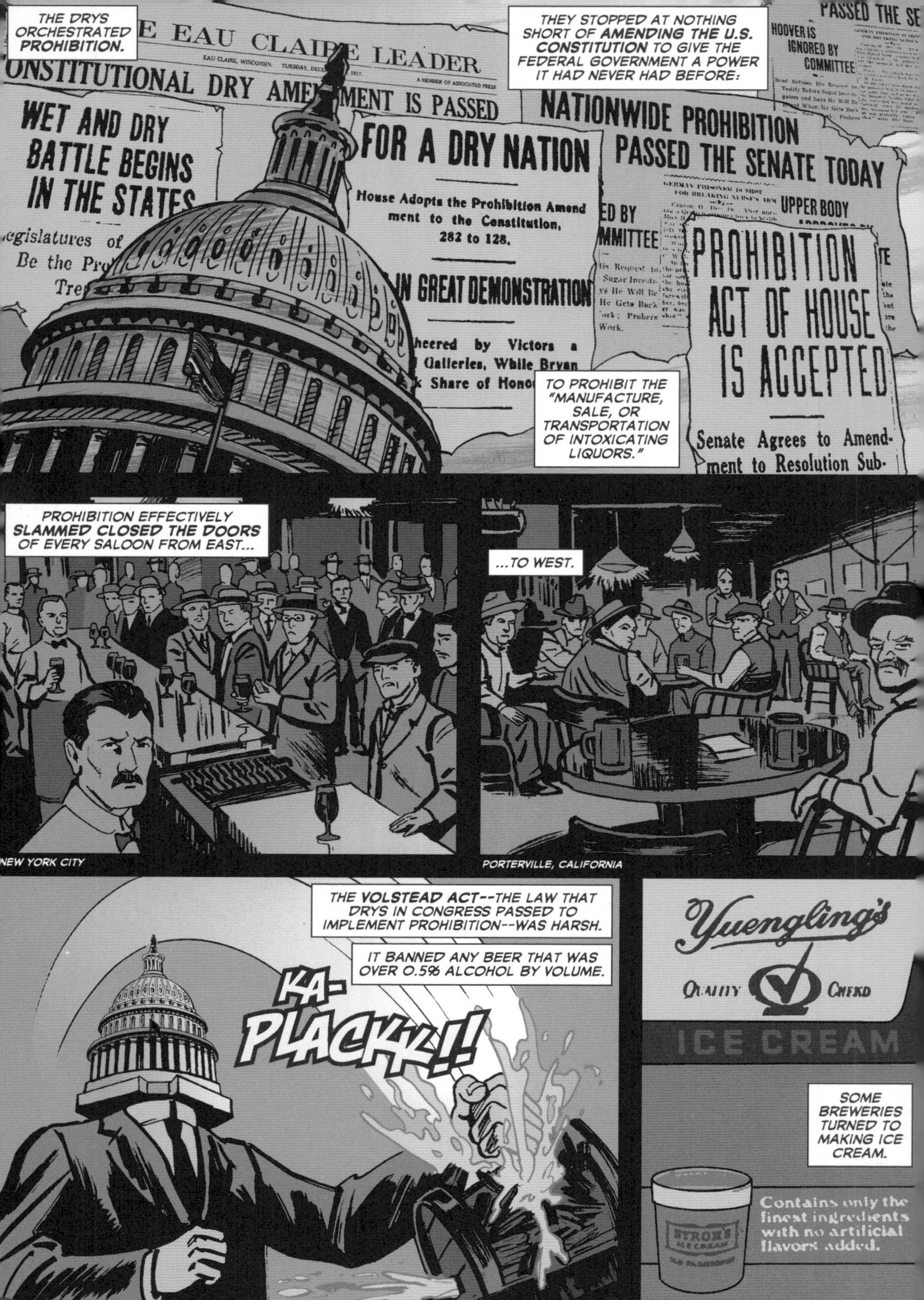
THE DRYS ORCHESTRATED PROHIBITION.
THE EAU CLAIRE LEADER
CONSTITUTIONAL DRY AMENDMENT IS PASSED
WET AND DRY BATTLE BEGINS IN THE STATES
FOR A DRY NATION
House Adopts the Prohibition Amendment to the Constitution, 282 to 128.
IN GREAT DEMONSTRATION
THEY STOPPED AT NOTHING SHORT OF AMENDING THE U.S. CONSTITUTION TO GIVE THE FEDERAL GOVERNMENT A POWER IT HAD NEVER HAD BEFORE:
PASSED THE SENATE
HOOVER IS IGNORED BY COMMITTEE
NATIONWIDE PROHIBITION PASSED THE SENATE TODAY
UPPER BODY
PROHIBITION ACT OF HOUSE IS ACCEPTED
Senate Agrees to Amendment to Resolution Sub-
TO PROHIBIT THE "MANUFACTURE, SALE, OR TRANSPORTATION OF INTOXICATING LIQUORS."
PROHIBITION EFFECTIVELY SLAMMED CLOSED THE DOORS OF EVERY SALOON FROM EAST...
NEW YORK CITY
...TO WEST.
PORTERVILLE, CALIFORNIA
THE VOLSTEAD ACT--THE LAW THAT DRYS IN CONGRESS PASSED TO IMPLEMENT PROHIBITION--WAS HARSH.
IT BANNED ANY BEER THAT WAS OVER 0.5% ALCOHOL BY VOLUME.
KA-PLACKK!!
Yuengling's
QUALITY CHEKD
ICE CREAM
SOME BREWERIES TURNED TO MAKING ICE CREAM.
STROH'S ICE CREAM
Contains only the finest ingredients with no artificial flavors added.

OTHERS PRODUCED GINGER ALE, BIRCH BEER, MALT EXTRACT, CORN SYRUP, AND SOMETHING CALLED "GRAPE BOUQUET."

THEY TURNED OUT DEALCOHOLIZED NEAR BEER, UNDER THAT BRUTAL 0.5% ABV.

PROHIBITION WAS A TOWERING FAILURE FROM THE START.

ENFORCEMENT WAS SPOTTY, UNDERFUNDED, AND RIFE WITH CORRUPTION AND BRIBERY.

AMERICANS STILL WANTED ALCOHOL. MOST TURNED TO ILLICIT HARD LIQUOR.

BUT A THIRST FOR BEER REMAINED.

PEOPLE SET UP WILDCAT BREWERIES ON THE SLY.

THEY ACQUIRED PHONY-BALONEY PRESCRIPTIONS FOR "MEDICINAL" BEER.

ORGANIZED CRIME LEAPT TO TAKE ADVANTAGE OF AMERICANS' THIRST.

ARE YOU FROM MIKE MERLO'S?

THE WANTONNESS AND VIOLENCE OF ORGANIZED CRIME DURING THIS PERIOD...

BLAM! BLAM! BLAM! BLAM!

THE 1924 MURDER OF DEAN O'BANION, CHICAGO CRIME BOSS. HE HAD SOLD RIVAL JOHNNY TORRIO AN ILLEGAL BREWERY THAT O'BANION ALLEGEDLY KNEW WOULD BE RAIDED BY FEDERAL AGENTS.

...ARE INFAMOUS.

Tat-Tat-Tat-Tat-Tat-Tat!!!

AMERICANS GRADUALLY CAME TO THEIR HEADS.

"WET" POLITICIANS BEGAN TO GET THEIR MESSAGE ACROSS:

PROHIBITION WAS ALL WASHED UP.

ROOSEVELT AND GARNER

SINGER AND RADIO PERSONALITY ERNEST HARE.

126

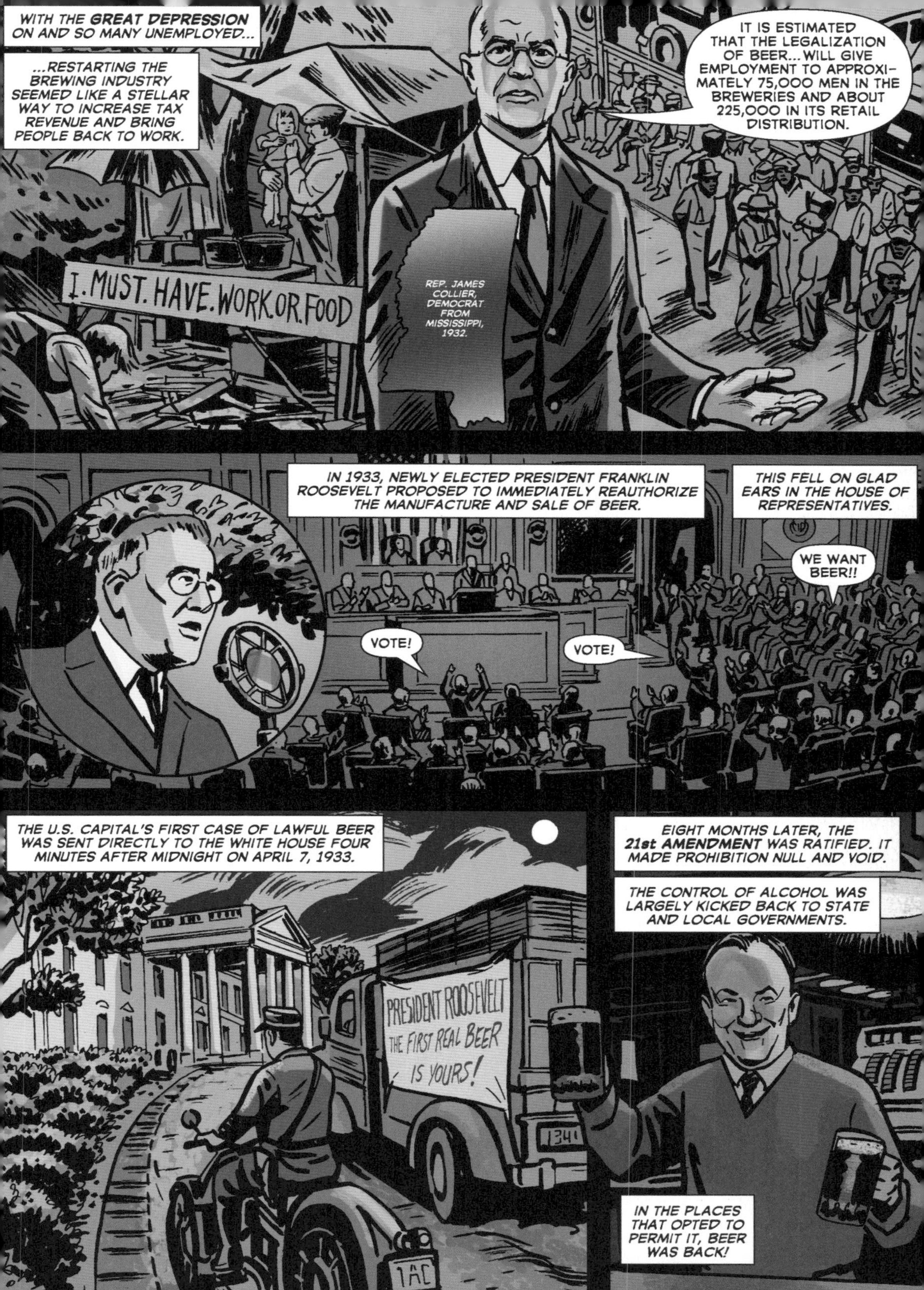

WITH THE **GREAT DEPRESSION** ON AND SO MANY UNEMPLOYED...
...RESTARTING THE BREWING INDUSTRY SEEMED LIKE A STELLAR WAY TO INCREASE TAX REVENUE AND BRING PEOPLE BACK TO WORK.
I. MUST. HAVE. WORK. OR. FOOD
REP. JAMES COLLIER, DEMOCRAT FROM MISSISSIPPI, 1932.
IT IS ESTIMATED THAT THE LEGALIZATION OF BEER... WILL GIVE EMPLOYMENT TO APPROXIMATELY 75,000 MEN IN THE BREWERIES AND ABOUT 225,000 IN ITS RETAIL DISTRIBUTION.
IN 1933, NEWLY ELECTED PRESIDENT FRANKLIN ROOSEVELT PROPOSED TO IMMEDIATELY REAUTHORIZE THE MANUFACTURE AND SALE OF BEER.
THIS FELL ON GLAD EARS IN THE HOUSE OF REPRESENTATIVES.
WE WANT BEER!!
VOTE!
VOTE!
THE U.S. CAPITAL'S FIRST CASE OF LAWFUL BEER WAS SENT DIRECTLY TO THE WHITE HOUSE FOUR MINUTES AFTER MIDNIGHT ON APRIL 7, 1933.
PRESIDENT ROOSEVELT THE FIRST REAL BEER IS YOURS!
1341
1AC
EIGHT MONTHS LATER, THE **21st AMENDMENT** WAS RATIFIED. IT MADE PROHIBITION NULL AND VOID.
THE CONTROL OF ALCOHOL WAS LARGELY KICKED BACK TO STATE AND LOCAL GOVERNMENTS.
IN THE PLACES THAT OPTED TO PERMIT IT, BEER WAS BACK!

BUT THINGS WEREN'T THE SAME.

EVEN WHEN THEY'D HAD PROHIBITION'S DECK STACKED AGAINST THEM, AMERICA'S INDUSTRIAL BREWING TITANS HAD HUNG ON.

BUT MANY SMALLER, LOCAL BREWERIES HAD NOT.

AFTER 13 LONG YEARS OF DORMANCY, THEY HAD FALLEN INTO DISREPAIR. THEIR STAFFS HAD DISPERSED. THEIR COFFERS WERE EMPTY.

BEFORE 1920, THE NUMBER OF AMERICAN BEER BRANDS HAD SOARED. EVERY GOOD-SIZED CITY HAD HAD DOZENS OF BREWERIES WITH HOMEGROWN LABELS.

BUT AFTER PROHIBITION, THE BIG DOGS AT THE TABLE GOT EVEN BIGGER...

...WHILE THE LITTLE GUYS WERE INCREASINGLY SQUEEZED OUT.

FORMERLY, SALOONS HAD PRETTY MUCH BEEN THE ONLY PLACE BEER WAS AVAILABLE--IN KEGS AND ON TAP.

ANHEUSER-BUSCH HAD BEGUN TO PRODUCE BOTTLED BEER AS FAR BACK AS 1876.

BUT IT WAS EXPENSIVE.

STARTING WITH A BREAKTHROUGH IN 1935, BEER STARTED BEING PACKAGED IN CANS.

ENJOY the NEW CONVENIENCE of a CONSERVADOR
Sold and Guaranteed by PHILCO

THE PRICE OF CANNED BEER AND HOME REFRIGERATORS FELL.

PEOPLE DRANK AT HOME MORE OFTEN.

LIKE THE FORMER BOUNTY OF BEER CHOICES...

...THE AMERICAN SALOON-- AND ALL THE MALE CAROUSING THAT WENT WITH IT--FELL INTO DECAY.

MEANWHILE, ACROSS THE ATLANTIC IN GERMANY, NOT EVEN THE COUNTRY'S GALLING DEFEAT IN WORLD WAR I COULD DISLODGE GERMAN BEER HALLS FROM THEIR PREEMINENCE.

BEER HALLS WERE A FAVORITE HAUNT OF ADOLF HITLER...

Süddeutsche Monatshefte

Heft 7. Jahrg. 21   April 1924

DER DOLCHSTOSS

Süddeutsche Monatshefte G. m. b. H., München

...THE BLUSTERY, KNOW-IT-ALL SON OF A MIDDLING CIVIL SERVANT NEAR THE AUSTRO-GERMAN BORDER.

HITLER BLAMED JEWS AND MARXISTS FOR GERMANY'S DEFEAT.

HITLER BECAME A RIGHT-WING LEADER.

ON NOVEMBER 8 AND 9, 1923, HE AND HIS SUPPORTERS GATHERED AT THE BÜRGER-BRÄUKELLER BEER HALL IN MUNICH.

Bürger Bräu Keller

IIA-263

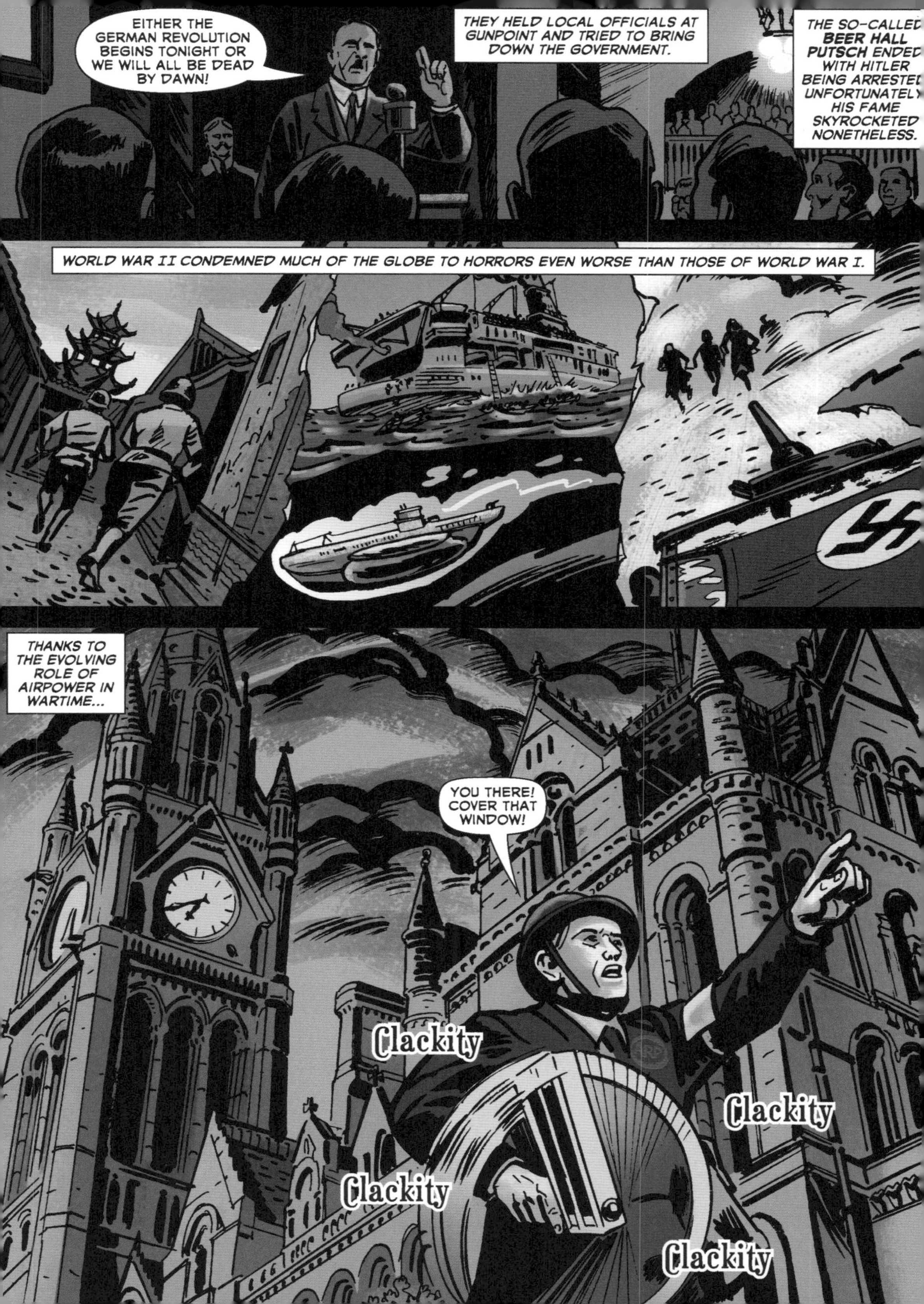

EITHER THE GERMAN REVOLUTION BEGINS TONIGHT OR WE WILL ALL BE DEAD BY DAWN!
THEY HELD LOCAL OFFICIALS AT GUNPOINT AND TRIED TO BRING DOWN THE GOVERNMENT.
THE SO-CALLED BEER HALL PUTSCH ENDED WITH HITLER BEING ARRESTED. UNFORTUNATELY, HIS FAME SKYROCKETED NONETHELESS.
WORLD WAR II CONDEMNED MUCH OF THE GLOBE TO HORRORS EVEN WORSE THAN THOSE OF WORLD WAR I.
THANKS TO THE EVOLVING ROLE OF AIRPOWER IN WARTIME...
YOU THERE! COVER THAT WINDOW!
Clackity
Clackity
Clackity
Clackity

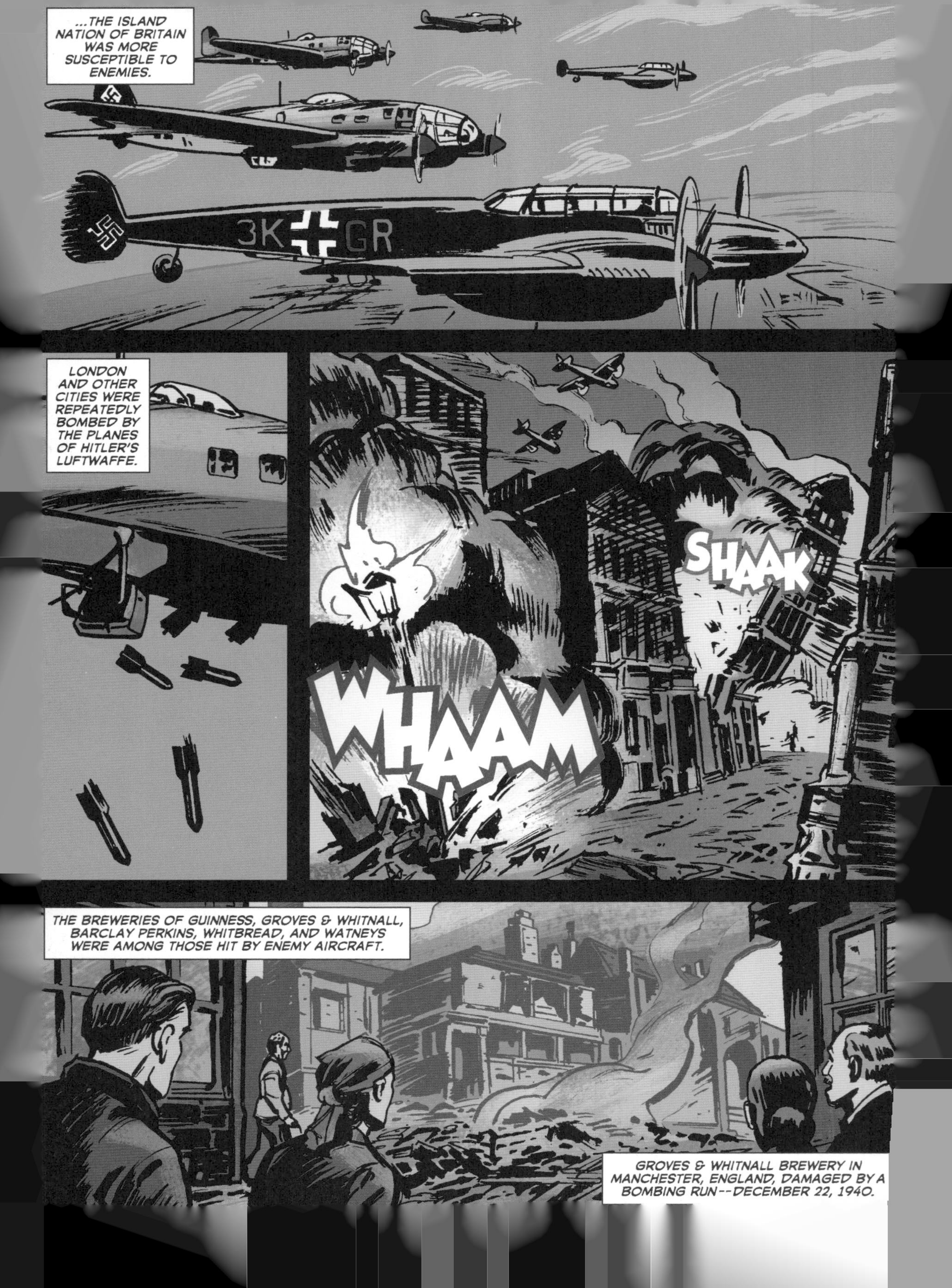
...THE ISLAND NATION OF BRITAIN WAS MORE SUSCEPTIBLE TO ENEMIES.
3K GR
LONDON AND OTHER CITIES WERE REPEATEDLY BOMBED BY THE PLANES OF HITLER'S LUFTWAFFE.
SHAAK
WHAAM
THE BREWERIES OF GUINNESS, GROVES & WHITNALL, BARCLAY PERKINS, WHITBREAD, AND WATNEYS WERE AMONG THOSE HIT BY ENEMY AIRCRAFT.
GROVES & WHITNALL BREWERY IN MANCHESTER, ENGLAND, DAMAGED BY A BOMBING RUN--DECEMBER 22, 1940.

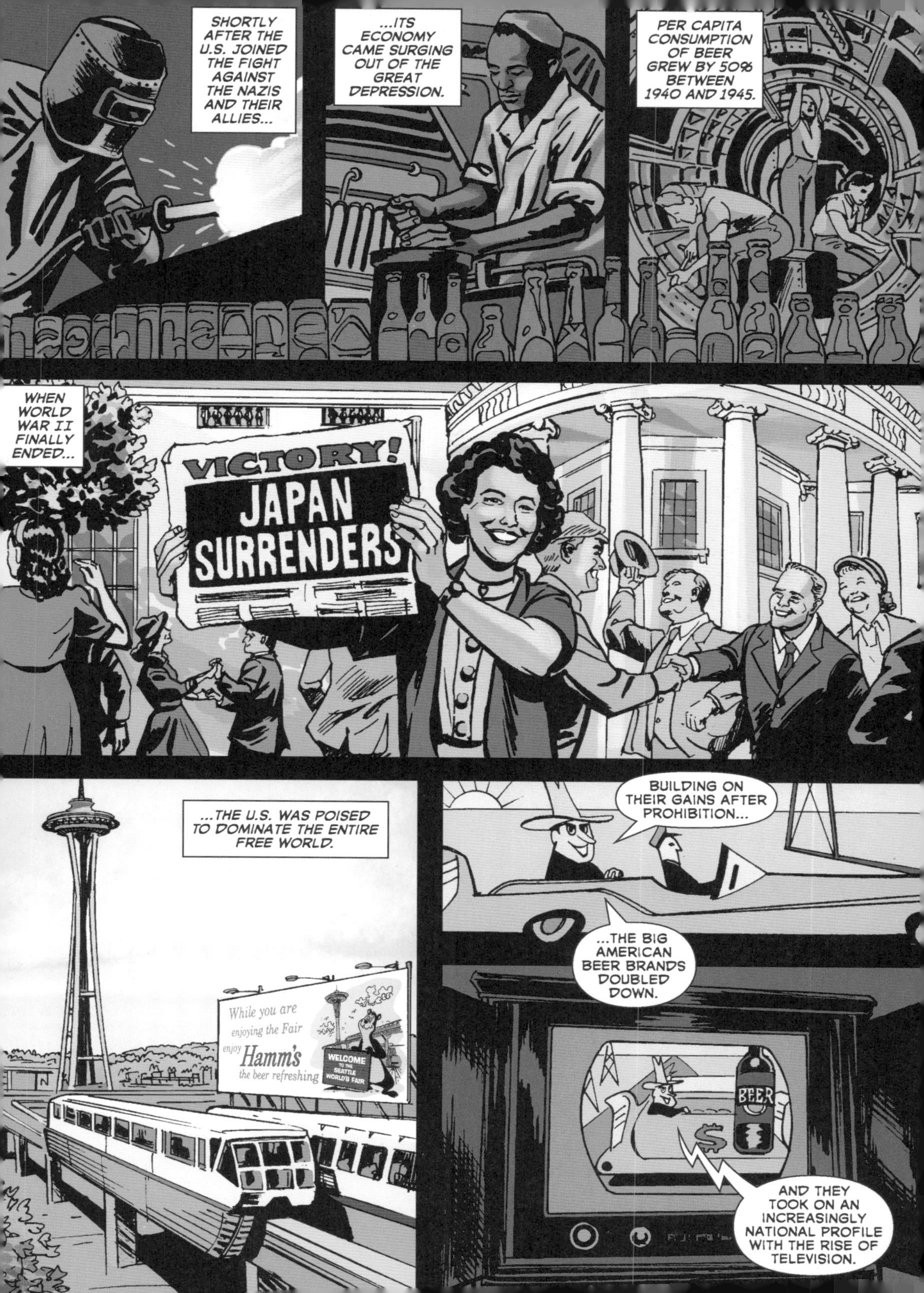

SHORTLY AFTER THE U.S. JOINED THE FIGHT AGAINST THE NAZIS AND THEIR ALLIES...
...ITS ECONOMY CAME SURGING OUT OF THE GREAT DEPRESSION.
PER CAPITA CONSUMPTION OF BEER GREW BY 50% BETWEEN 1940 AND 1945.
WHEN WORLD WAR II FINALLY ENDED...
VICTORY!
JAPAN SURRENDERS
...THE U.S. WAS POISED TO DOMINATE THE ENTIRE FREE WORLD.
While you are enjoying the Fair enjoy Hamm's the beer refreshing
WELCOME TO THE SEATTLE WORLD'S FAIR
BUILDING ON THEIR GAINS AFTER PROHIBITION...
...THE BIG AMERICAN BEER BRANDS DOUBLED DOWN.
BEER
$
AND THEY TOOK ON AN INCREASINGLY NATIONAL PROFILE WITH THE RISE OF TELEVISION.

IN 1953, AUGUST "GUSSIE" BUSCH--ADOLPHUS'S GRANDSON AND THEN BREWERY PRESIDENT--BOUGHT THE SAINT LOUIS CARDINALS BASEBALL TEAM.

THEIR STADIUM WAS OUTFITTED WITH THE FAMILY NAME AND FESTOONED WITH BUDWEISER ADS, PITCHING THEIR PRODUCT TO MILLIONS VIA TV.

Budweiser

THE BLUE-CHIP AMERICAN BREWERS CONSTRUCTED EVER-LARGER FACTORIES.

AUTOMATED AND, WITH TIME, COMPUTERIZED SYSTEMS HELPED THEM PRODUCE AND DISTRIBUTE ONCE UNTHINKABLY ENORMOUS QUANTITIES OF BEER.

THE DESIRES OF AMERICAN DRINKERS LED THEM REPEATEDLY TO THE SAME SORT OF PRODUCT:

AFTER AN EARLY, EXPERIMENTAL "DIET" BEER FIZZLED...

I COULDN'T DO ANYTHING ABOUT THE TASTE OF BEER, BUT I COULD DO SOMETHING ABOUT THE CALORIES.

GABLINGER'S BEER

BIOCHEMIST JOSEPH OWADES, INVENTOR OF LIGHT BEER.

INOFFENSIVE, MASS-PRODUCED BLONDE, LIGHT-BODIED, "DRINKABLE" LAGERS WITH LITTLE OR NO CUMULATIVE BITTERNESS.

...MILLER BREWING INTRODUCED LOW-CALORIE PRODUCT IN 1975

Everything you always wanted in a beer.
And less.

New Lite Beer from Miller.

COMING SOON!

REGARDLESS OF WHETHER "LIGHT" BREWS ACTUALLY HELP PREVENT BEER GUTS, THIS INNOVATION METEORICALLY SWELLED REVENUES--AND ADVERTISING BUDGETS

Meet The Beer: American Lager

LIGHT · AMBER · DARK · MILD · MODERATE · BITTER · WEAK · MODERATE · STRONG

Color: Very Pale Straw to Light Golden; 2 - 4 SRM

Bitterness: Mild; 8 - 15 IBU

Strength: Low to Moderate; 3 - 5.5% ABV

MALT

MALT CHARACTER: LIGHT IN BODY AND DRY FROM PRODIGIOUS USE OF NONMALT ADJUNCTS. SOMETIMES HAS A TOUCH OF CORN-LIKE VEGETAL SWEETNESS.

HOPS

HOP CHARACTER: HOP BITTERNESS JUST BARELY BALANCES THE MALT; ALMOST NO HOP AROMA.

FOOD

FOOD PAIRINGS: HOT DOGS, PEANUTS, AND CRACKER JACK.

CLASSIC EXAMPLES: BUDWEISER, MILLER, COORS

AMERICAN LAGER, YOU MIGHT SAY, IS MUCH MALIGNED.

BUT ALL THE SAME, THIS STYLE REMAIN THE MOST WIDELY CONSUMED BEERS BREWED IN THE WORLD.

OFTEN OSTENSIBLY DESCRIBED AS "PILSNER," AMERICAN LAGER USUALLY SHARES ONLY ITS LIGHT COLOR WITH ITS BOHEMIAN ANCESTOR.

WHILE ITS ROOTS REACH TO EARLIER TIMES, AMERICAN LAGER IS A PRODUCT OF THE AMERICAN 20th CENTURY. IT EVOLVED TO SUIT THE TYPICAL TASTES OF THE POSTWAR AMERICAN CONSUMER. IT IS, THEREFORE, A PRODUCT OF AMERICAN INDUSTRIALIZATION, CORPORATE CONSOLIDATION, AND ECONOMICS. THESE FACTORS HAVE TRUMPED THE USUAL DRIVING FORCES BEHIND A BEER STYLE: AGE-OLD TRADITIONS AND REGIONAL VARIATIONS.

AFTER PROHIBITION WINNOWED DOWN THE NUMBER OF BREWERIES IN THE U.S., THE SURVIVORS FOUND THAT THEIR MARKETS HAD EXPANDED, BUT ADVANCES IN DISTRIBUTION HAD MADE THOSE MARKETS MORE COMPETITIVE. BEER HAD BECOME A NATIONAL, RATHER THAN REGIONAL, PRODUCT.

AMERICAN BEER HAS LONG INCLUDED ADJUNCTS SUCH AS RICE AND CORN.

BUT AFTER WORLD WAR II, THE LARGE INDUSTRIAL AMERICAN BREWERS--FOR MOSTLY ECONOMIC REASONS--BEGAN TO INCREASE THE AMOUNT OF THESE ADDITIVES.

IN ADDITION TO MAKING BEER CHEAPER TO PRODUCE, THESE ADJUNCTS ALLOWED BREWERS TO DESIGN BEERS THAT WERE LESS CHALLENGING, WITH APPEAL FOR WIDER AUDIENCES.

MANY AMERICAN LAGER BREWERIES USE UP TO 40% CORN OR RICE IN THEIR BEERS. THEY ALSO ADD ONLY ENOUGH HOPS TO PROVIDE THE SMALLEST HINT OF BITTERNESS.

THE INOFFENSIVENESS OF AMERICAN LAGERS FOUND A READY ACCEPTANCE IN MANY GROUPS, INCLUDING WOMEN AND PEOPLE WHO DIDN'T HAIL FROM CENTRAL EUROPEAN ORIGINS. IN OTHER WORDS, PEOPLE WHO TYPICALLY WEREN'T CONSIDERED BEER DRINKERS.

MANY BEER GEEKS TEND TO DISMISS AMERICAN LAGER. THEY OFTEN SPEAK OF IT AS A COMMODITY--ONE DEVOID OF THE RICH MALT AND BITTER HOP CHARACTER THAT PREVIOUSLY DEFINED THE FLAVORS OF BEER.

IN FACT, IT WAS A REACTION TO AMERICAN LAGER'S UBIQUITY THAT SPARKED THE MODERN CRAFT BEER MOVEMENT.

AMERICAN LAGERS MAY NOT BE TO EVERYONE'S TASTE. BUT ONE THING ABOUT THEM IS UNDENIABLE: THEY ARE BREWED TO EXACTING STANDARDS.

THE BREWERS WHO MAKE AMERICAN LAGER ARE SOME OF THE MOST TECHNICALLY SOPHISTICATED ANYWHERE.

WITH PLUNGING NUMBERS AND NARROWING VARIETY THAT SEEMS TO CORRELATE WITH THE RISE OF FAST FOOD, IN 1979 AMERICAN BREWERIES FELL TO AN ALL-TIME LOW OF JUST 44 BREWERIES, PUMPING OUT AN *EVEN SMALLER NUMBER* OF BRANDS.

Breweries vs McDonald's - 1950 — 1980

McDonalds
Breweries

IN **THIS** LANDSCAPE OF CORPORATE LAGERS, SOME AMERICAN BEER LOVERS STILL LOOKED FOR DIAMONDS IN THE ROUGH: REGIONAL, HERITAGE BREWS, OR EUROPEAN IMPORTS.

THE FIRST OF THESE WAS FREDERICK LOUIS "FRITZ" MAYTAG III.

MAYTAG'S ENTREPREUNERIAL *FAMILY* HAD FOUNDED THE EPONYMOUS BRANDS OF WASHING MACHINES AND BLUE CHEESE.

MAYTAG'S MAKING WASHERS AGAIN!

WHILE LIVING IN BOHEMIAN SAN FRANCISCO IN THE 1960s...

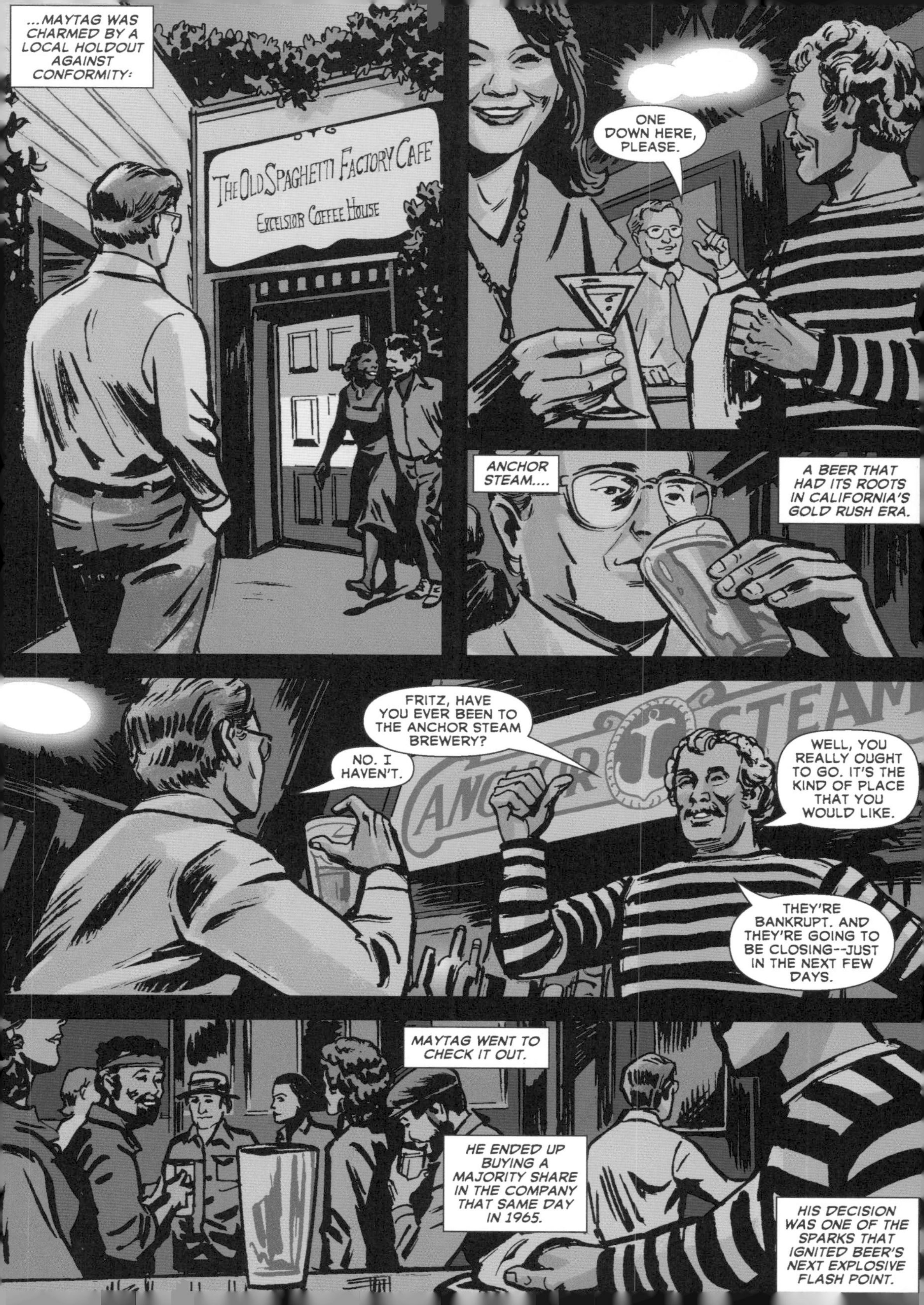

...MAYTAG WAS CHARMED BY A LOCAL HOLDOUT AGAINST CONFORMITY:
THE OLD SPAGHETTI FACTORY CAFE
EXCELSIOR COFFEE HOUSE
ONE DOWN HERE, PLEASE.
ANCHOR STEAM....
A BEER THAT HAD ITS ROOTS IN CALIFORNIA'S GOLD RUSH ERA.
FRITZ, HAVE YOU EVER BEEN TO THE ANCHOR STEAM BREWERY?
NO. I HAVEN'T.
WELL, YOU REALLY OUGHT TO GO. IT'S THE KIND OF PLACE THAT YOU WOULD LIKE.
THEY'RE BANKRUPT. AND THEY'RE GOING TO BE CLOSING--JUST IN THE NEXT FEW DAYS.
MAYTAG WENT TO CHECK IT OUT.
HE ENDED UP BUYING A MAJORITY SHARE IN THE COMPANY THAT SAME DAY IN 1965.
HIS DECISION WAS ONE OF THE SPARKS THAT IGNITED BEER'S NEXT EXPLOSIVE FLASH POINT.

Chapter Eight
DRINKING ON THE SHOULDERS OF GIANTS: BEER TODAY

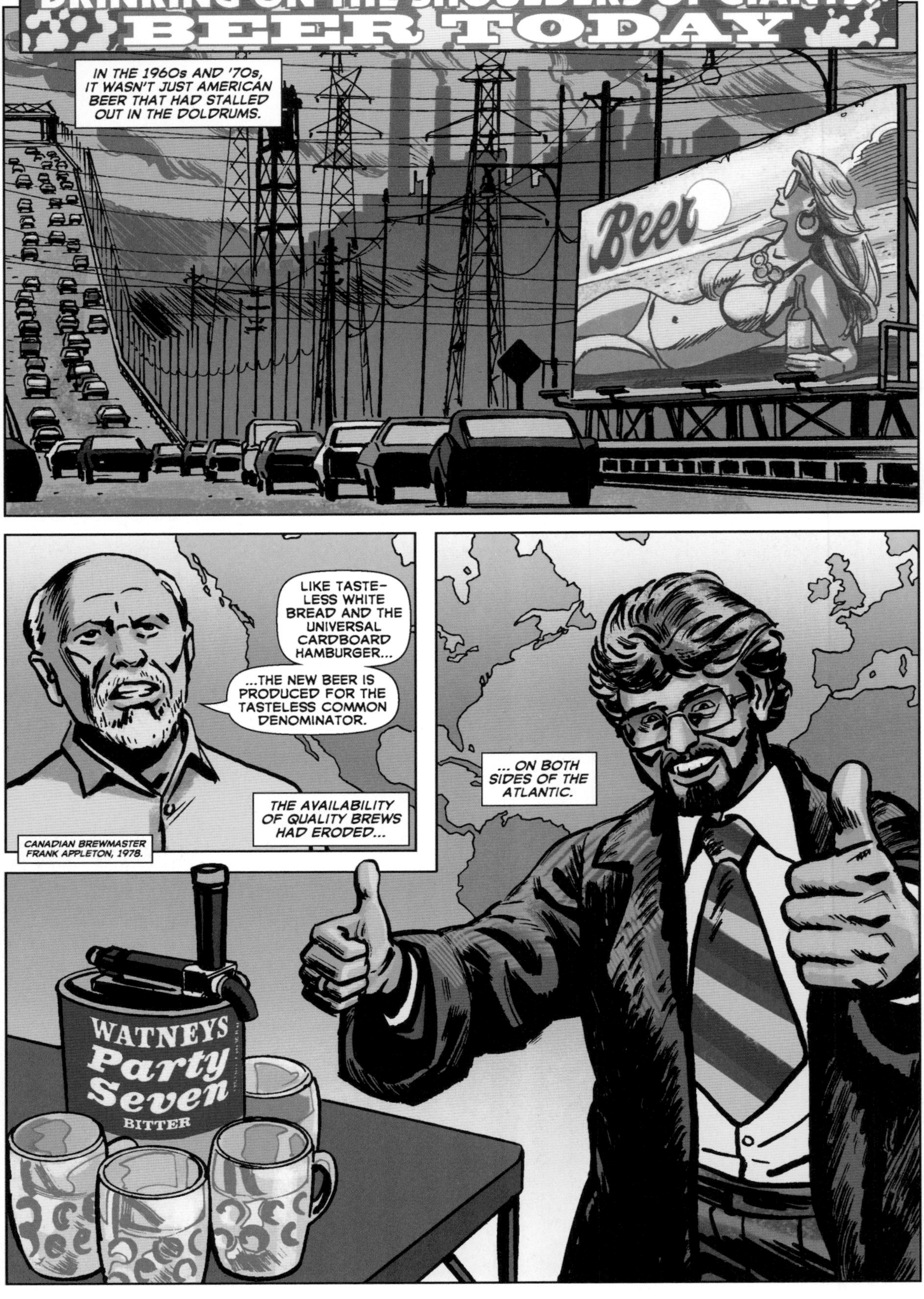
IN THE 1960s AND '70s, IT WASN'T JUST AMERICAN BEER THAT HAD STALLED OUT IN THE DOLDRUMS.
Beer
LIKE TASTE-LESS WHITE BREAD AND THE UNIVERSAL CARDBOARD HAMBURGER...
...THE NEW BEER IS PRODUCED FOR THE TASTELESS COMMON DENOMINATOR.
CANADIAN BREWMASTER FRANK APPLETON, 1978.
THE AVAILABILITY OF QUALITY BREWS HAD ERODED...
... ON BOTH SIDES OF THE ATLANTIC.
WATNEYS
Party
Seven
BITTER

IN MARCH 1971, FOUR FRIENDS FROM THE NORTH OF ENGLAND WERE ON A "BOOZING HOLIDAY."

THEIR ITINERARY OF INEBRIATION HAD TAKEN THEM TO THE WESTERN-MOST PUB IN EUROPE...

...KRUGER'S BAR, ON IRELAND'S DINGLE PENINSULA.

LIKE FRITZ MAYTAG, MICHAEL HARDMAN, BILL MELLOR, JIM MAKIN, AND GRAHAM LEES HAD HAD ENOUGH.

ALTHOUGH BRITISH BREWING HAD FACED WARTIME WOES, IT HAD CONTINUED UNIMPEDED.

AFTER ALL, A POLICY OF NATIONAL PROHIBITION WOULD HAVE BEEN UNTHINKABLE IN BRITAIN.

NEVERTHELESS, U.K. BEER PRODUCTION HAD BEEN MODERNIZED INTO MEDIOCRITY.

139

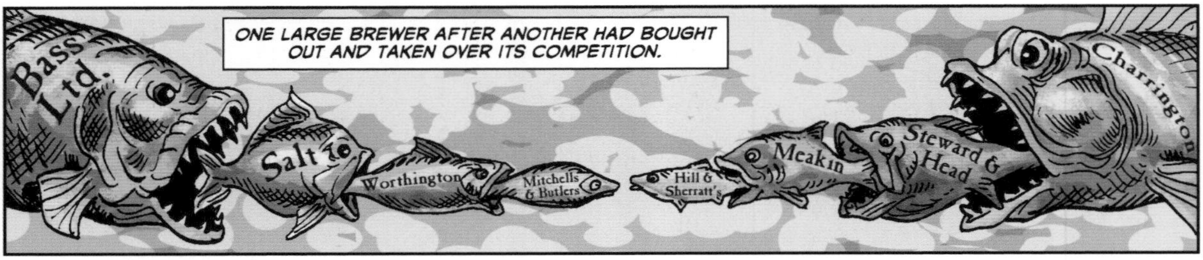
ONE LARGE BREWER AFTER ANOTHER HAD BOUGHT OUT AND TAKEN OVER ITS COMPETITION.
Bass Ltd.
Salt
Worthington
Mitchells & Butlers
Hill & Sherratt's
Meakin
Steward & Head
Charrington

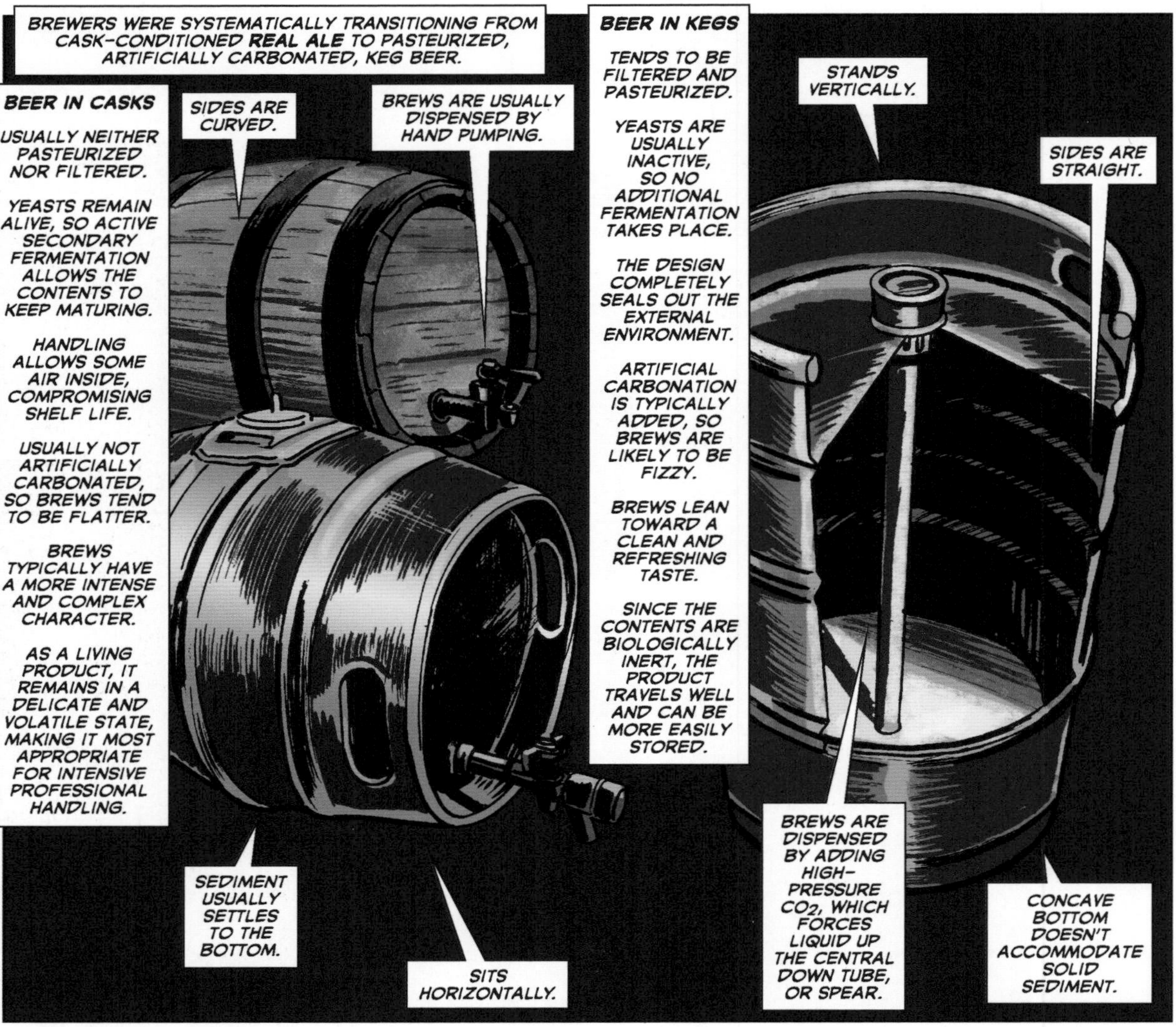
BREWERS WERE SYSTEMATICALLY TRANSITIONING FROM CASK-CONDITIONED **REAL ALE** TO PASTEURIZED, ARTIFICIALLY CARBONATED, KEG BEER.
BEER IN CASKS
USUALLY NEITHER PASTEURIZED NOR FILTERED.
YEASTS REMAIN ALIVE, SO ACTIVE SECONDARY FERMENTATION ALLOWS THE CONTENTS TO KEEP MATURING.
HANDLING ALLOWS SOME AIR INSIDE, COMPROMISING SHELF LIFE.
USUALLY NOT ARTIFICIALLY CARBONATED, SO BREWS TEND TO BE FLATTER.
BREWS TYPICALLY HAVE A MORE INTENSE AND COMPLEX CHARACTER.
AS A LIVING PRODUCT, IT REMAINS IN A DELICATE AND VOLATILE STATE, MAKING IT MOST APPROPRIATE FOR INTENSIVE PROFESSIONAL HANDLING.
SIDES ARE CURVED.
BREWS ARE USUALLY DISPENSED BY HAND PUMPING.
SEDIMENT USUALLY SETTLES TO THE BOTTOM.
SITS HORIZONTALLY.
BEER IN KEGS
TENDS TO BE FILTERED AND PASTEURIZED.
YEASTS ARE USUALLY INACTIVE, SO NO ADDITIONAL FERMENTATION TAKES PLACE.
THE DESIGN COMPLETELY SEALS OUT THE EXTERNAL ENVIRONMENT.
ARTIFICIAL CARBONATION IS TYPICALLY ADDED, SO BREWS ARE LIKELY TO BE FIZZY.
BREWS LEAN TOWARD A CLEAN AND REFRESHING TASTE.
SINCE THE CONTENTS ARE BIOLOGICALLY INERT, THE PRODUCT TRAVELS WELL AND CAN BE MORE EASILY STORED.
STANDS VERTICALLY.
SIDES ARE STRAIGHT.
BREWS ARE DISPENSED BY ADDING HIGH-PRESSURE CO_2, WHICH FORCES LIQUID UP THE CENTRAL DOWN TUBE, OR SPEAR.
CONCAVE BOTTOM DOESN'T ACCOMMODATE SOLID SEDIMENT.

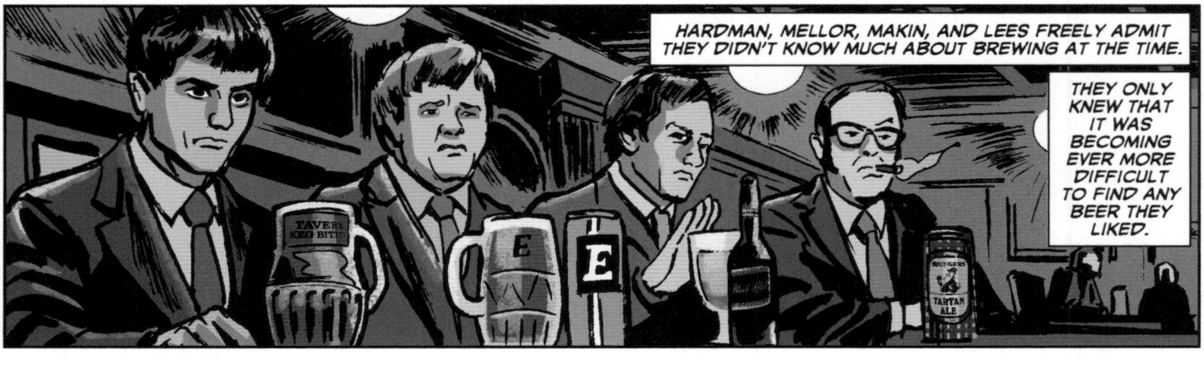
HARDMAN, MELLOR, MAKIN, AND LEES FREELY ADMIT THEY DIDN'T KNOW MUCH ABOUT BREWING AT THE TIME.
THEY ONLY KNEW THAT IT WAS BECOMING EVER MORE DIFFICULT TO FIND ANY BEER THEY LIKED.
E
E
TARTAN ALE

THE FOURSOME WENT ON TO FOUND ONE OF THE MOST SUCCESSFUL **CONSUMER REVOLTS** IN THE WORLD.

THIS WAS THE CAMPAIGN FOR REAL ALE, OR **CAMRA**.

CAMRA HAS BECOME A STAUNCH PROTECTOR OF BRITISH BREWING TRADITIONS -- AND THE PUBS IN WHICH THOSE PRODUCTS ARE SERVED.

CAMRA'S RANKS BEGAN TO SWELL.

OVER 2,000 PEOPLE JOINED IN ITS FIRST YEAR ALONE.

BY 1974, THE ORGANIZATION BEGAN ANNUAL PUBLICATION OF ITS INFLUENTIAL **GOOD BEER GUIDE**.

GOOD BEER GUIDE

The GREAT BRITISH BEER FESTIVAL

OFFICIAL SOUVENIR PROGRAMME

IN 1977, CAMRA ALSO INAUGURATED ITS YEARLY GREAT BRITISH BEER FESTIVAL.

BACK IN THE U.S., THE RESURGENCE OF DISTINCTIVE BEER WAS A BIT LESS ORGANIZED.

Beer

FRITZ MAYTAG WAS DETERMINED TO RESCUE THE TINY ANCHOR BREWERY FROM THE BRINK OF FAILURE.

ANCHOR BREWERY

HE AND A SMALL TEAM OF BREWERS HONED THEIR RECIPES.

THANKS BOTH TO PRAISEWORTHY PRODUCTS AND FRUGAL, DYNAMIC MARKETING...

...ANCHOR WAS ADEQUATELY SOLVENT TO BEGIN EXPERIMENTING. THE BREWERY PRODUCED:

A CHRISTMAS ALE   A HOPPY ALE   A BARLEY WINE   AND EVEN A PORTER, FIRST BREWED IN 1972.

BY THAT TIME, PORTER HAD BECOME VIRTUALLY EXTINCT EVEN IN ITS NATIVE LAND, GREAT BRITAIN.

QUALITY AND CHARACTER, RATHER THAN QUANTITY AND SLICK ADVERTISING, FUELED ANCHOR'S SUCCESS.

ANCHOR
SINCE 1896
BREWING
SAN FRANCISCO

THE UPSHOT? BREWERS DISCOVERED THAT SOME AMERICAN DRINKERS WERE WILLING TO PAY TOP DOLLAR FOR HANDMADE, FLAVORFUL, PREMIUM BEER.

MAYTAG'S TRIUMPH BECAME THE NUCLEUS OF A MOVEMENT THAT WOULD *CHANGE* AND *EXPAND* THE VERY NOTION OF WHAT BEER COULD BE.

THE WEST COAST OF THE U.S. HAD BECOME THE EPICENTER OF A *CRAFT BEER* REVOLUTION.

IN SONOMA, CALIFORNIA...

R-R-RUMBLE!!

...LIVED JACK McAULIFFE, A FORMER U.S. NAVY SUBMARINE MECHANIC.

WHILE STATIONED IN SCOTLAND, McAULIFFE'S TASTE BUDS HAD THRILLED TO THE TRULY REMARKABLE BEERS AVAILABLE IN THAT COUNTRY.

MCAULIFFE BEGAN BREWING IN HIS SPARE TIME. THE RESULTS PLEASED HIM.

MAN... I CAN GET RICH DOING THIS.

BUT WHEN HE RETURNED TO THE U.S., THE DIVERSE, FULL-FLAVORED BEERS HE'D COME TO LOVE WERE ALL BUT UNAVAILABLE.

FOR RENT

SO MCAULIFFE DECIDED TO TRY HIS HAND AT GOING COMMERCIAL.

UNLIKE MAYTAG, MCAULIFFE COULDN'T JUST GO OUT ON A LARK AND BUY A DISCOUNT BREWERY.

SO HE FIRED UP HIS WELDING TORCH.

SALVAGED DAIRY EQUIPMENT AND SODA SYRUP DRUMS BECAME A JURY-RIGGED BEERWORKS.

KZZZZZ-T!

new albion brewing company
SONOMA, CALIFORNIA
net conts. 12 fl. oz.
ALE

WITH A PARTNER, HE FOUNDED NEW ALBION,* AMERICA'S FIRST **MICROBREWERY**, IN 1976.

THEY TURNED OUT SMALL BATCHES OF ALE, PORTER, AND STOUT.

* NAMED AFTER SIR FRANCIS DRAKE'S 1579 CLAIM ON NORTHERN CALIFORNIA AS NOVA ALBION, OR NEW ENGLAND.

BUT NEW ALBION WAS TOO FAR AHEAD OF ITS TIME.

THERE WAS SCANT INFRASTRUCTURE TO SUPPORT THE TINY START-UP-- AND ONLY A SPOTTY MARKET FOR ITS DELICATE, LABOR-OF-LOVE PRODUCTS.

McAULIFFE HAD TO EXPAND, OR HIS VENTURE WOULD COLLAPSE.

new albion brewing compa
SONOMA, CALIFORNIA

UNABLE TO LOCK IN INVESTORS, NEW ALBION SHUT ITS DOORS IN 1983.

McAULIFFE'S DAUGHTER IS REVIVING THE NEW ALBION BRAND.

YET McAULIFFE PROVED THAT WITH LITTLE MORE THAN GRIT AND DETERMINATION, A WILD-EYED DREAMER...

Beer

...COULD START A SMALL BREWERY FROM THE GROUND UP.

HIS PIONEERING EXAMPLE ESTABLISHED THE DIY TEMPLATE FOLLOWED BY GENERATIONS OF CRAFT BREWERS TO COME.

Welcome to California
San Bernardino COUNTY LINE

AMERICAN PALE ALE

LIGHT · AMBER · DARK

MILD · MODERATE · BITTER

WEAK · MODERATE · STRONG

Color:
Pale to Deep Amber;
6 - 14 SRM

Bitterness:
Moderate to Hoppy;
30 - 50 IBU

Strength:
Moderate;
4.5 - 6% ABV

MALT

MALT CHARACTER: SOLID MALT BACKBONE, OFTEN WITH SUBTLE CARAMEL OVERTONES.

HOPS

HOP CHARACTER: CRISP AND HOP FORWARD BUT NOT OVERLY BITTER. PINEY AND CITRUSY HOP AROMAS FROM THE LIBERAL USE OF AMERICAN FINISHING HOPS.

FOOD

FOOD PAIRINGS: JUST ABOUT ANYTHING, ESPCIALLY PUB FARE LIKE NACHOS, CHEESE BURGERS, AND PIZZA.

CLASSIC EXAMPLES:
SIERRA NEVADA PALE ALE,
DESCHUTES MIRROR POND PALE ALE,
DALE'S PALE ALE

THE STORY OF AMERICAN PALE ALE IS LARGELY THE STORY OF KEN GROSSMAN.

GROSSMAN, A CALIFORNIA BICYCLE MECHANIC AND HOMEBREW EQUIPMENT PURVEYOR, WAS ALSO SPURRED ON BY THE MOVEMENT THAT CREATED FRITZ MAYTAG'S ANCHOR BREWING AND JACK McAULIFFE'S NEW ALBION.

RELYING ON HIS JACK-OF-ALL-TRADES SKILL SET ANDHELP FROM THE WEST COAST BREWING COMMUNITY, GROSSMAN SET UP SHOP IN THE COLLEGE TOWN OF CHICO.

IN 1981, GROSSMAN RELEASED SIERRA NEVADA PALE ALE.

SIERRA NEVADA BECAME THE GOLD STANDARD SPECIMEN OF AMERICAN PALE ALE--AND ONE OF THE BEST-SELLING CRAFT BEERS OF ALL TIME.

THE PIONEERING AMERICAN MICROBREWERS TENDED TO BASE THEIR BEERS ON THE ENGLISH, RATHER THAN THE GERMAN, MODEL: THEY BREWED ALES.

BECAUSE ALES REQUIRE NEITHER LONG LAGERING TIMES NOR EXTENSIVE CELLAR STORAGE, THEY COULD BE PUT UP FOR SALE MORE QUICKLY.

ALSO, BRITISH RATHER THAN GERMAN BREWING TEXTS WERE EASIER FOR AMERICANS TO ACQUIRE AND UNDERSTAND.

AMERICAN PALE ALE IS A BRASH REINVENTION OF ITS ENGLISH COUSIN.

AMERICAN PALE ALE IS BREWED WITH BOTH NEW-WORLD FLAIR AND NEW-WORLD INGREDIENTS, PARTICULARLY AROMATIC FINISHING HOPS GROWN IN THE CASCADE REGIONS OF OREGON AND WASHINGTON. CASCADE HOPS WERE DEVELOPED IN THE USDA HOPS BREEDING PROGRAM AND RELEASED IN 1971. THEIR GRAPEFRUIT AND PINEY OVERTONES BECAME A HALLMARK OF AMERICAN CRAFT BREWS.

BEFORE THE EMERGENCE OF AMERICAN VERSIONS OF IPA, AMERICAN PALE ALE WAS THE QUINTESSENTIAL MICROBREW. EVERY SMALL BREWERY HAD AN AMERICAN PALE ALE IN ITS PORTFOLIO.

NOT LONG AGO, THESE BREWS WERE CONSIDERED TO BE STARTLINGLY BITTER.

BUT THE PALATES OF AMERICAN CRAFT BEER DRINKERS SEEM TO HAVE EVOLVED IN TANDEM WITH HOPPING LEVELS, WHICH HAVE BEEN RATCHETED UP ALMOST EXPONENTIALLY. NOW, MOST DEVOTEES CONSIDER AMERICAN PALE ALE TO BE JUST MODERATELY HOPPY.

GOOD LUCK FROM **HUDDERSFIELD.**

ABOUT THIS SAME TIME, A BEER-LOVING CHAP (AND JOURNALIST) FROM THE NORTH OF ENGLAND...

...DID SOMETHING THAT CHANGED THE VERY WAY WE THINK ABOUT BEER.

THE BEER HUNTER

IN 1969, AN ASSIGNMENT BROUGHT MICHAEL JACKSON TO THE NETHERLANDS.

HE QUICKLY TIRED OF DRINKING HEINEKEN AND AMSTEL. IN SEARCH OF MORE INTERESTING BEER...

...JACKSON ABSCONDED TO THE SOUTHERN PROVINCES OF THE NETHERLANDS.

IT'S TERRIFIC.

THAT IS A TRAPPIST BEER.

IF YOU LIKE THAT SORT OF THING, YOU ARE IN THE WRONG COUNTRY.

THE MAN IN THE MASK TOLD JACKSON TO GO TO BELGIUM.

Buddens

VOLVO

73214 0R

THERE, HE WAS INTRODUCED TO VARIED AND DELECTABLE ALES.

Buddens

THE BELGIUM VISIT INSPIRED IN JACKSON A WHOLE NEW APPRECIATION FOR THE SUBTLE AND NOT SO SUBTLE DIFFERENCES IN THE CHARACTER OF BEER.

IN 1977, JACKSON PUBLISHED *THE WORLD GUIDE TO BEER*, FROTHING UP ITS PAGES WITH WIT, ELOQUENCE, AND PASSION.

JACKSON CODIFIED THE DIFFERENCES BETWEEN AND CREATED THE VERY CONCEPT OF STYLES OF BEER--A CONCEPT THAT THIS BOOK AND VIRTUALLY ALL CURRENT WRITING ABOUT BEER TAKE ENTIRELY FOR GRANTED.

THE WORLD GUIDE TO BEER

JACKSON BEQUEATHED UPON THE BEER-DRINKING PUBLIC A LEXICON AND FRAMEWORK FOR DESCRIB-ING BEER DOWN TO ITS MOST MINUTE DETAILS.

WITH PROLIFIC WRITINGS THAT FOLLOWED THE *WORLD GUIDE*, THIS BARD OF BEER...

...EARNED A SPOT AS CHAMPION AND SPIRITUAL LEADER OF THE CRAFT BREWING REVOLUTION.

MANY OF THE ELEMENTS OF THAT REVOLUTION WERE ALREADY IN PLACE...

...BUT JACKSON GAVE THE MOVEMENT A GOOD, HARD SHOVE.

MICHAEL JACKSON DIED IN 2007.

149

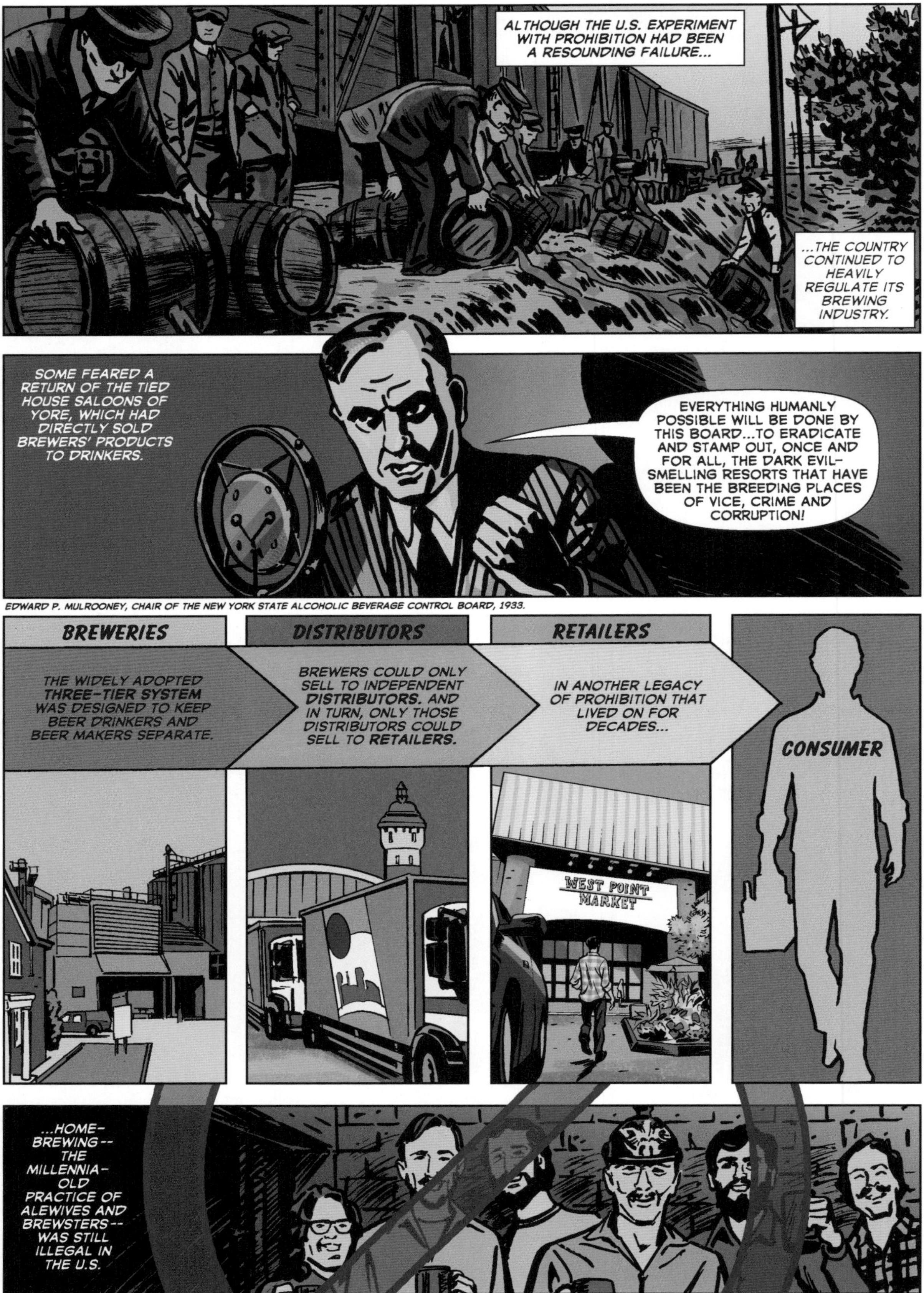

ALTHOUGH THE U.S. EXPERIMENT WITH PROHIBITION HAD BEEN A RESOUNDING FAILURE...
...THE COUNTRY CONTINUED TO HEAVILY REGULATE ITS BREWING INDUSTRY.
SOME FEARED A RETURN OF THE TIED HOUSE SALOONS OF YORE, WHICH HAD DIRECTLY SOLD BREWERS' PRODUCTS TO DRINKERS.
EVERYTHING HUMANLY POSSIBLE WILL BE DONE BY THIS BOARD...TO ERADICATE AND STAMP OUT, ONCE AND FOR ALL, THE DARK EVIL-SMELLING RESORTS THAT HAVE BEEN THE BREEDING PLACES OF VICE, CRIME AND CORRUPTION!
EDWARD P. MULROONEY, CHAIR OF THE NEW YORK STATE ALCOHOLIC BEVERAGE CONTROL BOARD, 1933.
BREWERIES
DISTRIBUTORS
RETAILERS
THE WIDELY ADOPTED THREE-TIER SYSTEM WAS DESIGNED TO KEEP BEER DRINKERS AND BEER MAKERS SEPARATE.
BREWERS COULD ONLY SELL TO INDEPENDENT DISTRIBUTORS. AND IN TURN, ONLY THOSE DISTRIBUTORS COULD SELL TO RETAILERS.
IN ANOTHER LEGACY OF PROHIBITION THAT LIVED ON FOR DECADES...
CONSUMER
WEST POINT MARKET
...HOME-BREWING--THE MILLENNIA-OLD PRACTICE OF ALEWIVES AND BREWSTERS--WAS STILL ILLEGAL IN THE U.S.

BUT THE **COUNTERCULTURE** THAT BEGAN IN THE 1960s WAS NO STICKLER FOR THE LETTER OF THE LAW.

ITS ADHERENTS GLORIFIED LIVING INDEPENDENTLY AND OFF THE GRID. THEY REBUFFED BOTH THE PRODUCTS AND THE VALUES OF CORPORATE CAPITALISM.

BIG BEER WAS NOT FOR THEM.

WE'RE A BUNCH OF RAW MATERIALS THAT DON'T MEAN TO...HAVE ANY PROCESS UPON US, DON'T MEAN TO BE MADE INTO ANY PRODUCT...

...THERE'S A TIME WHEN THE OPERATION OF THE MACHINE BECOMES SO ODIOUS, MAKES YOU SO SICK AT HEART, THAT YOU CAN'T TAKE PART!

AND YOU'VE GOT TO PUT YOUR BODIES UPON THE GEARS AND UPON THE WHEELS...UPON THE LEVERS, UPON ALL THE APPARATUS, AND YOU'VE GOT TO MAKE IT STOP!

NEW SUPER STORE

MONEY IS AN UNNECESSARY EVIL

FEED IN

DIGGER FREE STORE

ILLEGAL HOMEBREWING BECAME AN ALTERNATIVE FOR ANYONE JONESING FOR A BEER OTHER THAN THE STANDARD AMERICAN LAGER.

BUT FEW OF THOSE UNDERGROUND ACTIVISTS HAD A GOOD STOREHOUSE OF BREWING WISDOM, AND IT SHOWED IN THE SOMETIMES INCONSISTENT QUALITY OF THEIR BATCHES.

THE HOW-TOS OF BREWING WERE PASSED ALONG BY WORD OF MOUTH OR, AT BEST, THROUGH A HANDFUL OF IMPORTED BRITISH MANUALS.

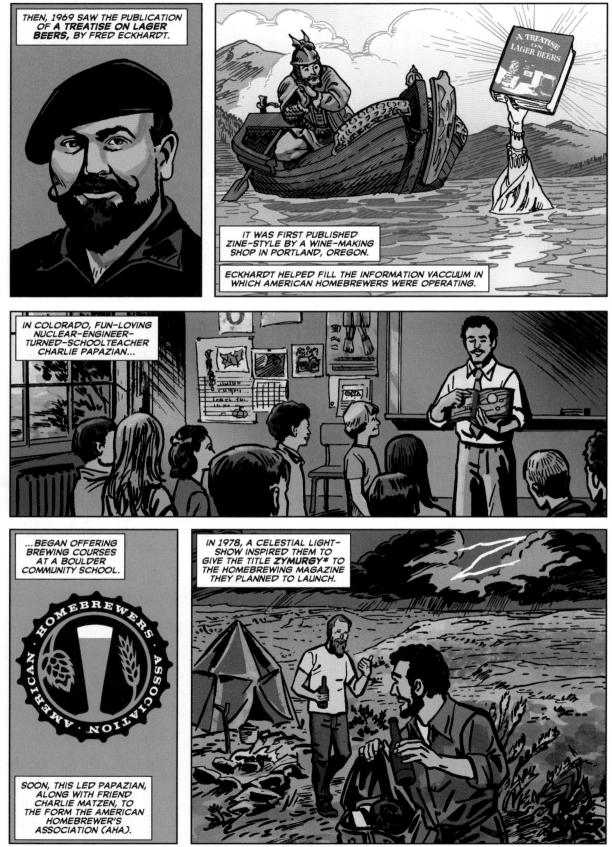

THEN, 1969 SAW THE PUBLICATION OF *A TREATISE ON LAGER BEERS*, BY FRED ECKHARDT.

IT WAS FIRST PUBLISHED ZINE-STYLE BY A WINE-MAKING SHOP IN PORTLAND, OREGON.

ECKHARDT HELPED FILL THE INFORMATION VACCUUM IN WHICH AMERICAN HOMEBREWERS WERE OPERATING.

A TREATISE ON LAGER BEERS

IN COLORADO, FUN-LOVING NUCLEAR-ENGINEER-TURNED-SCHOOLTEACHER CHARLIE PAPAZIAN...

...BEGAN OFFERING BREWING COURSES AT A BOULDER COMMUNITY SCHOOL.

· AMERICAN · HOMEBREWERS · ASSOCIATION ·

SOON, THIS LED PAPAZIAN, ALONG WITH FRIEND CHARLIE MATZEN, TO THE FORM THE AMERICAN HOMEBREWER'S ASSOCIATION (AHA).

IN 1978, A CELESTIAL LIGHT-SHOW INSPIRED THEM TO GIVE THE TITLE *ZYMURGY** TO THE HOMEBREWING MAGAZINE THEY PLANNED TO LAUNCH.

* NAMED FOR THE SCIENCE OF FERMENTATION. FUN FACT: YOU'LL OFTEN FIND *ZYMURGY* AS THE LAST WORD IN AN ENGLISH DICTIONARY.

PAPAZIAN WENT ON TO PUBLISH *THE COMPLETE JOY OF HOMEBREWING...*

...AND ORGANIZE THE FIRST *GREAT AMERICAN BEER FESTIVAL.*

MEANWHILE, HOMEBREWERS IN CALIFORNIA (WHERE ELSE?) STARTED PUSHING FOR LEGALIZATION OF THEIR HOBBY.

IN SENATOR ALAN CRANSTON, HOMEBREWERS FOUND AN ALLY IN WASHINGTON.

CRANSTON INTRODUCED A BILL TO LEGALIZE HOME PRODUCTION OF BEER FOR PERSONAL CONSUMPTION.

"(e) BEER FOR PERSONAL OR FAMILY USE.—Subject to regulation prescribed by the Secretary, any adult may, without payment of tax, produce beer for personal or family use and not for sale... ag-gregate amount of beer exempt from tax under this subsection with respect to any household shall not exceed—

ON OCTOBER 14, 1978, PRESIDENT JIMMY CARTER SIGNED THE LEGISLATION.*

* IT WAS OFFICIALLY AND POETICALLY ENTITLED "AN ACT TO AMEND THE INTERNAL REVENUE CODE OF 1954 WITH RESPECT TO EXCISE TAX ON CERTAIN TRUCKS, BUSES, TRACTORS, ET CETERA, HOME PRODUCTION OF BEER AND WINE, REFUNDS OF THE TAXES ON GASOLINE AND SPECIAL FUELS TO AERIAL APPLICATORS, AND PARTIAL ROLLOVERS OF LUMP SUM DISTRIBUTIONS."

HOWEVER, THE 21st AMENDMENT STILL EMPOWERED INDIVIDUAL U.S. STATES TO CONTINUE THE BAN.

THE LAST TWO HOLDOUTS, MISSISSIPPI AND ALABAMA, LEGALIZED HOMEBREWING ONLY AS OF JULY 1, 2013.

ALABAMA YELLOWHAMMER

MOCKINGBIRD STATE BIRD OF MISSISSIPPI

HOMEBREWING IS NOW FINALLY LEGAL IN ALL 50 STATES!

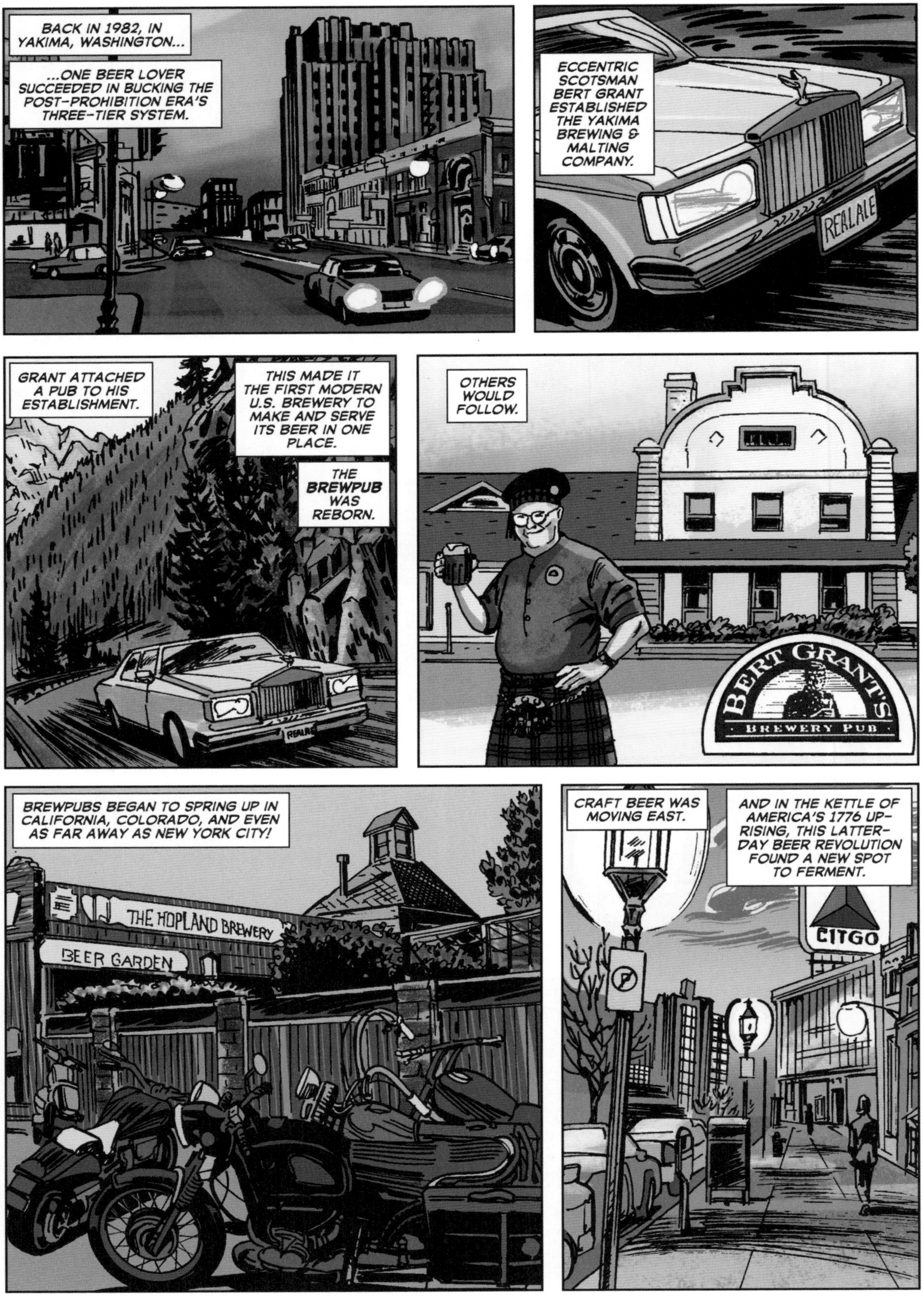
BACK IN 1982, IN YAKIMA, WASHINGTON...
...ONE BEER LOVER SUCCEEDED IN BUCKING THE POST-PROHIBITION ERA'S THREE-TIER SYSTEM.
ECCENTRIC SCOTSMAN BERT GRANT ESTABLISHED THE YAKIMA BREWING & MALTING COMPANY.
REALALE
GRANT ATTACHED A PUB TO HIS ESTABLISHMENT.
THIS MADE IT THE FIRST MODERN U.S. BREWERY TO MAKE AND SERVE ITS BEER IN ONE PLACE.
THE ***BREWPUB*** WAS REBORN.
OTHERS WOULD FOLLOW.
BERT GRANT'S
BREWERY PUB
BREWPUBS BEGAN TO SPRING UP IN CALIFORNIA, COLORADO, AND EVEN AS FAR AWAY AS NEW YORK CITY!
THE HOPLAND BREWERY
BEER GARDEN
CRAFT BEER WAS MOVING EAST.
AND IN THE KETTLE OF AMERICA'S 1776 UPRISING, THIS LATTER-DAY BEER REVOLUTION FOUND A NEW SPOT TO FERMENT.
CITGO

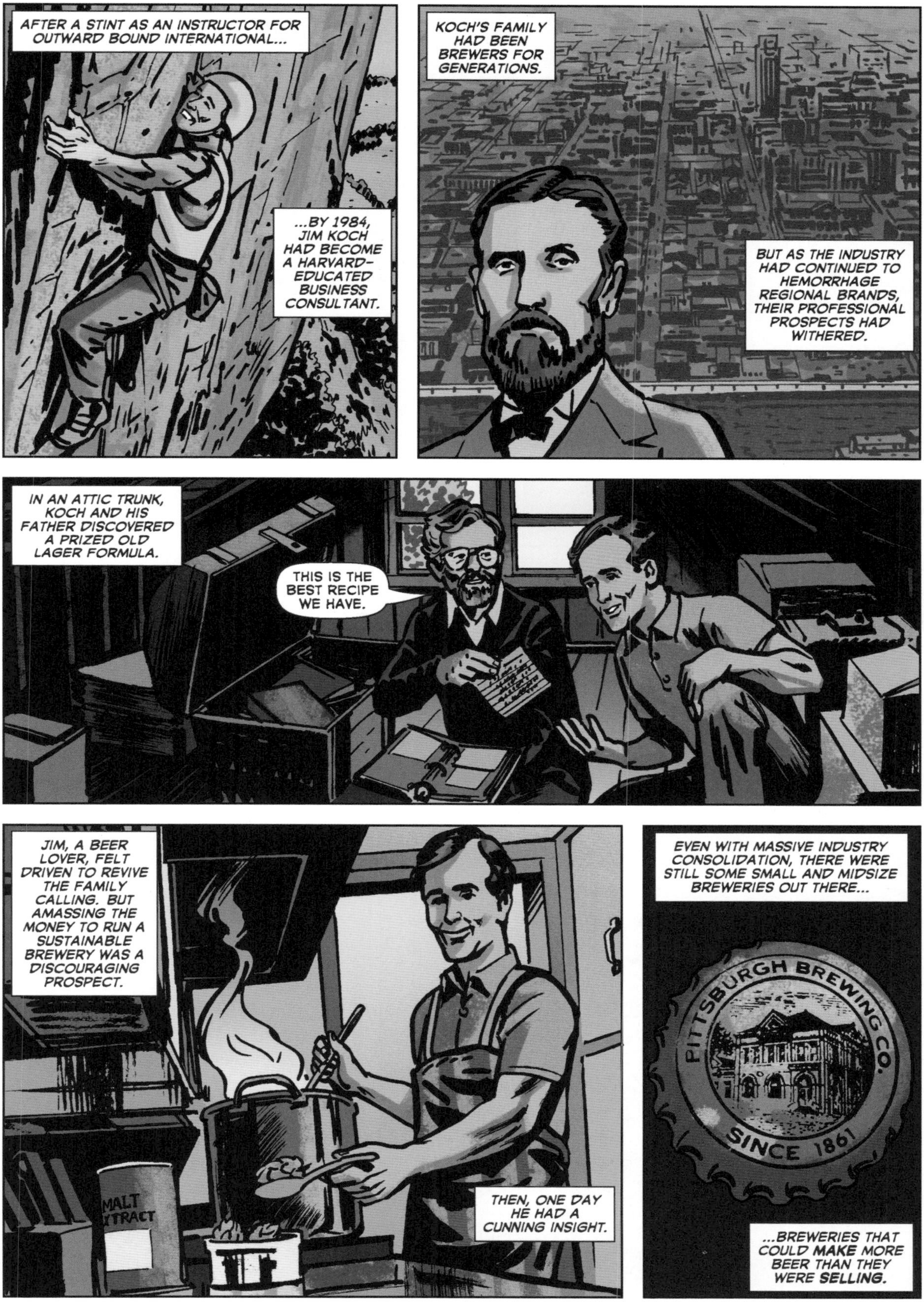
AFTER A STINT AS AN INSTRUCTOR FOR OUTWARD BOUND INTERNATIONAL...
...BY 1984, JIM KOCH HAD BECOME A HARVARD-EDUCATED BUSINESS CONSULTANT.
KOCH'S FAMILY HAD BEEN BREWERS FOR GENERATIONS.
BUT AS THE INDUSTRY HAD CONTINUED TO HEMORRHAGE REGIONAL BRANDS, THEIR PROFESSIONAL PROSPECTS HAD WITHERED.
IN AN ATTIC TRUNK, KOCH AND HIS FATHER DISCOVERED A PRIZED OLD LAGER FORMULA.
THIS IS THE BEST RECIPE WE HAVE.
JIM, A BEER LOVER, FELT DRIVEN TO REVIVE THE FAMILY CALLING. BUT AMASSING THE MONEY TO RUN A SUSTAINABLE BREWERY WAS A DISCOURAGING PROSPECT.
MALT EXTRACT
THEN, ONE DAY HE HAD A CUNNING INSIGHT.
EVEN WITH MASSIVE INDUSTRY CONSOLIDATION, THERE WERE STILL SOME SMALL AND MIDSIZE BREWERIES OUT THERE...
PITTSBURGH BREWING CO.
SINCE 1861
...BREWERIES THAT COULD **MAKE** MORE BEER THAN THEY WERE **SELLING**.

KOCH NEGOTIATED A CONTRACT TO HAVE HIS ATTIC RECIPE BREWED ON A COMMERCIAL SCALE.

HE ESSENTIALLY HIRED AN UNDERUTILIZED FACILITY TO BREW FOR HIM.

DR. JOSEPH OWADES, BREWERY CONSULTANT

INSIDE A YEAR, KOCH'S SAMUEL ADAMS BOSTON LAGER WAS LAUDED AT THE GREAT AMERICAN BEER FESTIVAL.

SAMUEL ADAMS BOSTON LAGER

THE BOSTON BEER COMPANY REMAINS THE LARGEST CRAFT BREWERY IN THE U.S.

KOCH'S BUSINESS MODEL IS STILL VIABLE, ALLOWING TODAY'S START-UP BREWERS TO GET THEIR WARES TO MARKET AT A FRACTION OF FORMER COSTS.

SAMUEL ADAMS

CRAFT BREWING PIONEERS PROPELLED THE MOVEMENT INTO THE 1990S WITH EVER-INCREASING DIVERSITY.

BARLEY

STYLES SUCH AS PORTER, VIENNA LAGER, AND BELGIAN WIT HAD VIRTUALLY DIED OUT IN THEIR NATIVE LANDS.

BUT AMERICANS BROUGHT THEM BACK FROM OBSCURITY.

Meet The Beer:
Belgian Wit

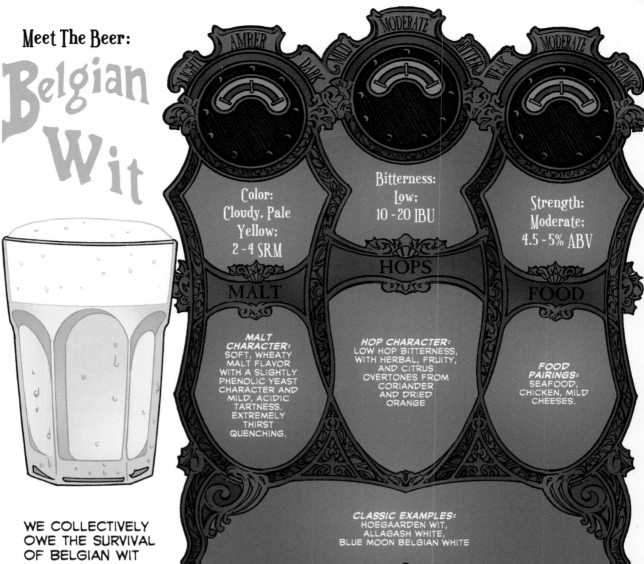

Color:
Cloudy, Pale
Yellow;
2 - 4 SRM

Bitterness:
Low;
10 - 20 IBU

Strength:
Moderate;
4.5 - 5% ABV

MALT

MALT CHARACTER:
SOFT, WHEATY MALT FLAVOR WITH A SLIGHTLY PHENOLIC YEAST CHARACTER AND MILD, ACIDIC TARTNESS. EXTREMELY THIRST QUENCHING.

HOPS

HOP CHARACTER:
LOW HOP BITTERNESS, WITH HERBAL, FRUITY, AND CITRUS OVERTONES FROM CORIANDER AND DRIED ORANGE

FOOD

FOOD PAIRINGS:
SEAFOOD, CHICKEN, MILD CHEESES.

CLASSIC EXAMPLES:
HOEGAARDEN WIT,
ALLAGASH WHITE,
BLUE MOON BELGIAN WHITE

WE COLLECTIVELY OWE THE SURVIVAL OF BELGIAN WIT TO A MILKMAN FROM FLANDERS.

A DECADE BEFORE THE CRAFT BREWING MOVEMENT BEGAN IN THE U.S., A MILKMAN FROM THE ANCIENT BREWING VILLAGE OF HOEGAARDEN (PRONOUNCED "WHO-GARDEN") SINGLE-HANDEDLY RESCUED A BEER STYLE THAT HAD NEARLY VANISHED. THAT STYLE HAS SINCE BECOME POPULAR THE WORLD OVER.

THE WIT ("WHITE") BEERS OF HOEGAARDEN WERE NOTED FOR THEIR HAZY, VERY PALE APPEARANCE, CHARACTERISTICS THAT RESULTED FROM THE USE OF UNMALTED WHEAT AND SOMETIMES OATS. WIT BEERS ALSO FEATURED A CITRUSY PERFUME DUE TO THE ADDITION OF CORIANDER AND DRIED, BITTER CURAÇAO ORANGE PEEL.

THE LAST WIT BREWERY IN HOEGAARDEN SHUT ITS DOORS IN 1957.

IT HAD BEEN A VICTIM OF PILSNER LAGER'S POPULARITY.

BUT IN 1966, LAMENTING THE LOSS OF THE TOWN'S SIGNATURE BEER STYLE, THE AFOREMENTIONED MILKMAN--PIERRE CELIS-- OPENED *BROUWERIJ CELIS*. AFTER A MOVE AND EXPANSION, HE LATER RENAMED THIS CONCERN *DE KLUIS* (THE CLOISTER).

IN 1985, A FIRE RAVAGED THE *DE KLUIS* BREWERY. TO FUND REPAIRS, THE UNDER-INSURED CELIS WAS FORCED TO SELL A STAKE TO THE BELGIAN BREWING GIANT INTERBREW. BUT CELIS AND INTERBREW COULDN'T AGREE ON HOW TO MANAGE *DE KLUIS*.

SO CELIS SOLD HIS REMAINING SHARES IN THE BREWERY, PULLED UP STAKES, AND MOVED ALL THE WAY TO TEXAS.

CELIS CHOSE AUSTIN, TEXAS, AS HIS NEW, ADOPTED HOMETOWN. THE AREA WAS ATTRACTIVE

TO HIM FOR SEVERAL REASONS: ITS MINERAL-RICH WATER, THE AVAILABILITY OF LOCALLY GROWN WINTER WHEAT, AND THE FACT THAT THE SLOW DRAWL OF THE LONE STAR STATE'S SPEAKERS WAS EASIER FOR THE BELGIAN TO UNDERSTAND!

IN 1992, CELIS OPENED A NEW BREWERY TO MAKE HIS WIT BEER. IT BECAME A HIT. UNFORTUNATELY, SUCCESS LED TO OVEREXPANSION. IN 2000, THE BREWERY WAS BOUGHT OUT AND SHUTTERED.

CELIS WIT INSPIRED MANY IMITATIONS. IT BECAME ONE OF THE MOST EMULATED STYLES ON THE AMERICAN CRAFT BREWING SCENE. EVEN BREWING GIANT COORS BEGAN TO BREW THE STYLE, AND COORS' BLUE MOON BRAND CAN NOW BE FOUND ACROSS THE U.S.

SADLY, THE MAN WHO BROUGHT NEW LIFE TO A BYGONE BREW OF OLD PASSED AWAY IN 2011 AT THE AGE OF 86.

BUT THE WIT BEER PIERRE CELIS RESURRECTED CONTINUES TO LIVE ON.

A GENUINE *BEER CULTURE* EMERGED--OR REEMERGED--IN THE U.S.

AND AS IN THE AMERICAN TRADITION OF JAZZ MUSIC, AMERICAN CRAFT BREWERS, FREE FROM OLD-WORLD RESTRICTIONS...

...RIFFED ON AND REINVENTED OLDER STYLES.

IPAS MADE WITH DARK MALTS OR FERMENTED WITH FRUITY BELGIAN YEASTS APPEARED.

SO DID BEER AGED IN WHISKEY BARRELS OR FLAVORED WITH EXOTIC INGREDIENTS-- OR BOTH.

...MAKING THEM "FUNKY" WITH WILD YEAST AND OTHER MICROORGANISMS THAT PREVIOUSLY WOULD HAVE BEEN ABHORRED IN THE STERILE CONFINES OF FERMENTATION CELLARS.

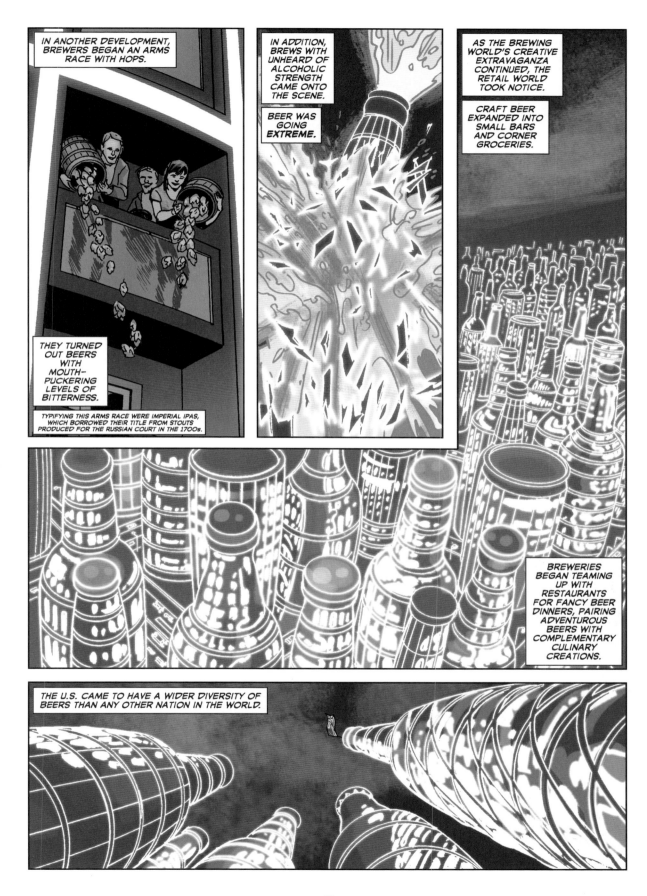

IN ANOTHER DEVELOPMENT, BREWERS BEGAN AN ARMS RACE WITH HOPS.

THEY TURNED OUT BEERS WITH MOUTH-PUCKERING LEVELS OF BITTERNESS.

TYPIFYING THIS ARMS RACE WERE IMPERIAL IPAS, WHICH BORROWED THEIR TITLE FROM STOUTS PRODUCED FOR THE RUSSIAN COURT IN THE 1700s.

IN ADDITION, BREWS WITH UNHEARD OF ALCOHOLIC STRENGTH CAME ONTO THE SCENE.

BEER WAS GOING EXTREME.

AS THE BREWING WORLD'S CREATIVE EXTRAVAGANZA CONTINUED, THE RETAIL WORLD TOOK NOTICE.

CRAFT BEER EXPANDED INTO SMALL BARS AND CORNER GROCERIES.

BREWERIES BEGAN TEAMING UP WITH RESTAURANTS FOR FANCY BEER DINNERS, PAIRING ADVENTUROUS BEERS WITH COMPLEMENTARY CULINARY CREATIONS.

THE U.S. CAME TO HAVE A WIDER DIVERSITY OF BEERS THAN ANY OTHER NATION IN THE WORLD.

BY TURNS, AMERICAN BREWERS' INTREPID, INNOVATIVE SPIRIT REVERBERATED AROUND THE WORLD.

AMERICAN-STYLE ALES BEGAN SHOWING UP IN DUBLIN'S BARS.

MORE RECENTLY, ITALIAN BREWPUBS STARTED CREATING SIGNATURE BEERS WITH LOCAL CHESTNUTS OR MEDITERRANEAN HERBS.

CENTURIES-OLD BELGIAN BREWERIES ARE PRODUCING PUNGENT IPAS MADE WITH IMPORTED AMERICAN HOPS.

CRAFT BREWERIES ARE POPPING UP EVERY-WHERE FROM CHINA TO SOUTH AFRICA; FROM PALESTINE TO PALAU TO PERU.

WE NOW INHABIT A WORLD WHERE CRAFT BEER IS MAINSTREAM.

AS OF 2015, THERE ARE OVER **3,200** BREWERIES IN THE U.S.

AND MORE THAN 2,000 ARE REPORTED TO BE IN PLANNING!

IF YOU LOOK BACK AT 1979'S ALL-TIME LOW OF 44 BREWERIES IN AMERICA. THE RATE AND **DEGREE** OF CHANGE ARE ASTONISHING.

NOW THE SUCCESS OF CRAFT BREWING, ALONG WITH THE LOCAVORE AND SLOW FOOD MOVEMENTS, IS SPAWNING NEW INDUSTRIES, SUCH AS ORGANIC AND "MICRO-MALTING" OPERATIONS. SMALL HOPS FARMS ARE SPROUTING UP ACROSS THE U.S. TO SUPPLY THE GROWING MULTITUDE OF SMALL BREWERIES WITH LOCAL HOPS, OFTEN UNKILNED FOR FRESH-HOP ALES.

REVOLUTION

THE WORD REVOLUTION DOES NOT SIGNIFY THE SUDDEN APPEARANCE OF SOMETHING NEW AND UNPRECEDENTED. INSTEAD IT INDICATES A RETURN — LIKE OUR PLANET COMPLETING ITS ORBIT AROUND THE SUN.

WORLDWIDE
NORTH WEST SOUTH EAST

Revolution is a homecoming to what's old, pure, and foundational. It's a journey back to and reinstatement of the uncorrupted first principles

THAT WERE ALWAYS MEANT TO BE.

THE CONTEMPORARY STATE OF BEER BEAUTIFULLY EMBODIES THIS UNDERSTANDING OF THE TERM REVOLUTION.

THE WORLD TODAY DRINKS AND PRODUCES

MORE BEER

THAN EVER. THE MAJORITY OF IT MAY STILL BE RENDERED ON A MASSIVE SCALE AND MAY UTILIZE LONG-ESTABLISHED AND SAFELY CROWD-PLEASING RECIPES.

BUT BEER'S REVOLUTION IS SOMETHING OF A RETURN TO FIRST PRINCIPLES BECAUSE BEER ONCE AGAIN IS WIDELY MADE BY ARTISANS RATHER THAN INDUSTRIALISTS.

CRAFT BREWING AND HOMEBREWING REDEEM BEER AND RESTORE IT TO ITS ORIGINAL STATE: SMALL-BATCH, HAND-HEWN CREATIONS OF COUNTLESS KETTLES AND HEARTHS.

The brewing revolution is also a boomerang shot to its

Beginnings

for redoubling legions, Beer is once again a product made and enjoyed in a specific native habitat.

THIS IS A RETURN TO HOW THINGS HAD BEEN FOR THE LONG CENTURIES WHEN PEOPLE SAVORED THE YIELD OF THE TOWN BREWERY, THE YONDER COUNTRY HOUSE, THE QUIET MONASTERY ON THE RIDGE ABOVE THE FIELDS, THE FUSSING WIDOW IN THE EARTHEN HOVEL DOWN THE LANE, OR THE TEMPLE-DWELLING SERVANTS OF THE HIGH PRIESTESS.

FOR EVER MORE

PEOPLE

IN EVER MORE PLACES, BEER CAN BE—LIKE IT FIRST WAS— A TASTE OF HOME.

AS AN EXPRESSION OF THE LOCALE (OR *TERROIR* IF YOU *WANT* TO GET FANCY) THAT BIRTHED IT, BREWS CAN BE BUILDING BLOCKS OF OUR *VERY* IDENTITIES.

THOSE IDENTITIES MAY BE OUR OWN. OR, SINCE DEVOTEES OF BEER ARE KNOWN TO BOTH TRAVEL FROM PLACE TO PLACE AND DELIGHT IN BREWS THAT HAVE THEMSELVES CROSSED BORDERS, THE SHADES OF IDENTITY THAT BEER CAN IMPART CAN BE SOMETHING TO TRY ON.

Like Clothes or Costumes,

NEW BEERS CAN HELP US IMAGINE SOMEONE ELSE WE MIGHT HAVE BEEN OR COULD YET BECOME.

Beer has come full circle in one additional and most meaningful way.

OUR ANCESTRAL BEER LOVERS

DID NOT PARTICIPATE IN ANY KIND OF RIGID DEFINITION OF WHAT BEER IS. THEIR DRINK MAY OR MAY NOT HAVE BEEN AROMATIZED WITH HOPS, SWEETENED WITH BERRIES, OR MADE PUNGENT WITH A PANOPLY OF PLANT MATTER.

THEIR DRINK MIGHT HAVE BEEN FIZZY OR FLAT. AND WHETHER BASED IN BREAD OR STAND-ALONE MALTED CEREAL GRAINS, IT COULD HAVE ARISEN FROM ANY COMBINATION OF GRAINS, CULTIVATED OR EVEN WILD (SOME OF WHICH MAY NOW EVEN BE EXTINCT).

BEER'S MODERN REVOLUTION ONCE AGAIN BRINGS US BACK TO THAT ANCIENT, INCLUSIVE, AND, ABOVE ALL, FUZZY DEFINITION OF WHAT BEER IS.

SOCIAL MEDIA

and the INTERNET

HAVE CREATED AN EXPLOSION OF KNOWLEDGE ABOUT BREWING TECHNIQUES AND APPRECIATION. AND TO STAND OUT FROM THE TEEMING THRONG OF COMPETITORS, SOME BREWERS ARE PULLING OUT ALL THE STOPS. MORE THAN A FEW BATTER AT BEER'S TRADITIONAL BOUNDARIES SOLELY FOR THE SAKE OF EXPERIMENTATION. OTHERS MAY JUST WANT TO GRASP AT THE DIGITAL STRAWS OF ELECTRONIC PUBLICITY. BUT AS OUTLANDISH AS THE WARES OF THESE PROFESSIONALS AND HOBBYISTS MIGHT BE, THEY REMAIN, AT LEAST IN A TECHNICAL SENSE, BEERS.

SO IN THE THROES OF Revolution

Beer has rebounded from a barley-water-hops-yeast elixir to its purest essence: an alcoholic drink made from fermented grain.

It has become a virtually blank canvas for both auteur and dilettante artists.

WE ARE ASTONISHINGLY

LUCKY

TO FIND OURSELVES DRINKING BEER AT THE BEST TIME TO DO SO IN ALL OF HUMAN EXISTENCE!

BEER HAS SURVIVED THE PLUNGING OF CIVILIZATION INTO THE DARK AGES. IT HAS SURVIVED THE BLACK PLAGUE, WORLD WARS, AND PROHIBITION — AS WELL AS THE INNUMERABLE, UNKNOWABLE PERILS FACED BY EARLY HUMANITY.

AND MAYBE, JUST MAYBE, THE CONVERSE IS TRUE: THAT HUMANITY SURVIVED THOSE SLINGS AND ARROWS...

...Because of Beer!

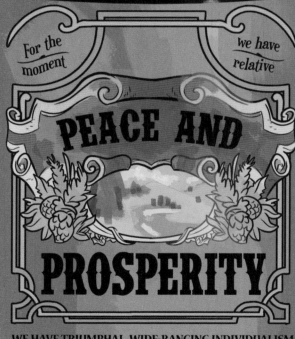

For the moment

we have relative

PEACE AND

PROSPERITY

WE HAVE TRIUMPHAL, WIDE-RANGING INDIVIDUALISM AND TECHNICAL KNOW-HOW, WHICH HAVE ALLOWED SO MANY TO JOIN THE RANKS OF BREWERS. TRADE AND TECHNOLOGY (AND PROFITS) HAVE BROUGHT BEERS FROM AROUND THE GLOBE TO OUR DOOR.

LET US GO TO THEM.

WE CAN AND SHOULD BE FREE TO ENJOY BEER...

...WITHOUT ANALYZING IT TO DEATH.

STILL, BEER HAS A LONG, COMPLEX, AND STAGGERINGLY COLORFUL STORY.

IF WE ACCEPT THE INVITATION TO KEEP THAT STORY IN MIND...

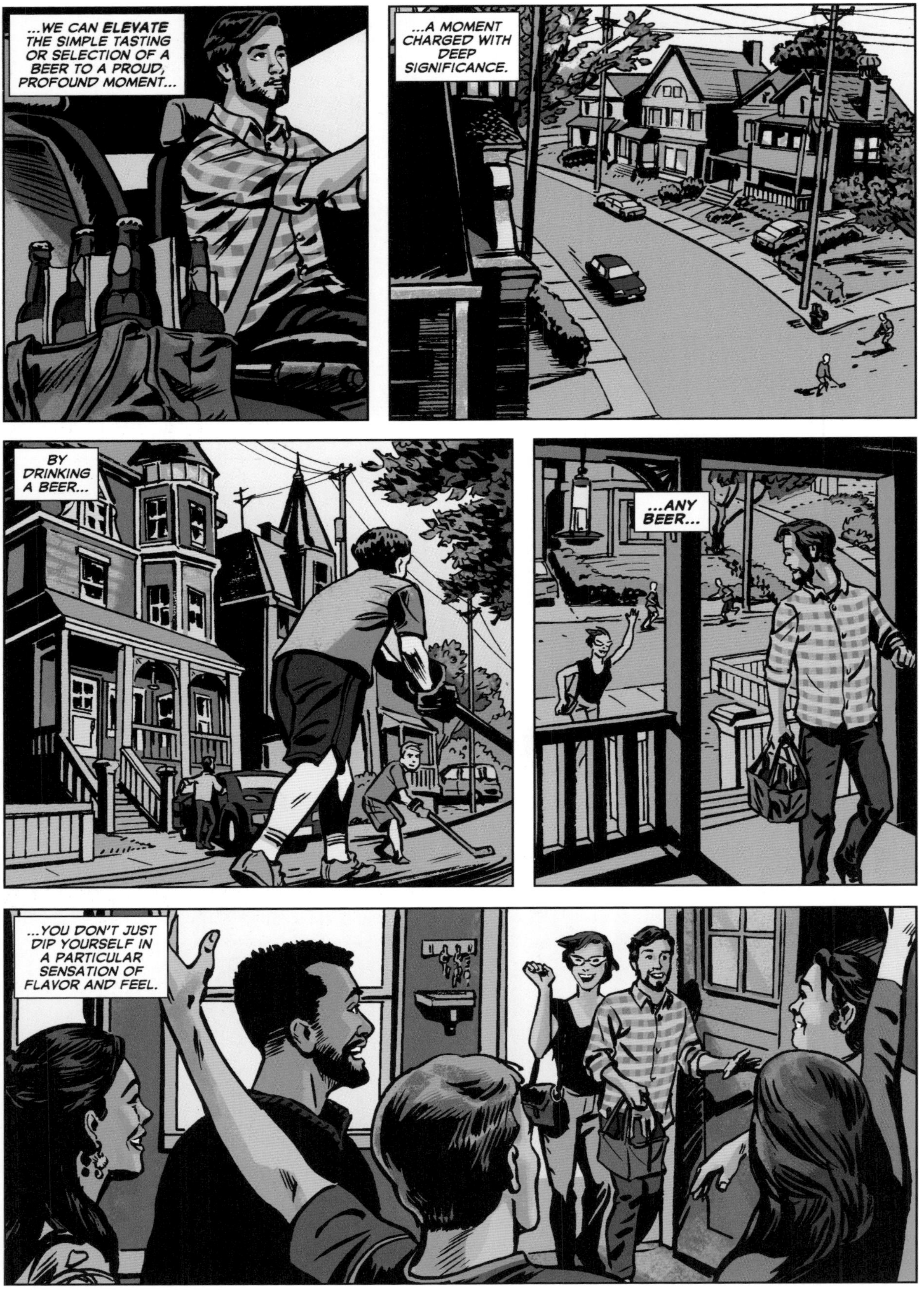
...WE CAN ELEVATE THE SIMPLE TASTING OR SELECTION OF A BEER TO A PROUD, PROFOUND MOMENT...
...A MOMENT CHARGED WITH DEEP SIGNIFICANCE.
BY DRINKING A BEER...
...ANY BEER...
...YOU DON'T JUST DIP YOURSELF IN A PARTICULAR SENSATION OF FLAVOR AND FEEL.

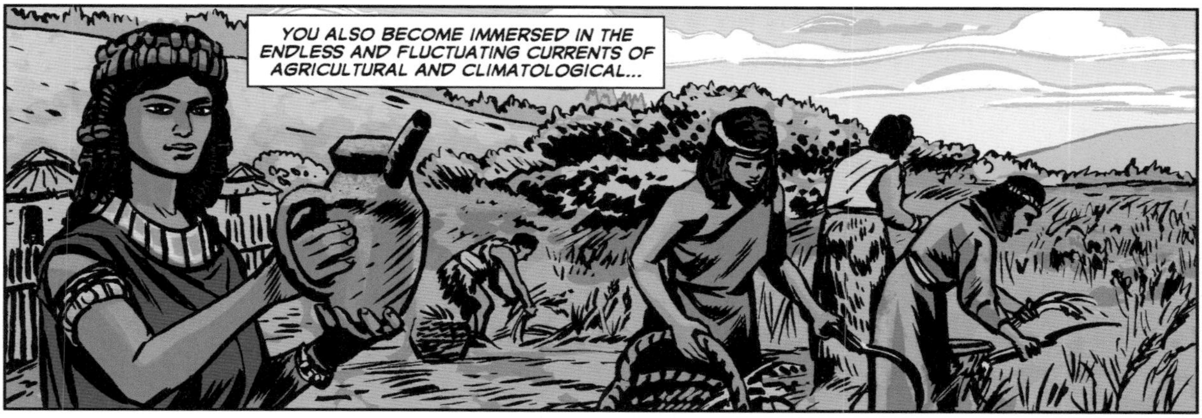
YOU ALSO BECOME IMMERSED IN THE ENDLESS AND FLUCTUATING CURRENTS OF AGRICULTURAL AND CLIMATOLOGICAL...

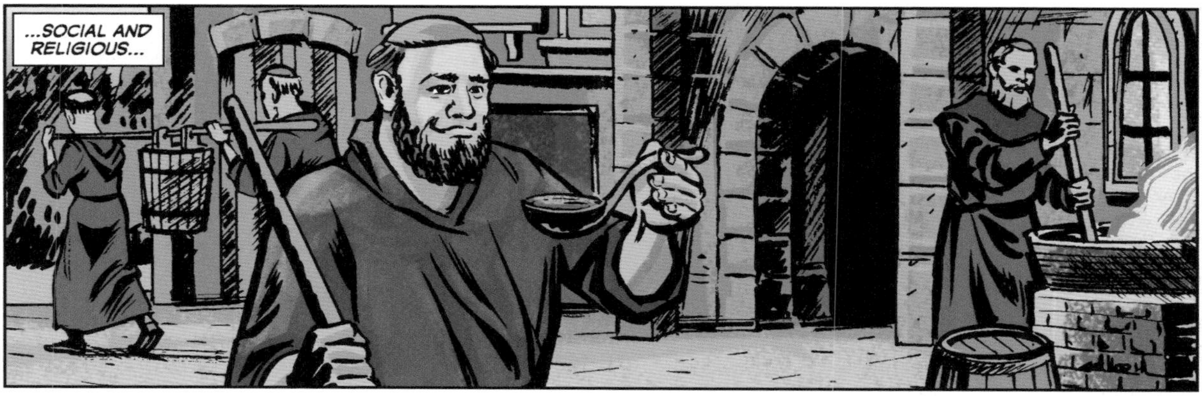
...SOCIAL AND RELIGIOUS...

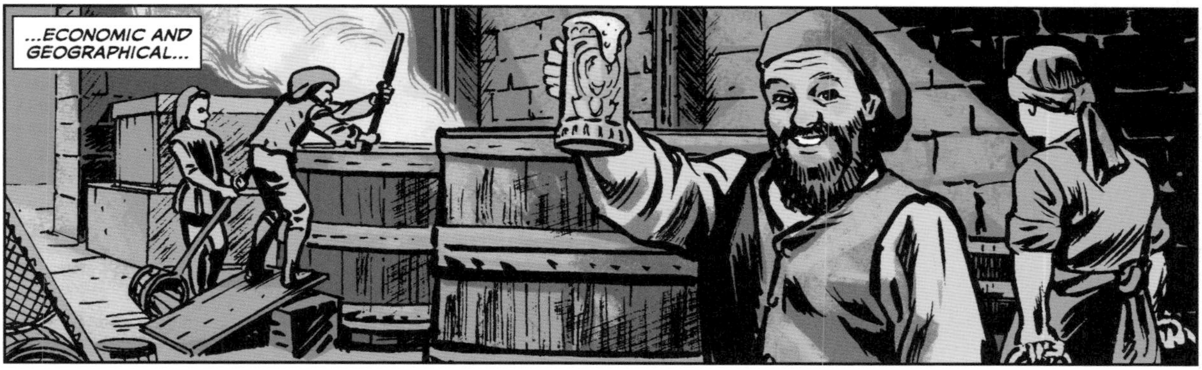
...ECONOMIC AND GEOGRAPHICAL...

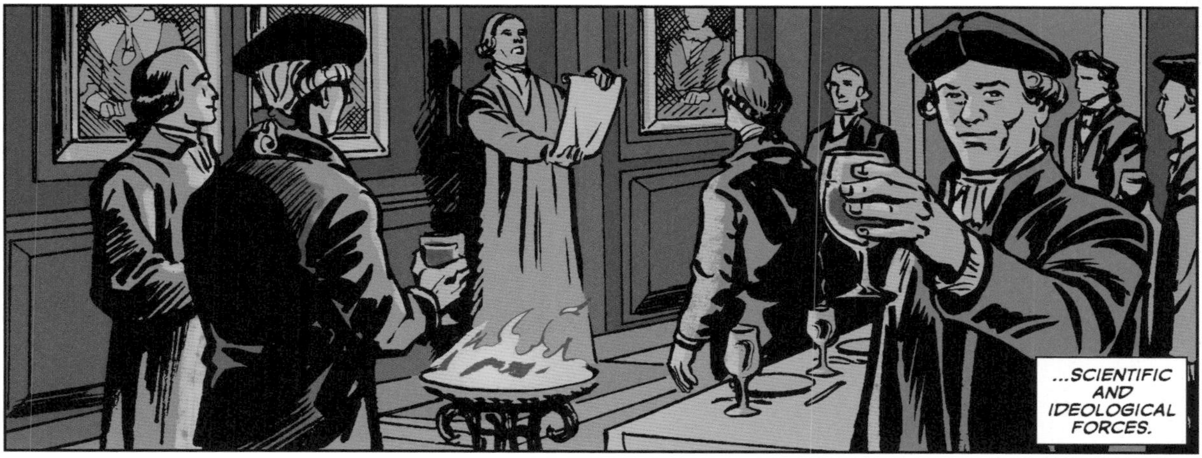
...SCIENTIFIC AND IDEOLOGICAL FORCES.

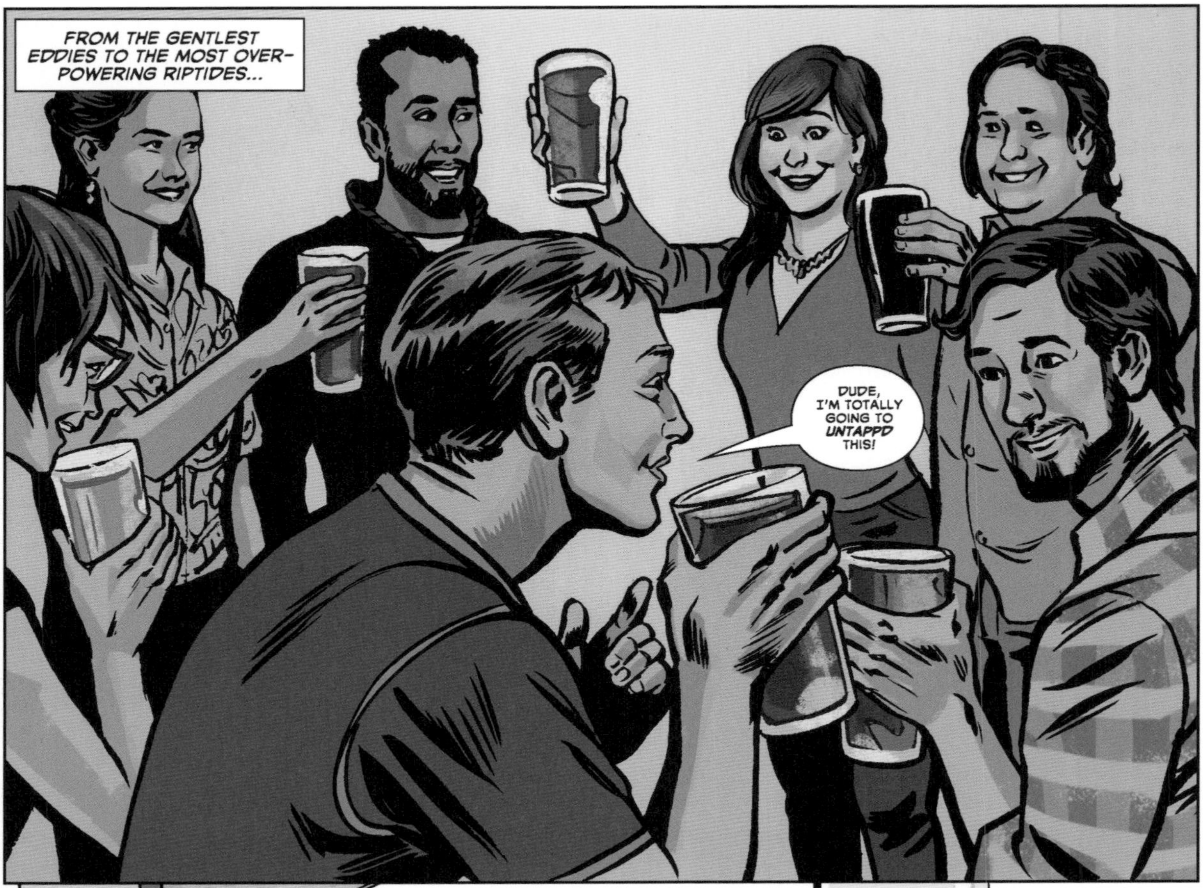
FROM THE GENTLEST EDDIES TO THE MOST OVER-POWERING RIPTIDES...
DUDE, I'M TOTALLY GOING TO UNTAPPD THIS!

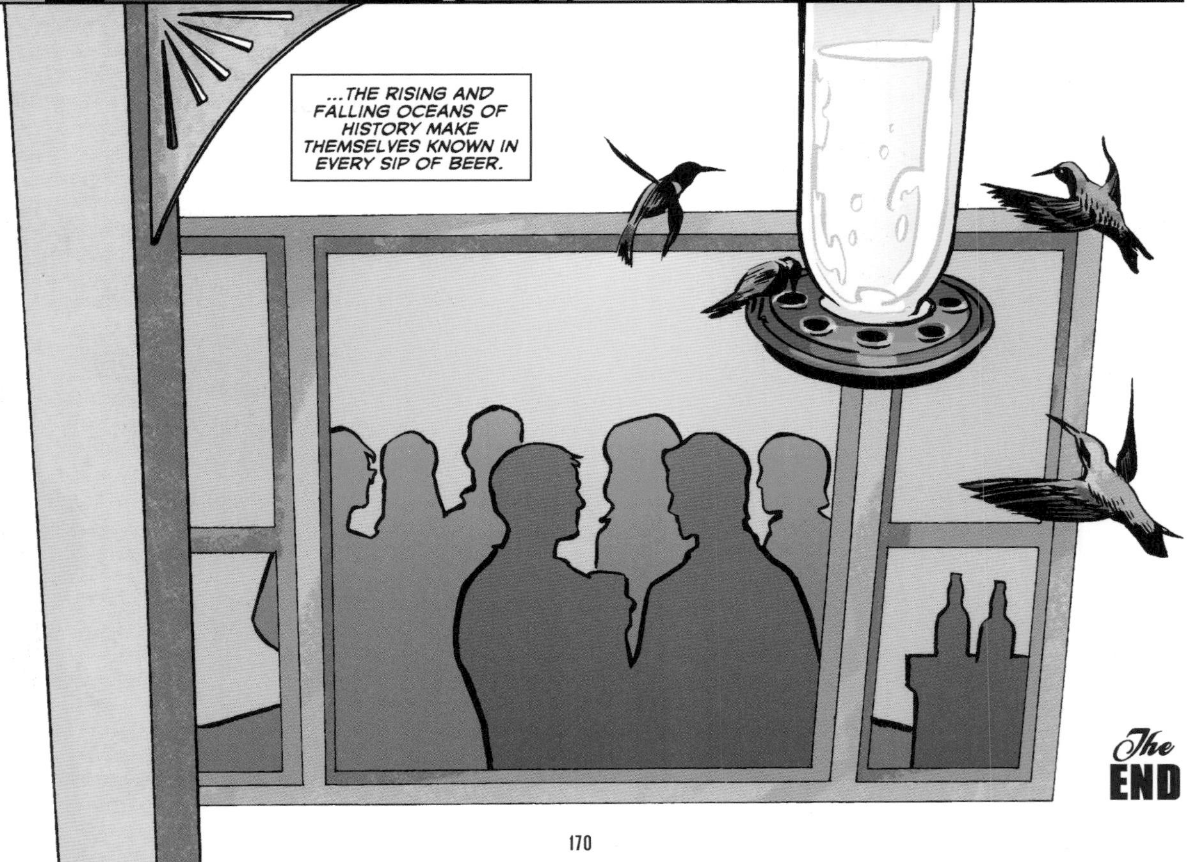
...THE RISING AND FALLING OCEANS OF HISTORY MAKE THEMSELVES KNOWN IN EVERY SIP OF BEER.

The END

Acknowledgments

The creators wish to thank the following for invaluable aid and support in the making of this book. In the art department: additional original art and design by Erica Henderson; color art by Lucy Bellwood and Matthew Bogart, with additional color art from Jon Siruno, Ruby McConnell, and Dan McConnell; additional design by Ashley Hoffman. In the source material and inspiration department: Byron Burch; Natalie and Vinnie Cilurzo; Renée DeLuca; Ray Dobens; Fred Eckhardt; Teri Fahrendorff; Paddy Gunningham, her daughter Sam Hopkins, and the late, great Michael Jackson; Lynne Hennessey; Richard Hennessey; Steve Kleiman; Jim Koch; Mike Marques of Mike Marques Photography; Charlie Matzen; Fritz Maytag; Ann McConnell; Dr. Patrick McGovern; Charlie Papazian; Alan Pugh; Jay Savage; Mal Sharpe; William Farley; Charlie Storey; Ian Thomas. In the breweries and brewing institutions department: Anchor Brewing Co.; Avery Brewing Co.; the entire staff of Back East Brewing; Boston Beer Company; BrewDog; Dogfish Head Craft Brewery; the entire staff, past and present, of Harpoon Brewery; New Albion Brewing Co.; Russian River Brewing Co.; and the Beer Judge Certification Program for style guidelines employed throughout. In the research institution department: Case Western Reserve University Library, Occidental College Library, University of Akron Library, Fuller Theological Seminary Library, Los Angeles Public Library, San Francisco Public Library, Library of Congress. We also must extend hearty gratitude to literary agent Jason Yarn and the deep recesses of talent and diligence at Ten Speed Press—including but not limited to our editor Patrick Barb, Chloe Rawlins, and Melissa Moore.

And now a brief section of dedicatory statements. Mike: I would like to thank my lovely sweetheart, Kristina Kozak, my mother Anne, and the rest of my wonderful family for all of their support and encouragement. I would also like to thank all the brewers and beer scribes who have generously shared their knowledge along the way and Jonathan Hennessey for making this whole project happen. I would like to dedicate this effort to my father, Bernard Donnelly Smith, who was always proud of "his son the brewer." Aaron: To my grandmother, Virginia Lee Pitts (1926-2014), for her love and support. Jonathan: To my darling wife, Annie. She may have no great affection for either beer or comics. But love she has in spades—and works wonders with it. To the undervalued historians, ancient and modern, whose work lights the way, and for Aaron, whose hand refracts that light on every page. And to Mike Smith, as the idea for this book germinated from his faultless cheer, mastery of the art of the anecdote, and impassioned pursuit of good work.

Index

A

Adams, Samuel, 90
Adjuncts, 38, 113, 135
Aeschylus, 30
Agriculture, invention of, 14–19
Alcohol, 116–17, 124, 159
American Homebrewer's
    Association (AHA), 152
American lagers, 135
American Pale Ale, 146
American Revolution, 90–91
Amici, Giovanni Battista, 113
Amsterdam, 74
Amylases, 40
Anchor Brewing, 137, 142, 146
Anheuser, Eberhard, 111
Anheuser-Busch, 112, 129, 134
Appleton, Frank, 138

B

Bappir, 21
Barley, 33, 35, 113
Beer
    alcohol in, 116–17, 124, 159
    ale vs., 81–82
    in the ancient world, 11–32
    brewing process for, 33–49
    Christianity and, 52–56
    definition of, 33
    etymology of, 5
    as food, 6–7
    health benefits of, 7–8, 17,
        62–63, 116
    ingredients in, 35, 81
    in kegs vs. casks, 140
    oldest, 11–13
    origins of, 13–20
    popularity of, 5
    significance of, 166–70
    as social lubricant, 8–9
    women and, 28, 61, 80
    See also Beer styles;
        Craft beer movement;
        Homebrewing
Beer Hall Putsch, 131

Beer styles
    American lager, 135
    American Pale Ale, 146
    Belgian wit, 157
    bock, 83
    Imperial IPA, 159
    India Pale Ale, 96, 97
    lambic, 60
    pilsner, 106–9
    porter, 93, 94
    stout, 94
    Trappist dubbel, 65
    Vienna lager, 104
Belgian wit beers, 157
Benedict, Saint, 64
Beowulf, 55
Bible, 21, 28–29
Black, William, 98
Black Death, 75–78
Blatz, Valentin, 111
Bock, 83
Bread
    beer as liquid, 6–7
    beer brewed from, 21–22
Brewpubs, 154
Brigit, Saint, 56
Budweiser, 109, 112, 113, 124,
    134, 135
Burton-on-Trent, 91, 97, 99,
    100, 101
Busch, Adolphus, 111–12, 113, 123
Busch, August "Gussie," 134

C

Caesar, Julius, 31
Cagniard de la Tour,
    Charles, 113
CAMRA (Campaign for
    Real Ale), 141
Canned beer, 129
Carbonation, 47
Carlsberg Brewery, 115–16
Carter, Jimmy, 153
Casks vs. kegs, 140
Catherine the Great (empress
    of Russia), 92

Celis, Pierre, 157
Chicha beer, 87
Christianity, 52–56, 82
Collier, James, 127
Columba, Saint, 57
Conditioning, 46–47
Coors, 124, 135, 157
Craft beer movement, 135,
    143–45, 149, 154–56, 158–65
Cranston, Alan, 153

D

Decoction, 41–42
Dioscorides, 31
Dreher, Anton, 99–101, 104
Dryhopping, 47
Dwades, Joseph, 134

E

East India Company, 96, 97
Eckhardt, Fred, 152
Egypt, ancient, 24–26
Einbeck, 83
Elizabeth I (queen of
    England), 86
Enfield, John, 79
Epic of Gilgamesh, 26–27

F

Fermentation, 45–46
Flocculation, 46
Francke, Kuno, 123
Franklin, Benjamin, 89
Fraunces Tavern, 88

G

Gambrinus, King, 54
Gibbon, Edward, 52
Goodwin, Henry, 93
Grant, Bert, 154
Great Depression, 127
Greece, ancient, 29–31
Grist, 39
Groll, Josef, 107, 108, 109
Grossman, Ken, 146
Groves & Whitnall
    Brewery, 132

Gruit, 67–68, 72, 74
Gueuze, 60
Guilds, 79–80
Guinness, 94, 96, 132
Guinness, Arthur, 96

H

Hamburg, 69–70, 73, 74
Hanseatic League, 73–74, 83
Hansen, Emil Christian, 115, 116
Hardman, Michael, 139–41
Hare, Ernest, 126
Hitler, Adolf, 130–31, 132
Hodgson, George, 97
Homebrewing, 150–53
Hops, 43–44, 47, 71–72, 81, 108, 159, 161
"Hymn to Ninkasi," 20–21, 23

I

IBUs (International Bittering Units), 44
Imperial IPA, 159
India Pale Ale (IPA), 96, 97
Industrial Revolution, 93, 95
Infusion mashing, 41
Ireland, 55–57, 96, 139

J

Jackson, Michael, 147–49
Jansz, Hendrick, 88
Jefferson, Thomas, 90, 119
Jesus, 52, 53, 64
Jiahu, 11, 13

K

Kegs vs. casks, 140
Koch, Jim, 155–56
Kruger's Bar, 139
Kützing, Friedrich, 113

L

Lagers, 101, 103–5
Lambics, 60
Lautering, 41
Lees, Graham, 139–41
"Light" beers, 134
Linde, Carl von, 105
Livesey, Joseph, 117, 119
Lübeck, 73
Luther, Martin, 82, 84

M

Machrie Moor, 12
Makin, Jim, 139–41
Malt, 36–39

Mashing in, 39–41
Matzen, Charlie, 152
Mayflower, 85
Maytag, Frederick Louis "Fritz," III, 136–37, 139, 142–43, 146
McAuliffe, Jack, 143–45, 146
McGovern, Patrick, 26
Mellor, Bill, 139–41
Meux, Henry, 95
Miller, Frederick, 111, 113
Miller Brewing, 134, 135
Monasteries, 57, 63–66, 102
Mulrooney, Edward P., 150
Munich, 80, 83, 102, 104–5, 130–31

N

Nation, Carry A., 120
New Albion, 144–45, 146

O

O'Banion, Dean, 126
Odin, 55
Oktoberfest, 104–5
Osiris, 24

P

Pabst, Frederick, 111, 113
Papazian, Charlie, 152–53
Pasteur, Louis, 114–15, 116
Pasteurization, 115
Patrick, Saint, 56
Penn, William, 89
Peter I (czar of Russia), 91
Pichler, Elias, 83
Pilgrims, 84–85, 87
Pilsner, 106–9
Plato, 30
Plzeň, 106–7
Porters, 93, 94
Printing press, invention of, 78
Prohibition, 124–28, 135, 150
Pubs, evolution of, 61, 82

R

Refrigeration, mechanical, 105
Reinheitsgebot, 80–81
Rice beer, 23
Rome, ancient, 29–32, 47, 50–52, 58
Roosevelt, Franklin, 126, 127

S

St. Louis, 111, 134
Samoset, 87
Samuel Adams, 156
Schaefer, Frederick, 111, 113
Schlitz, Joseph, 111
Schwann, Theodor, 113
Sedlmayr, Gabriel, 99–101, 104, 115
Sekhmet, 24–25
Shakespeare, William, 82
Sierra Nevada, 146
Spanish Armada, 86
Spaten, 104, 105
Spent grain, 42
SRM, 38
Stouts, 94
Stroh, Bernhard, 111
Sumeria, 20–21, 23

T

Temperance movement, 117–21, 123–24
Theodosius (Roman emperor), 53
Theophrastus, 31
Torrio, Johnny, 126
Trappist ales, 65
Trumbull, John, 89

V

Vienna lager, 104
Volstead Act, 124
Vorlaufing, 42

W

Washington, George, 90
Whitbread, Samuel, 93
William III (count of Holland), 72
Wit beers, 157
World War I, 121–23, 130
World War II, 131–33

Y

Yakima Brewing & Malting Company, 154
Yeast, 45–46, 102–3, 113, 115

Z

Zymurgy, 152

Check out thecomicbookstoryofbeer.com for detailed chapter notes, additional material, news, reccomendations for futher reading, and more.

Library of Congress Cataloging-in-Publication Data
Hennessey, Jonathan, 1971-
  The comic book story of beer / by Jonathan Hennessey and Mike Smith ;
artwork by Aaron McConnell. — First edition.
    pages cm
  Includes bibliographical references.
1. Beer—History—Comic books, strips, etc. 2. Brewing—History—Comic books, strips, etc.
3. Graphic novels. I. Smith, Mike, 1971- II. McConnell, Aaron, 1976- III. Title.
  TP577.H457 2015
  663'.42—dc23

                              2014044184

Trade Paperback ISBN: 978-1-60774-635-5
eBook ISBN: 978-1-60774-636-2

Printed in China

Design by Chloe Rawlins

10 9 8 7 6 5 4 3 2 1

First Edition